Animals of AFRICA

Josef Vágner

OCTOPUS BOOKS

N 16935

Text and photographs by Josef Vágner
Edited by Steve Parker
Line drawings by Eva Hašková
Maps by Jiří Hedánek
Translated by Jiří Krojzl
Graphic design by Antonín Blažek

Designed and produced by Artia for The Hamlyn Publishing
Group Ltd., a division of the Octopus Publishing Group PLC,
Michelin House, 81 Fulham Road, London SW3 6RB.

© 1989 Artia, Prague

ISBN 0 7064 3332 7

Printed in Czechoslovakia by Svoboda
3/99/54/51—01

Animals of
AFRICA

CONTENTS

A word of introduction 7
The transitory nature of animal species 8
Africa — theatre of animal drama 10
How Africa was discovered by Europe 13

THE LARGEST DESERT
IN THE WORLD 18
From the shores of the Mediterranean
across the Sahara
Civet predators 26   Monitors 28
Camels 30   Eagles 30

THE SILENT VOLCANOES 34
The Ethiopian highlands
Baboons 35   Gazelles 40
Hyaenas 47   Bushbuck 48

THE ENDLESS STEPPE 50
The Sudanese savannah belt
Ostriches 54   Cheetahs 54
Oryxes 55

THE HORN ON THE BROW OF
AFRICA 62
The Somalian promontory
Locusts 65   Antelope 70

THE LAND BURNED BY FIRE 74
The Guinea savannah
Hartebeest 78   The Tsetse fly 80
Vervet Monkeys 80

WHERE THE WHITE NILE FLOWS 84
The Upper Nile basin
Hippopotami 87
Herons, Shoebils and Hammerheads 96
Storks and ibises 97   Crocodiles 99

THE INHOSPITABLE WILDERNESS 102
The East African bush
Duikers and other dwarf antelope 104
Rock Hyraxes (Rock Badgers) 106
Poisonous snakes 107

THE PLAINS FULL OF ANIMALS 110
The East African grasslands
African Wild Dogs 115   Lions 117
Wildebeest 121

WHERE THE SUN
NEVER PENETRATES 124
The tropical rain forest
Hogs 127   Okapis 128
Pangolins 129   Chimpanzees 130
Gorillas 131   Pygmies 134

THE LAND CALLED MIOMBO 138
The great southern savannah
Giraffes 142   Secretary Birds 144
Reedbuck and waterbuck 146   Termites 148

GLACIERS ON THE EQUATOR 150
The East African mountains
Elephants 154   Pythons 163
Rhinos 164   African Buffalo 167

THE LAND OF LAKES
AND VOLCANOES 170
The Great Trench Depression
Flamingoes 174
Pelicans, cormorants and anhingas 175

THE SUN-SCORCHED BUSHVELD 180
The southern savannah and bush
Zebras 184   Antelope 189
Jackals 190   Vultures 192

FROM THE DRAKENBERG
MOUNTAINS TO LEMURIA 194
The southern mountains and coast,
and Madagascar
Porcupines 197   Chameleons 197
Lemurs and other prosimians 198
Leopards 198

THE LAND OF RED SAND 202
The southern deserts and bushvelds
Scorpions 205   Weavers 207
Albatrosses and petrels 209
Aardvarks 210   Caracals 212
Servals 213

THE CAPTURE AND TRANSPORTATION
OF ANIMALS 217
Safari without gunpowder and bullets
My first giraffe 220   An Elephant calf 225
A Rhinoceros mother 226
Treacherous terrain 231   Capturing zebras 234
The obstinate Monitor 237

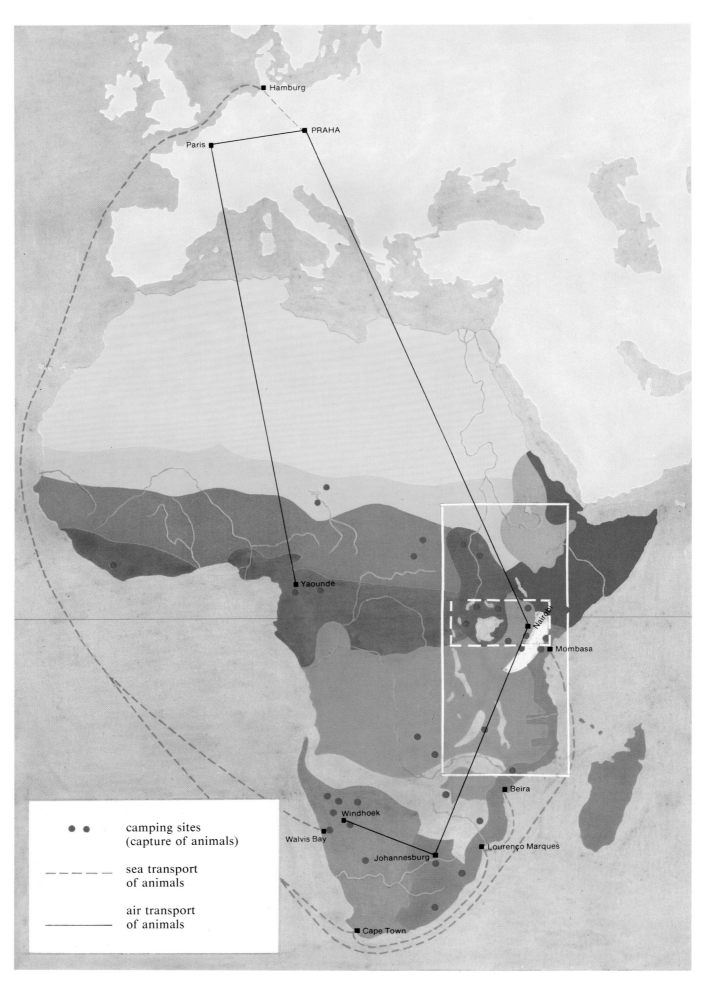

camping sites
(capture of animals)

sea transport
of animals

air transport
of animals

Hamburg

PRAHA

Paris

Yaoundé

Nairobi

Mombasa

Beira

Windhoek

Walvis Bay

Johannesburg

Lourenço Marques

Cape Town

A WORD
OF INTRODUCTION

This book is dedicated to all those struggling to make a contract with nature, the sun and the universe, so that our world does not become a dead planet. For no one ever gave Mankind the right to destroy the air, water, flora and fauna of the Earth.

I am standing on the deck of a ship sailing at full steam towards the Canary Islands. Looking behind us, the coast of Africa, flooded in sunlight, is slowly disappearing. An adventure has come to an end, the animals we have captured are sailing towards their new homeland, and the African wilds are now already far behind us.

On my expeditions to Africa I always take with me two books: a large book of Czech fairy tales and a book containing old maps of Africa. I often peruse these maps and compare them with reality. The travellers of old only knew the coast of Africa at all well. This they were able to draw exactly; the places in the interior of the continent, which they did not know, were simply filled in with drawings of elephants, rhinos, ostriches and giraffes. They could do this with a clear conscience, as in those times such animals were to be found almost everywhere. Pick up any of the books by the great travellers, such as Bruce, Livingstone, Speke, Baker, Stanley, Wissmann, Chapman, Böhm, Holub or Thomson, and you constantly come across passages dedicated to descriptions and observations of African animals. Even hunters were often excellent naturalists and superb observers. Many of them, for example Burchell, Selous, Le Vaillant, Schillings and Roosevelt, laid the foundations on which we now base our contemporary knowledge of African fauna.

Africa is remarkable for the fact that on this continent lives the largest number of hoofed mammals in the world, 90 species in all. Asia, including the Japanese islands, the Philippines and Indonesia, has 70 species of hoofed mammals; South and Central America have 16, Europe 13 and North America 12 species. In Africa, Man himself also appeared early, and the fossil evidence and research so far support the idea that mankind in fact originated in Africa.

Man the hunter had almost the same effect on wild animals as that of his rivals the lion, the African wild dog or the hyaena. He was a component of the ecosystem of those times, helping to maintain the natural balance, and together with other carnivores he prevented the over-reproduction of herbivores. As the primitive hunter, however, he never threatened the existence of wild animal species. The killing of animals in large numbers occurred only when people began to use firearms. From the beginning of the 18th century, not only colonizers but also the natives, equipped with modern weapons, hunted down hundreds of thousands of animals. Elephant tusks, rhino horns, as well as zebra and antelope hides, were (and still are) important items of merchandise. Even a number of scientists caused disaster when they tried to exterminate the tsetse fly by wiping out all wildlife. Disastrous diseases, mainly cattle fever, were disseminated among wild animals by way of domestic cattle. This situation, which came close to producing a major catastrophe, brought about attempts to repair the damage. The first national parks, protected reservations and areas with controlled hunting began to be established. Free African states, in spite of great internal political and economic difficulties, take great care of their reservations and national parks.

Even if the protection of many species of plants and wild animals is proceeding successfully for the time being in these extensive reservations, I nevertheless fear that the time of African wildlife is slowly but inexorably coming to an end. Virgin nature changes quickly in the civilized environment. Herds of animals living in the wild are dwindling, and the existence of some of their species is seriously threatened. If we permit the extinction of any wild animal or plant species, we permit something rare to depart from our world which can never be replaced. For this reason it is essential to recognize and research into the causes of the extinction of so many species. One species of animal dies out on our planet every few days. Why do we devastate the earth to the extent that we do?

When writing this book, it was my intention to make at least some contribution towards clarifying these issues. I wanted to present in a simple way a comprehensible account of the current situation of African wildlife, and to present it convincingly in terms of its past, as well as of its future prospects. Hopefully the reader will be able to understand that the conservation of nature and the living environment today is identical with that of the protection of Man himself.

The transitory nature of animal species

Records which have been preserved in fossil form give evidence of the fact that countless genera and species of animals have existed on earth, appearing and then disappearing in the endless flow of time. After a period of remarkable fish, including many species which had become extinct much earlier in the age, came the period of amphibians. Their reign culminated with the clumsy Stegocephalia. After these followed an incredible number of both small and giant reptiles, until, at the dividing line between the Triassic and Jurassic periods, there appeared mammals. Inconspicuous at first, they reached their greatest proliferation in the Eocene period. Many of these, however, were to follow extinct fish and reptile species into the realm of non-existence.

Still earlier, well before Man appeared with his first axes and spears, whole orders of animals disappeared which were unable to adapt to the changing environment. From fossils we can see that many animals of prehistoric times were very different from those of today. Diverse forms not only followed one upon the other, but often existed side by side, each developing to its own peak. Some species which were developmentally resistant, for example the Tuatara (*Sphenodon punctatus*) or opossums (Didelphidae) have survived throughout the ages until the present time, while others quickly disappeared, to be replaced by species better equipped for the changed environment. From the earliest periods there has been a predominance of invertebrate animal species. The vertebrates began to win their important position in the world of animals only in more recent times.

No animal species lasts forever. As soon as natural conditions change to the point where the species is no longer able to live in them, it dies out and disappears. The Koala Bear (*Phascolarctos cinereus*), for example, feeds almost exclusively on eucalyptus leaves. If, for any reason, eucalyptus trees begin to die out, the Koala will also begin to disappear. Animals dependent upon the environmental conditions in the African forests do not have to be hunted at all in order to disappear. It is enough for the forest to be gradually cut down, destroyed or burned down — which is what is occurring at present — and their fate is sealed.

Since 1600 AD at least 40 mammal species of the 4,200-odd in existence have disappeared, and nearly 100 bird species out of the existing 8,700 or so species. Only in the case of every fourth species was this due to natural causes. One whole per cent of mammal and bird species have become extinct in less than 400 years, whilst a further three per cent of other species are in danger of the same thing happening very shortly. We cannot deny that the chief culprit

here is Man. His large and capable brain, dexterous hands and considerable size and strength have given him the opportunity to accomplish magnificent things. The taming of fire, the development of tools and implements, agricultural cultivation and the domestication of cattle, speech, communication technology, modern means of transport and the ability to produce more food than people need, have all made it possible for human life to exist in large agglomerations. The gigantic spread of human population and habitation has extended to almost all areas of the earth.

Man has learned to hunt down animals with a thoroughness no other predator in the world can match. He has also been able to change the

Lechwe in the swamps of the River Kafua in Zambia, at sunset.

Africa — theatre of animal drama

In the southern corner of Uganda's Ruwenzori National Park, by the River Ishasha which forms the frontier between Zaire and Uganda, one can regularly find Lions resting in favourite trees. Up here they have no interruptions, and fewer problems with flies than on the ground. They also have shade and breeze to cool them.

face of the earth to such a degree that it has proved catastrophic for many animal and plant species. Modern Man unscrupulously squanders irreplaceable natural resources, whilst using replaceable resources with unprecedented wastefulness. He also has limitless faith in the power of technology and chemistry. We believe ourselves capable of solving every problem even without nature and the natural environment to which we belong and in which we originated. Man nevertheless is, and always will be, dependent upon the enormous biological complexity of the earth. For this reason a superhuman task lies ahead of us, if what still remains undisturbed in nature is to be conserved for future generations.

In the beginning there was no such place as Africa, only a vast continent called Pangea, surrounded by the Pantalasa super-ocean. With the splitting up of Pangea, two supercontinents were formed: Lesser Laurasia consisted of present-day North America, Greenland, and those parts of Eurasia lying north of the Alps and Himalayas; the larger supercontinent of Gondwana contained what were to become South America, Africa, India, Australia and the Antarctic. This is how it was hundreds of millions of years ago. During the Triassic period, over 200 million years ago, these supercontinents began to break up. Long before the beginning of the disintegration of Gondwana, however, in the Permian period and on the territory of present-day southern Africa, the mammal-like reptiles (Therapsida), the direct predecessors of mammals, began to appear.

At the beginning of the Mesozoic, in the Triassic period, Madagascar separated from the African continent. Africa itself separated from Eurasia, the waters began to subside and deserts, covered only with sparse bushes, extended over the dry land. The majority of the mainland was hot and arid. About 140 million years ago, in the Jurassic period, Africa moved still farther away from South America and the ocean cut farther into the mainland — less in the case of Africa, however, than in that of Eurasia. Forests spread over the African lowlands, swamps came into being, lakes started to form and rivers meandered. Water plants appeared and reptiles were more numerous, mainly crocodiles (belonging to the sub-order Protosuchia) in southern Africa; pterodactyls (Pterosauria) had appeared in northern Africa. Mammals were small, living both on the ground and in trees.

The earliest mammals known are from the transition between the Jurassic and the Triassic, roughly from the period around 190 million years ago. In the later Mesozoic, by the Cretaceous period, South America moved far to the West and Africa became a vast island surrounded by water on all sides. The climate gradually cooled down and coniferous trees appeared. The evolution of insects accelerated, and life both on the land and in the sea was dominated by large reptiles. These disappeared relatively quickly towards the end of the Mesozoic era, with only crocodiles remaining. Mammals were still inconspicuous. At the end of the Jurassic period the first birds of the genus *Archaeopteryx* appeared, as well as hesperornitids and ichthyornitids in the following Cretaceous period, and the first species of several orders still living to this day.

At the end of the Cretaceous, bird species included representatives of the divers and loons (*Gaviiformes*). By the beginning of the Tertiary era, 65 million years ago, many other bird species had evolved. They included members of the grebe order (Podicipediformes); the Pelecaniformes which today includes majestic seabirds such as the tropicbirds, gannets, boobies, cormorants and frigatebirds as well as pelicans and darters; and the Ciconiiformes — herons, egrets, storks, ibises and flamingoes. We also know from this period the first viviparous (live-bearing) mammals, these being the insectivore placentals, the prosimians from among the pri-mates, and the now-extinct early hoofed species (condylarths).

In the earliest period of the Tertiary, the Palaeocene, the ocean subsided again to reveal the dry land connections between Africa and Arabia, with Eurasia. This connection enabled various animal species from elsewhere to reach Africa. Around 45 million years ago, in the middle Eocene period, the moderate conditions continued. Tropical vegetation extended far to the south and north. Volcanic eruptions gave the Atlantic and Indian Oceans their present form. A great spurt of evolution began among mammals.

The first elephants, rhinos, hogs, horses and other hoofed mammals appeared. The first apes

Two male White Rhinos with a one-year-old calf in the Meru National Park in Kenya. The species was brought from the South Africa Umfolozi Reservation and successfully acclimatized to Kenya. This calf was born in the new homeland.

In the middle of a Giraffe herd is a large white male. This was the only white specimen sighted during an aerial survey of the left bank of the River Tana, from the Somali border as far as the town of Isiolo in Kenya.

and more birds, among them ostriches and pelicans, also started to develop. Insects appeared in all the groups living today, and the majority of fish also had their present-day form. During the Oligocene period, 35 million years ago, the ocean level dropped markedly, the climate cooled and the dry seasons caused the forests to be replaced by savannah. The subsidence of the African Great Trench Depression (Rift Valley) began. Among elephants, a species with four tusks (*Tetralophodon*) appeared, and some elephants acquired trunks.

At the start of the Miocene, 26 million years ago, the amount of precipitation increased, causing widespread erosion. Africa cooled down, but was still warmer than at present. The majority of African vegetation was already similar to that of today. The dry-land bridges across the Red Sea, Sicily and the Straits of Gibraltar joined Africa and Arabia with Eurasia. The surface of considerable parts of eastern and southern Africa was raised to heights of around 1,200 metres, and the majority of the continent was once again covered by forests. More herbivore species appeared, particularly the giraffes and wild cattle. Antelopes began to evolve, and the first sabre-toothed cat predators appeared. The first ape-men (Hominidae) also began to appear. About seven million years ago, at the start of the Pliocene, all the continents had virtually their present-day form. A drier climate caused the forests to recede again. Mount Kenya rose

above the equator and Kilimanjaro began to erupt. The surface of eastern and southern Africa was raised to a height of 1,800 metres, while the Ruwenzori Range could boast a height of over 5,000 metres. The Congo was covered by a vast lake. Some of the hominids began to walk upright, while rhinos and elephants attained their present form.

During the Pleistocene period, which began two million years ago, the leopards appeared, as well as the Caracal (*Felis caracal*) and zebras, while sabre-toothed cats began to disappear. The Giraffe (*Giraffa camelopardalis*) assumed its present form, although other giraffe species died out. Then, one and a half million years ago, present-day hyaena species appeared and Lake Victoria began to rise to 100 metres above its present level; the other great lakes of Africa began to form. Lake Turkana (formerly Lake Rudolf) was three times longer than it is today, submerging almost the whole of the Trench Depression in Kenya. The Ruwenzori range continued to rise.

One million years ago in eastern Africa, a hog as large as a rhino appeared, and a baboon as large as a gorilla. Over 60 species of bovine animals were living. By 400,000 years ago the majority of present-day animal species were in existence. By 200,000 years ago the Great Trench Depression attained its present form, and Lake Victoria became a swamp. About 70,000 years ago a worldwide drop in temperature caused the first Ice Age. Temperatures began to fall even in tropical Africa, and glaciers started to form in the East African mountains. By 12,000 years ago Africa had warmed up, but 10,000 years ago it cooled down again slightly. Large areas south of the Sahara dried out. Then, 8,000 years ago, the African climate warmed up and the atmosphere became more humid. Large animals were living in the Sahara: elephants, hippopotami and giraffes. Man began agricultural cultivation and domesticated a number of animals. Finally, 7,500 years ago, the civilization of the Ancient Egyptians began.

In spite of the alternate warming and cooling which has taken place in Africa over the last millennia, it remains a hot continent, being situated between 37° north and 34° south in latitude. From the zoo-geographical point of view, Africa can be divided up into three regions:

- North Africa (the Atlas countries, Egypt and the Sahara), which belongs, together with Europe and the northern part of Asia, to the Palaearctic region;
- the remainder of Africa south of the Sahara, which together with the south of the Arabian peninsula forms the Ethiopian region;
- Madagascar and the nearby islands in the Indian Ocean, which form a separate Malagasy region.

In this book the division of Africa into separate regions is based roughly on that made by Dr. Leslie Brown.

How Africa was discovered by Europe

The first European reference to Africa is the legacy left to us by a Greek historian of the 5th century BC. The Egyptian king Nekos commanded the Phoenicians to circumnavigate

Africa from the Persian Gulf and to sail back to Egypt via the Columns of Hercules — that is, the Straits of Gibraltar. In the third year of their voyage they did indeed sail back to Egypt via the Columns. Thus the first sighting of Africa came about.

The Carthaginians were also navigators who tried to circumnavigate Africa. After them, the Greeks set off on voyages of discovery, and later the Romans, who incorporated North Africa into their Empire and penetrated farther south, and to Ethiopia. The Arabs established themselves on the East African coast, where they organized prosperous mercantile centres and thus became the lords of East Africa until, in the 15th century, the Portuguese arrived, driven by their desire for gold. Portuguese power in Africa was not threatened until the 17th century, when the profitable slave trade began to interest Holland, Britain and France. At the end of the 17th century the Portuguese lost their position and their place was taken by the

Africans are well aware of the pricelessness of wild animals and unviolated nature. Here is the entrance gate to the Meru National Park in Kenya, one of the many superbly-organized reservations in which large numbers of different animals live under exemplary protection.

Boehm's Zebra with foal on the plains of the Serengeti National Park in Tanzania.

14

In extensive areas of the Garissa district in Kenya the inhabitants have lived since time immemorial in harmony with nature. They protect their dwellings and domestic cattle from predators using thorny enclosures.

British. When the era of slavery came to an end, interest in Africa continued for completely different reasons. The Industrial Revolution in Europe required new sources of raw materials and markets for its surplus production. Africa began to interest scientists of almost all persuasions.

One day in 1722 the slender Swede, Carl Peter Thunberg, set foot on the summit of Table Mountain. He was already professor at the University of Uppsala, at the age of only 28. Thunberg had been a pupil of the excellent Carl Linné, 'father of botany'. The flowers that attracted his attention on this spot were the Blue Orchids (*Disa longicornis*). This event probably

Contemporary Makonde art has its origins in ancient popular myths and superstitions, being based on tribal tradition. It admirably conveys the hard life of the Africans. Artists from the Meru foothills in Tanzania spend months patiently shaping beautiful figural and abstract carvings out of heavy black mahogany.

Cape Buffalo in the Kabalega National Park in Uganda, cooling themselves in the noonday heat in the mud. This also helps to protect them from the enormous numbers of biting insects.

marked the beginning of the scientific study of African nature.

In Europe at that time, strange rumours were circulating about African fauna. It was believed that a lion had such hard bones that it was possible to use them instead of flint and steel. A rhino was said to live by the River Orange, which killed people and then scraped the meat off their bones with its rough tongue. A wildebeest was supposed to have the head of a bison and the rump of a deer, and it was assumed that the hyaena was an hermaphrodite (male and female). About elephants, it was maintained that before drinking from a pool they first disturbed the water with their trunks, because they could not endure the sight of their own ugly faces.

With the beginnings of critical science in the 18th century, the prepared skulls and hides of slaughtered animals, as well as pressed flowers, were becoming increasingly sought-after commodities. Ever greater numbers of hunters set off for Africa to obtain animals for scientific purposes. In 1788 the Society for the Study of the African Interior was founded in London. In 1795 the first modern explorer, Mungo Park, set out for the African interior. The British naturalist William Burchell studied South African flora and fauna with great care, collecting 63,000 various specimens.

In 1822 Hugh Clapperton became the first European to set foot in the large merchant town of Kano, in northern Nigeria. The Frenchman René Caillié was the first to reach Timbuctoo and return alive. Richard Burton and John Speke discovered Lake Tanganika in 1858. In 1866 Speke and James Grant discovered the sources of the Nile, where the great river flows from Lake Victoria. At the beginning of the 1880s Joseph Thomson walked the length of the

Great Trench Depression as far as Uganda, and it was only because he became enemies with the Masai that he had to give up his intention to climb Mount Kenya. This mountain was first climbed by a European in September 1899, by the British geographer Mackinder.

The most famous of all explorers were David Livingstone, who worked in Africa as a missionary, and Henry Stanley, the American reporter who set out to look for Livingstone, and who later worked with him.

At the beginning of the 19th century Africa was gradually divided among the then European powers and states — the maritime nations of Britain, France, Spain, Portugal, Belgium, Holland and Germany. It was not until 150 years later, in the 1960s, when the independence of individual countries and the abolition of the colonial system became widespread.

The Victoria Falls on the River Zambezi were discovered for the West by the British explorer David Livingstone. The flow of the river, 1,700 metres wide, falls a depth of 128 metres through a ravine ranging between 44 and 100 metres wide. The largest continuous fall is 109 metres. This photograph was taken during a period of relatively low water level, so that it is possible to see far into the rocky ravine.

THE LARGEST DESERT IN THE WORLD
From the shores of the Mediterranean across the Sahara

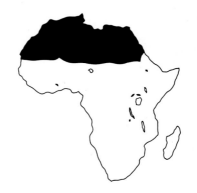

The Mediterranean, with its blue-green waves rolling between southern Europe and North Africa, has, since the earliest times, more joined these two continents than separated them. The weather is equally glorious on both north and south coasts, and the natural beauty of one shore can hardly be distinguished from that of the other. How many times in the course of history did the Greeks, Romans, Vandals and Vikings penetrate North Africa and, in reverse, the Carthaginians and Moors make inroads into Europe? As a result the cultures and races of both shores were already intermixed thousands of years ago. Greek traders voyaged far to the south of the Red Sea and the superbly organized Roman legions, after conquering Carthage, ruled over hundreds of kilometres of the North African coast. The Romans did not dare to push farther to the south, however. This was already wild country — *Terra incognita* — which was marked on their maps with *'Hic sunt leones'* — 'Here are lions'.

Only a little way from the Roman border strongholds lay the unexplored Atlas Mountains, a feared place associated with legend and fable; beyond was the endless Sahara desert, where wild men with dark skins lived. The Mediterranean African belt resembles Europe more than it does the rest of Africa. Today it is a narrow coastal strip but in the past it extended over 1,500 kilometres into the interior of the Sahara. This strip is continually retreating before the desert, so that today the Sahara touches the sea in some places. This coastal belt begins in the west at the Atlantic Ocean and extends across the Atlas Range and Tunisia as far as Tripoli in Libya. Farther to the east, the Sahara stretches as far as the coast, apart from the two more humid regions of Cyrenaica and the Nile Delta.

The Mediterranean climate is pleasant and benevolent. Winter there somewhat resembles a wet European summer. After winter comes a mild spring, when most flowers burst into bloom, only to fade and dry out in the long summer, when the land is scorched by the sun. A cooler, short autumn then sets in, followed by winter once again. The typical Mediterranean landscape is scrub, grown over with bushes, known as macchie (maquis). This dense, wild shrub cover is composed of woody-stemmed Tree Heather (*Erica arborea*), Laburnums, gorse (*Ulex*), oaks (*Quercus*), the Nut-pine (*Pinus pinea*), Salicornia saltbush, sedges (*Phragmites*) and the Mediterranean Palm (*Chamaerops humilis*). Among these grow opuntia cacti from America, and eucalyptus from Australia which are successfully used in sand afforestation.

The Egyptian Mongoose is an excellent snake hunter. Animals which we kept for years at our hunting camp in Namibia knew us and became very friendly.

A large group of Banded Mongeese lived in our hay and food barn next to the enclosures. The mongeese came to know us and our dogs. As soon as a strange dog strayed into the camp they would attack it and drive it off.

On the sandy dunes along the Atlantic coast magnificent flowering fig-marigolds (*Mesembryanthemum*) grow in large numbers, originating from South Africa. In high positions by the coast grows the Haleb Pine (*Pinus halepensis*), as well as the remaining stands of Atlas Cedar (*Cedrus atlantica*).

In spring and autumn, enormous flocks of migrating birds fly across the Straits of Gibraltar. The large birds like to stop during their travels on the Spartel Cape, where the Atlantic Ocean meets the Mediterranean. South of this headland the sand dunes begin, stretching for hundreds of kilometres along the coast. Streams flow through the dunes, overflowing during the winter rains and forming extensive swamps behind the dunes. There ducks and geese like to stay, having flown down from Europe in the autumn. In spring the edges of the swamps are covered with an enormous number of plants, most frequently salicornia and sedge. Above these soar Lapwings (*Vanellus vanellus*) and Curlews (*Numenius arquata*), while over the meadows and small pools White Storks (*Ciconia*

The largest desert in the world—the Sahara—has an area of more than 9 million square kilometres. Pure sandy plains with dunes occupy one fifth of the region. The face of the sandy desert is constantly changing due to the effect of winds, unlike rocky and gravel deserts.

ciconia) and Cattle Egrets (*Bubulcus ibis*) pace up and down in a dignified manner.

The drier regions are usually sandy or gravelly. Sometimes they are cultivated, sometimes herds of sheep graze them, and only here and there are they forested with imported eucalyptus. The farther south one goes, the more rocky the coast becomes, although the rocks are not particularly high. Typical plants for this rocky country are the spurges (*Euphorbia*), which slightly resemble a giant cactus. Farther into the interior the hilly terrain slowly changes into the Atlas Mountains, and to the north it becomes the Rif Range. Among the narrow valleys of the mountains rivers wind and twist, creating numerous creeks and marshy places.

19

The coastal lowlands have been densely populated since the earliest times. The wild game animals for hunting, with the exception of Wild Boars (*Sus scrofa*), were exterminated long ago. Only small bird life, as well as ravens, rodents, mongeese and kestrels, which have been able to adapt to human settlements, have remained. Jackals are abundant there, and in places porcupines are also found. There are sparse cultivated olive groves, and small clusters of Cork Oaks (*Quercus suber*) growing wild. In the cork forests of Morocco lives the Imperial Eagle (*Aquila heliaca*), which is not found anywhere else in Africa.

From the Spartel Cape as far as Tunisia the mountain range extends directly to the sea, and the shores are rocky and picturesque. The landscape along the coastline is shrubby and in spring bursts into flower with yellow laburnum and gorse, completed by oaks with dark green

The Barbary Ape has a slender body, a wrinkled face and hands, and the coat is reddish-tinged olive. The young have black coats and light faces. The Barbary Ape is very hardy, being able to tolerate heat of over 40 °C and up to 12 °C of frost.

leaves and white and red rock roses (*Cistus*). The Wild Lavender (*Lavandula pedunculata*) has an overpowering fragrance and the rocks are full of yellow-flowering marguerites (*Bellis*). A large number of goats and sheep graze among the shrubs. In times past, Mediterranean Seals (*Monachus monachus*) lived along this coast, but these have been almost completely hunted to

Young warriors of the Dinka tribe leading a Zeba-like bull to a celebration. The tribe lives along the White Nile in southern Sudan, numbering approximately two million people. The bull will be sacrificed at the grave of the founder of the family, on the anniversary of his death.

extinction — only a few thousand remain along the Atlantic coast.

The Rif Mountains in northern Morocco form a unique climatic, botanic and zoo-geographic region. High in the mountains grows the magnificent Atlas Cedar, interspersed with Spanish Firs (*Abies pinsapo*) and Haleb Pines. In the lower belt various types of oak also grow, particularly the Holm Oak (*Quercus ilex*) and the Cork Oak, and Wild Boars and foxes live there. South of the Rif is the Central Atlas range, vegetated at the lower levels with oak forests and in the higher places with conifers. In winter, when the forests are buried in snow, it is difficult to imagine that this is Africa. Still farther to the south extends the High Atlas range. In its coniferous forests the Pinaster (*Pinus pinaster*) is the most common tree. In the forests of the Central Atlas, Barbary Apes (*Macaca sylvanus*) can be seen. These are the only monkeys that also live in Europe — in fact on the Rock of Gibraltar, where the Carthaginians and Romans brought them from North Africa in ancient times.

The narrow strip of land along the Nile is barely able to support the local cattle in the dry season. A few trees afford a little shade in the noonday heat for both animals and people. Wild animals have been hunted to extinction here. Just beyond this narrow belt of shrubs, grass and trees, there is nothing but endless desert.

Long ago, the Leopard (*Panthera pardus*) hunted Barbary Apes and other wild animals in the Atlas; now there are less than 50 of these big cats left in the whole Atlas region. They are still hunted mercilessly, which makes it probable that they will disappear from this region altogether in the near future. As late as the beginning of this century Lions lived in the African Mediterranean region. After the wild hoofed mammals had been hunted to extinction, however, the Berber Lions began to hunt domestic animals, thus coming into conflict with humans and losing in the unequal struggle. In this region one can still find small predators such as the genets (*Genetta*) and mongeese (*Herpestes*). Apart from hogs there also used to be in this region the most numerous groups of hartebeest;

A Marabou Stork has tried to catch a Nile Monitor. As soon as the Marabou approached, the monitor lashed it with its tail and withdrew into deeper water until able to swim away.

however, they were defeated in their competition with domestic cattle. Among the mountain ridges of the Atlas, large numbers of Atlas Gazelles (*Gazella cuvieri*) were also once in evidence, but now only a few dozen remain. Here it is still possible to find the Bearded Vulture (*Gypaetus barbatus*). And here, as everywhere in North Africa, lives the famous Sacred Scarab Beetle (*Scarabaeus sacer*), which played an important part in the religion of the ancient Egyptians: they worshipped it as a sun god. Scarabs made from semi-precious stones or precious metals were placed into sarcophagi, and it was expected that they would speak for the deceased to the lord of the kingdom of the dead.

To reach farther into the interior from this

I caught my first Nile Monitor at Lake Victoria.

blessed maritime country one passes through oak forests, later travelling along paths by winding rivers, densely bordered by oleanders. The higher you travel, the more the landscape alters. The trees recede and in their place thorny shrubs appear; then suddenly everything is covered with snow, with small flocks of ravens circling above. Continuing over the summit and down, the dense snow clouds begin to clear, and after a few minutes one emerges into a landscape flooded in sunlight and full of reddish rocks, without a single plant as far as the eye can see. This is where the Sahara begins, extending for hundreds of kilometres to the south and east.

Sahara, or As-Sahra, is an Arabic word meaning desert in the general sense. Across the world, however, this word has come to be synonymous with the largest desert on the planet. It spreads across the whole of North Africa, from the Atlantic coast to the Red Sea. The Sahara forms part of the Great Palaearctic Desert, which covers not only North Africa but also a significant proportion of the Middle East, including the Arabian peninsula, and part of India. From coast to coast the Sahara is approximately 5,000 kilometres wide, and from north to south over 1,600 kilometres. For centuries it has formed an impenetrable barrier between Europe and the African interior.

In the Sahara there are three main types of desert; erg, reg and hamad. Erg is an extensive area of sandy dunes, such as the Libyan desert or the Great Western Erg. Reg is a practically flat plain, its surface consisting of coarse sand, gravel or stones, over which wind blows constantly. Hamad is the upper flatland bounded by dried-up streams, its surface made of slabs and rocks. In the Sahara there are great mountain ranges as well as endless sandy, stony and gravel plains. Large sand dunes make travel impossible. Oases with water, in some places pure, in others salty or bitter, in yet others even poisonous, are scattered here and there in the endless wasteland. Burning heat alternates with considerable cold. Strong winds, originating from these changes between hot and cold, stir up the sand and dust and persecute all living things; they alternate with periods of absolute quiet, in which not an animal, bird or insect sound disturbs the silence.

The Sahara covers almost a third of the African mainland. It is there simply because there is insufficient precipitation to balance the evaporation caused by the sun's rays. Nowhere in the Sahara is precipitation higher than 250 millimetres each year. Scientists are not in agreement as to the real boundaries of the desert, or where the desert ends and the semidesert or steppe begins. Some maintain that a landscape cannot be considered as desert if there is any vegetation on it; others place the boundary where plants specially resistant to dryness begin to predominate. The northern boundary of the Sahara is formed by a row of depressions known as the Saharan Fault. Some animals and

The Nile Monitor differs from other monitors chiefly in its distinctly tapered tail, which has a ridge on the upper side. Monitors up to two metres long live on the little rocky islands of Lake Victoria, near Entebbe.

A young Egyptian Vulture trying to break a large ostrich egg with a sharp-edged stone. After several attempts it invariably succeeds. This vulture is common in the Egyptian region.

plants never cross over this ecological barrier. The Date Palm (*Phoenix dactylifera*), for example, does not flourish behind the Fault. The Puff Adder, (*Bitis arietans*), which occurs south of the Fault, does not appear on its northern side. Indeed, even some birds such as ravens do not fly over this boundary. The southern Saharan boundary is even more difficult to determine, undoubtedly amongst other things because of the fact that the Sahara is constantly extending southwards and growing inexorably larger.

This great desert has many faces, changing according to whether there is underground water, how the surface is formed and how much precipitation it receives. In mountainous regions almost all rainfall flows down the smooth rocks or evaporates on them immediately. On the flat sandy plains the water quickly drains into the ground. As soon as it seeps deeper than 30 centimetres into the sand it cannot be lost either by evaporation or by flowing away.

The radiation of the sun has different effects on sand and on rock. Individual grains of sand are separated from one another by a layer of air, so that the surface of the sand dunes in the daytime is unbearably hot — but it quickly cools down at night. In rocky desert, however, heat accumulates during the day and the rocks are hot even at night. For this reason, living conditions among the rocks are even more severe than among the sand dunes.

The Barbary Sheep differs from goats in that it does not have a beard, and males in the mating season do not smell. Its horns are triangular in cross-section, and its broad chin is tipped forwards.

In the western Sahara there are a number of large massifs: the Ahaggar Mountains, the High Tibesti Mountains and the lower Air, Tasili and Adrar Ranges. The summits of the mountains have been uncovered by long-term erosion down to the rock itself. The lower slopes form hamads — undulating ridges of extended platforms between the valleys. Precipitation from the hamads flows down as if from a pitched roof into the valleys, carrying with it large amounts of stones and mud, which in the closed-off depressions can cause destructive floods.

The climate of the Sahara has been that of a desert throughout almost every age. Only in the recent ice ages did the Sahara have a moist climate, and the desert at that time existed only in small areas. This is how Mediterranean plants and animals from the north were able to mix with Sudanese fauna and flora to the south. To this day the Southern Freshwater Catfish (*Clarias lazera*) lives in several rivers in the northern part of the Sahara, and in the same region lives the Egyptian Cobra (*Naja haje*). During the ice ages, crocodiles lived even at the foot of the Tibesti and Ahaggar Mountains. The Sahara has only a few small areas with water — oases, rivers, lakes. Several small rivers have their sources in the Atlas and flow until their water is lost in the sand of the desert. Oases always have water, either from outflowing sources or from wells. Water is strictly managed in oases and its use is usually subject to law. In the majority of oases the original shrubby vegetation has been replaced by useful date palms and fruit trees, and even grain is cultivated here and there. Saharan wildlife may be divided into those species which can only exist close to water and those which can survive in the open desert. Even out there, where it does not rain for several years at a time, it is possible to find at least bacteria and fungi. In isolated dry regions lives the 20-centimetre long burrowing lizard called the Common Skink (*Scincus scincus*), which was well known in Europe even in the Middle Ages (it was believed that its meat was medicinal). The inhabitants of the oases hunt this skink, skin it and dry the meat. They then grind the dried meat into a powder which they mix with date jam, and sell this delicacy to passing camel caravans.

All animals are either directly or indirectly dependent upon plants. Plants in the desert must not only accommodate to lack of water, but they must also protect themselves against animals which are desperately hungry and craving water. It is quite amazing how these problems are resolved. Desert rain showers are heavy, but seldom. Part of the water collects in pools, the remainder sinking deep into the sand and mud. In such places tall trees and smaller perennial plants can grow. Where there is underground water, large acacias grow and African Palm Trees (*Hyphaene thebaica*) may also be found, as well as low shrub vegetation. These, however, are not true desert plants. The latter must retain water in their fibrous tissue.

Two ways in which grass vegetation can spread: a) by means of horizontal surface roots, which put small roots into the ground; and b) by means of underground connecting roots, out of which grow grass stalks above the ground.

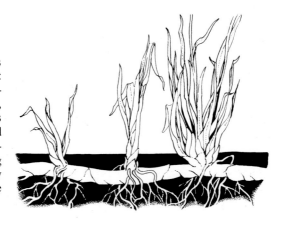

They achieve this by storing water in underground corms or in roots, or by reducing evaporation by having a waxy coating or a hairy, thorny or wrinkled surface, or by growing close to the surface of the ground so that they are not dried out by the wind. Mainly, however, they have an enormous root system stretching for many metres. In the hamads of the southern Atlas lives a remarkable plant called the Anabasia (*Anabasis arctyoides*). This forms pale green cushions similar to moss, but which are as hard as stone. Little greyish green stars on the surface serve the function of leaves. Drifting sand falls into the gaps among the little stars and in time the grains are absorbed by the plant. These particles bring about its hardness and resilience.

Animals have the same survival problems. Erg forms a better environment than either reg or hamad, mainly because erg is soft and animals can dig themselves in quickly and easily. Some animals such as the Fennec Fox (*Fennecus zerda*), and Sand Fox (*Vulpus rueppelli*), or the Egyptian Jerboa (*Jaculus jaculus*), live mainly in erg, where they are able to dig holes for themselves.

Interestingly there are frogs and toads in the desert, but they spend only a small proportion of their lives in water. When pools form during showers the water is often swarming with toads within hours. Their growth is much faster than elsewhere, the tadpoles losing their tails and becoming adults before the pool dries up. They then dig themselves into the ground or crawl in-

When crossing the Nile, camels protect herdsmen from the large Nile Crocodile. Crocodiles would never attack such a large herd.

to crevices between stones. In this way they avoid the burning heat of the sun, breathing slowly and sleeping for much of the time. They can lose incredible amounts of water — up to 60 per cent — without dying. As soon as it begins to rain they revive and lay their spawn.

Those animals best adapted for life in the desert are reptiles which mostly hunt insects and small vertebrates. Their prey is their source of water, and they are able to retain moisture longer than warm-blooded animals, since they have a dry skin covered with scales and do not perspire. The main problem facing these reptiles is not to be eaten themselves, because they are hunted by raptors (birds of prey). Birds and larger mammals solve the problem of survival in the desert by means of their greater mobility. They travel to find water. Even so, only rarely in the Sahara do you encounter truly desert animals — the Dorcas Gazelle (*Gazella dorcas*) and Loder's or Rhim Gazelle (*Gazella leptoceros*). On the southern edges of the Sahara the Dama Gazelle (*Gazella dama*) sometimes appears.

Some birds fly enormous distances for water. The Chestnut-bellied Sand Grouse (*Pterocles exustus*) in particular needs water quite regularly. When drinking, it stands in the water and dips its plumage as far as the lower part of the body. I once observed a Sand Grouse soaking its

The Imperial Eagle is dark brown, has two large white spots on its shoulders and a shortish tail finished with a narrow darker band. The young are light-coloured with yellow-brown plumage speckled with brown.

The Crowned Eagle remains faithful to its nesting place, returning there even if the tree and the nest have been knocked down or destroyed by fire.

plumage and offering the drops to its young, so that they could drink. The birds which can live farthest away from water are two species of lark, the Hoopoe (*Alaemon alaudipes*) and the Desert Lark (*Ammomanes deserti*). The Hoopoe, about 23 centimetres long, is an excellent runner. It feeds predominantly on beetle larvae, which it can dig out of the sand with its beak from depths of five centimetres or more. How it manages to find a larva cannot be explained, but it must know where they are because it hardly ever sticks its beak into the sand without finding one. The sand-coloured Desert Lark is smaller and is an inquisitive bird, unafraid of people.

Large animals are mobile and can travel far in search of water, but they are not able to dig themselves into the sand. The most noteworthy is the Addax (*Addax nasomaculatus*), which lives in small herds right in the middle of erg desert. It is approximately the same size as a donkey and has unusually large hooves which enable it to run well in the shifting sand. It has been hunted to extinction in the northern part of the Sahara, but still lives wild in small numbers scattered between the Rio de Oro and Sudan. The African Wild Ass (*Equus africanus*) also lives there in small numbers; it is the predecessor of the domestic donkey. On the southern slopes of the Atlas, in Tibesti, Ahaggar and Air, the Barbary Sheep (*Ammotragus lervia*) is found. This is a timid mountain animal which can only be observed with great difficulty. During the day it hides in rocky clefts and shady caves, coming out to graze only at night. The natives assert that if pursued it is able to dive headlong from the rocks, land on its head and horns without injury of any kind, and then make its escape.

CIVET PREDATORS

The first description of the African Civet (*Viverra civetta*) was by the famous Renaissance scholar Alpinus, who visited Cairo in 1580. The typical civet is similar to a large cat. It has an elongated head, short legs, and differs chiefly from cats in the possession of an anal musk gland. This secretes a scented substance known as 'civet' which is used in cosmetics. The civet marks out its hunting ground with its scent, which tells other civets: 'Warning! Do not enter here, or there will be trouble!' In Ethiopia and Egypt civets have been kept for centuries as domestic animals. The scent is removed by fastening the animal to the bar of its cage and pressing the secretion out of the gland into a prepared container. At first it is a white mucous substance, but later it turns brown and loses its musky scent to a certain extent. Each animal produces up to 20 grammes of civet scent a week. Civets live on small mammals, birds, frogs, insects and worms, but will also eat fruit. Occasionally they may attack a small, young antelope. In order to produce the civet secretion abundantly they must be fed on a predominance of meat.

The Spotted Genet (*Genetta genetta*) is found from the Cape region as far as the North African coast, and even in Spain and France. It hunts at night, stealing from one thicket to the next, following scents, listening carefully and ready to jump out at any small animal that breaks the silence. This genet moves easily, elegantly and noiselessly, its body extended in a straight line, its legs placed wide apart. When it jumps on its prey, it strangles and eats it on the spot. In Africa there are nine species of genet, all of which can easily be tamed. This animal mates twice a year, in March and August. During mating both male and female make mewing noises. The young are born after a period of 12 weeks' gestation.

The Egyptian Mongoose (*Herpestes ichneumon*), one of the many mongoose species, is a small but courageous animal. The earliest illustrations of this mongoose come from the early Empires in Egypt (2800—2150 BC), on the walls of tombs in Thebes and Sakkar. Its method of fighting snakes has given rise to many fables. Even the Greek philosopher Aristotle wrote about these battles. The term *ichneumon* means 'tracker', and the animal was named on account of its truly excellent sense of smell. It hunts during the day and will devour any animal it is capable of overpowering. It hunts lizards, insects, birds up to the size of a duck and mammals up to the size of a hare.

I once observed a fight between an Egyptian Mongoose and a large poisonous snake. The almost black cobra slithered out of a pile of cut thorny branches and the mongoose, which was crawling out of a stream, bumped into it . They saw each other at almost the same instant. The cobra raised itself and gave out a warning hiss; the mongose, immobile, watched with its head lowered and extended. The cobra made a strike and the mongoose raised itself and backed off a little. It approached the cobra again. The cobra tried another strike and the mongoose provoked it in this way several times. Then, all of a sudden, the mongoose itself attacked like lightning. It leapt forward, jumping high into the air. The cobra twisted away to defend itself, but not once was it able to bite the mongoose. The snake was beginning to tire and lowered its head, at which point the mongoose dived in and bit the cobra on the nape, close to its head. The cobra curled up and thrashed with its tail, but the mongoose did not let go. The snake's writhing gradually stopped and it remained completely motionless. Even now the mongoose remained cautious. It released the snake, retreated a short distance and then it bit it once again. Only when the cobra no longer moved did it begin to eat contentedly.

When the Banded Mongoose (*Mungos mungo*) wants to frighten its adversary it adopts a menacing posture by turning its back on its opponent, swinging the rear part of its body on

The Scimitar-horned Oryx is a beautiful sandy-white Saharan antelope, with its transversely-notched horns curved into an arch on both males and females. These antelopes are popular in zoos since, among themselves, they are not as aggressive as other oryxes and they are modest, unfussy about food and good breeders in captivity.

The Berber Lion has been hunted to extinction in the Atlas countries. Those kept in captivity come from the renowned Moroccan lion houses. They are a large variety with long gold and black manes, often extending as far as the abdomen and rear legs.

fully extended legs, lowering its head and stamping its hind feet powerfully. Banded Mongeese are very gregarious animals. They settle in whole groups in abandoned termite mounds, holes and various little caves. They also hunt in groups, preying on snakes, lizards, worms, snails, mice and frogs. These creatures are easy to tame and for this reason they are often kept in workshops and storehouses, where they get rid of pests.

MONITORS

The ancient Greek historian Herodotus called the Desert Monitor (*Varanus griseus*) the 'dry-land crocodile', and the ancient Egyptians often depicted and perhaps even venerated the Nile Monitor (*Varanus niloticus*). As a group, monitor lizards have long bodies and tails, and their well-developed limbs are equipped with small rounded scales which are arched and surrounded by a circle of fine granular scales. These lizards can move quickly, being able to catch small mammals and running birds, and are also able to swim well and dive. Protracted stays under water are made possible by means of two large cavities inside the upper part of the nose; these are filled with air and are connected to the nostrils, which can be closed by means of their mobile edges.

Monitors plunder the nests of birds and crocodiles; they also hunt other lizards, snakes, birds up to the size of a crow, mice, rats and fish, and will even devour carrion which is already decaying. These reptiles are not able to bite their food: their sharp teeth serve only to catch and hold their prey. The food itself they gulp and swallow whole.

Desert Monitors live in the driest regions of North Africa and like to hunt on the sandy plains among rocky heights. Nile Monitors live near almost all African rivers and lakes. They have their dens in the exposed roots of riverside trees, or else they settle in abandoned termite nests. Monitors defend themselves against their adversaries by turning to one side, swinging their tails, hissing and trying to jump on the enemy. The females of some species lay as many as 50 eggs, which they bury in the ground. Monitor eggs are regarded as a delicacy by some people, and differ from birds' eggs in that the albumen (white) does not coagulate when heated.

A diagram of the feeding relationships between African animals.

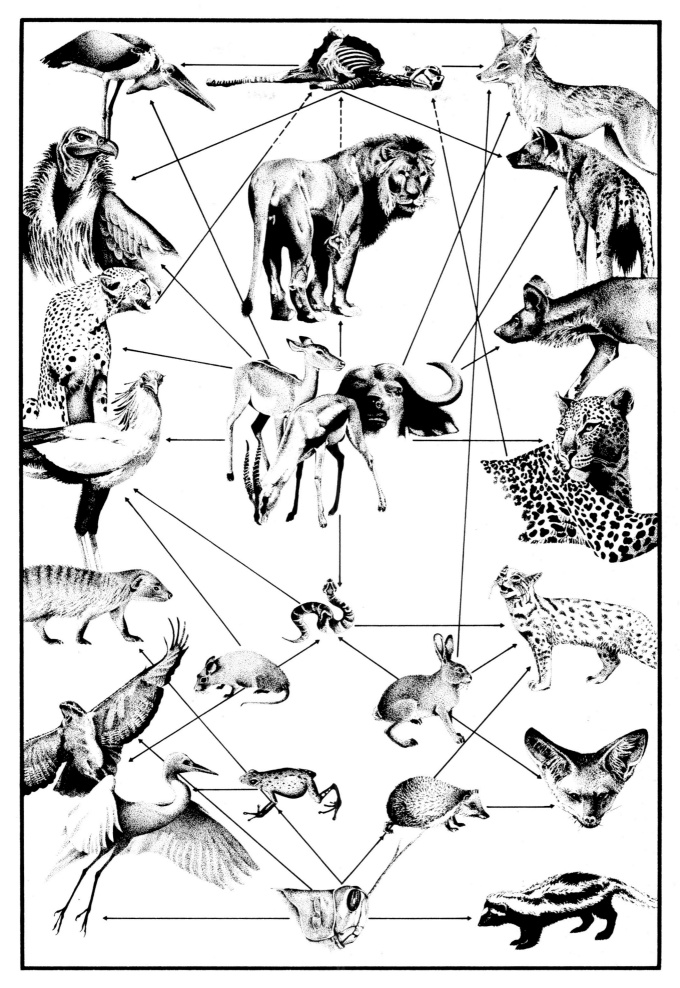

CAMELS

An Arab requires three things from a good Dromedary (single-humped) Camel (*Camelus dromedarius*): it must have a soft back, should be able to run without needing to be spurred on by the whip, and should not be noisy when getting up. A first ride on a camel is an unnerving experience. When the camel is walking the rider is thrown about in upward curving movements, forwards and backwards, and is at the same time pitched and tossed to the sides. As soon as the camel begins to trot, however, this swinging stops, and if the rider leans against the high seat the jolting is no worse than when riding a horse.

The voice of a camel is scarcely possible to describe, being an unearthly mixture of groaning, grunting, whining and roaring. A camel can frequently be stubborn to the point of driving an inexperienced rider to despair. This is appreciated to the full extent only when the rider has been thrown, walked over, spat at and left in the desert by his camel, after it has been disobedient day in and day out until it has completely exhausted his patience. In addition to all this, one must take into account the camel's unique smell; compared to it, the odour of a male goat is a pleasant fragrance . . .

Camels are amblers. A trained riding camel can cover up to 140 kilometres each day; a pack animal with a load of 150 kilogrammes can travel at the most 50 kilometres in a day. Camel's milk is thick and fatty and the meat of young camels is regarded as a delicacy. Even camel dung is valued in the desert, being dried and used as fuel. This amazing desert creature can last a week without water. In the sun it begins to sweat only when its body temperature reaches 40 °C. The secret of the camel's ability to last for such a long time without water, compared to a human being, lies in the water content of the blood. Humans and camels have in their blood approximately one-twelfth of all the water contained in the body. If a camel loses, through breathing and sweating, a quarter of its own weight, the water content of the blood reduces by only one tenth. The blood therefore remains at almost the same concentration as before. In the same situation a human would lose one-third of the water from his blood, which becomes so thick that it is able to flow through the body only with difficulty. It is also unable to dissipate the rising temperature of the inner body to the skin, with the result that the internal temperature rises and the person dies of heatstroke. A thirsty camel which has not drunk for several days is

able to consume one-quarter of its own weight in water at one session.

EAGLES

Eagles are large, robust, broad-breasted birds. Their musculature indicates that they are excellent fliers. All eagles have one characteristic feature: a strong beak, with the upper mandible extending over the lower one, and its sharp edge bent into a hook at the end. The beak looks somewhat compressed when viewed from the side, and is always taller than it is wide. These raptors live on other wild animals, which

they hunt either on the wing with a direct attack from above or by surprising the prey with a low flight, and in fact not hesitating even to take a victim on the ground. There are specialist eagles, some of which hunt fish, others snakes or monkeys.

The construction of the eagle's foot is to a certain extent adapted for hunting. The foot is equipped with four large talons, usually the most powerful on the first and second toes, and hollow underneath, so that the sharp edges protrude over the sides. In this way the foot can be an invaluable tool for catching and killing prey. Sometimes eagles kill their victims with their beaks, occasionally beating them on the ground.

In the Sahara the annual average rainfall is less than 50 millimetres, and in some places there is no rain at all for several years. Life concentrates around the oases that have artesian wells. Saharan vegetation, which favours both dry and salty conditions, occurs only sporadically.

Eagles which are predominantly fish-hunters have a sharp horn-like protrusion on the lower part of the toes which enables them to grip the fish in their claws and tear at it with their beaks. Birds are often plucked before being devoured.

The food first enters the crop, where it is partially digested. From the crop it is carried to the stomach, which has two parts. The first is a thin-walled, glandular section and the second,

The purple blossoms of the Scrophulariaceae family, which have grown here among a thorny acacia bush and are protected by it.

squirrel or dove, it flies like an arrow through the thick shrubs and catches the victim in its claws.

The Crowned Eagle (*Stephanoaetus coronatus*) hunts mainly monkeys, particularly vervets, in the tropical rain forests. It keeps watch, motionless in the crown of a tree. As soon as the eagle spots its prey it swoops down from above, digs its talons into the head and chest, kills the monkey and quickly eats it.

The Martial Eagle (*Polemaetus bellicosus*) is the strongest African eagle. It defends its territory scrupulously, driving all other eagles away. This species mostly prefers to hunt in the mornings and evenings, its prey consisting of hares, jungle fowl and small antelopes.

The Booted Eagle (*Hieraaetus pennatus*) spends the summer in Europe or Asia, flying to Africa for the winter. It is a skilful aerobat. It likes to sit in the crown of a tree, preferring dry forests, both on the plains and in the mountains. It defends its hunting ground courageously and takes birds up to the size of a pigeon and

at the rear, is a strong, muscular stomach, which is situated close to the body's centre of gravity. Like all birds eagles have no teeth, so that the food is ground up in the muscular stomach. The large intestine is short and without a rectum. After a certain period of time undigested remains, such as feathers, hair and bones, are regurgitated in the form of cone-shaped 'pellets'. It is possible, by means of analysing the contents of pellets, to determine what the eagle lives on.

Are eagles harmful or useful creatures? Taking into consideration the relations between living creatures in their own natural habitats, it is never possible to divide them into harmful or useful categories. Eagles are neither bloodthirsty nor cruel. Instinctively, they hunt predominantly sick or otherwise vulnerable animals. Even the look of its eyes is not cruel, although it may seem so to us because of the protruding bone on the upper edge of the eye socket, which forms a strange hood over the eye. The eagle, which has been called the king of birds, is moreover no more fearless than other, often much smaller, birds of prey.

The Long-crested Hawk Eagle (*Lophoaetus occipitalis*) has a striking crest on its head. It does not like dry places and prefers to live in forests near lakes and rivers. It sits quietly in the tree-top, shaking and spreading the feathers of its crest and looking absent-minded. As soon as it spots something to eat, such as a mouse,

A Long-crested Hawk Eagle regularly visited our Nabiswa camp in the Karamoja region of Uganda. It would sit on a tall tree and watch camp life for hours at a time. When we brought back and skinned a hunted antelope many vultures, Marabou Storks and kites would gather on the remains. The eagle, however, would remain aloof; it never ate this carrion.

mammals as big as a rabbit. This eagle often flies low over the ground and also likes to sit in the middle of a small meadow, where it can catch grasshoppers and mice. It uses the nests of another bird, most often a kite, which it drives away mercilessly before rearing its own young.

The Golden Eagle *(Aquila chrysaetos)* lives on rocky steppes and the dry rocky mountains of North Africa, as well as in the mountainous and forested regions of Europe, Asia and North America. It hunts largish animals up to the size of a fox. Burying its talons into the head and back of its prey, this huge bird then beats its victim to death with powerful pecking movements. It partly plucks a bird before eating warily, looking around constantly as it discards the entire intestines, beak and sometimes even the legs of its food. This species builds a nest on an inaccessible rocky promontory usually covered with shelter. In the lowlands it may make its nest in a large old tree. A pair frequently use the same nest for several years, progressively enlarging it. Young eagles look like downy round balls. From the beginning the parents feed them with partly digested food from their crop, later giving them prey which has been torn into pieces. When the young are able to move safely about the nest they are given the prey whole and learn to tear it up themselves. In some areas the Golden Eagle can be kept and trained for hunting.

The Imperial Eagle (*Aquila heliaca*) is slightly smaller than the Golden Eagle. It inhabits open country in Morocco, where leafy forests alternate with grasslands on the extensive plains. It

builds large untidy nests in the crowns of high dense trees, and hunts in a similar manner to the Golden Eagle. It too is easy to tame.

The African Fish Eagle (*Haliaetus vocifer*) ranges across almost the whole of Africa south of the Sahara along rivers, by lakes and on the coastline. It lives predominantly on fish, although it also hunts birds, mammals, amphibians and reptiles, and will not refuse carrion. It calls with a beautiful, clear, bell-like voice. African Fish Eagles often rest in pairs in tree crowns, greeting every eagle that flies nearby with a call, during which they raise their heads backwards and spread their tails.

The Bateleur Eagle (*Therathopius ecaudatus*) is also widespread south of the Sahara throughout almost the whole of Africa. It has a thickset body, short neck and large head with a small beard. In flight it looks as if it has no tail at all, hence its Latin name *ecaudatus* — tail-less. The natives revere this eagle and tell many fables and tales about it. An excellent flier and aerobat, it sails through the air and dashes to and fro, playing, looping the loop, falling like a stone or flitting like a butterfly. It catches mainly snakes and lizards.

A large flock of Tree Ducks (*Dendrocygna viduata*), the most common duck of the southern Sahara area, on one of the many ponds of the Lake Chad water system.

THE SILENT VOLCANOES
The Ethiopian highlands

Africa does not have large mountain ranges such as, for example, the Alps or the Himalayas. But in East Africa, in particular, there are solitary large mountains of volcanic origin, connected to extensive, considerably lower upland plains. The most extensive and interesting highlands in Africa are in Ethiopia. This massif stands like an island between the broad belts of vegetation running across Africa from west to east. The highlands are divided by the Great Trench Depression (Rift Valley). The mountain ridges are separated from one another by long strips of undulating landscape, the upland plateaux lacerated by ravines and large rivers. Some of the mountain ranges, in Semien for example, are so isolated from the others that different species of the same type of animal live on them.

This forbidding landscape is affected by moist winds blowing fresh from the Indian Ocean. The climate is considerable damper than that of neighbouring countries. On the highest summits there is sometimes snow. The alluvial soil in the Nile basin and Nile delta, which made Egyptian civilization possible, is the result of erosion on the slopes of the Ethiopian volcanoes. At the present time the human population is causing this erosion to proceed apace and, within a few years, only bare rocks will remain.

Water has cut through the upland plateaux, forming numerous abysses and canyons. The Blue Nile flows through the largest of these passes. It has its source in the Damot Mountains, flows through Lake Tana and creates one of the most magnificent waterfalls in Africa at the lake's outflow. The Blue Nile canyon is over 1,000 kilometres long and approximately 2,400 metres deep. Large troops of Gelada Baboons live on the plateaux up to heights of 4,000 metres, along with the little-known Abyssinian Jackal, (*Simenia simensis*), a most interesting hunter of small animals, mainly rats, which are abundant everywhere. On the rocks live Abyssinian Mountain Ibex or Walia Ibex

The timid Abyssinian Jackal is a swift hunter of small animals. Its main diet consists of rats and small rodents, although it occasionally eats various berries.

The Walia Ibex or Abyssinian Mountain Ibex is a highly-gifted climber and jumper. It is able to open its small hooves up to three times their normal width, so that it can walk over the steep rocks safely in any direction. It is threatened with extinction.

The Green Monkey is easily recognized by the long white whiskers that frame its face. It lives in Sudan and Ethiopia.

Large numbers are exported every year to America and Europe, where they are used for laboratory experiments.

(*Capra ibex wallie*), very timid animals which feed by biting off pieces of heather. A common bird in the region is the Thick-billed Raven (*Corvus crassirostris*) which lives around mountain villages. In the Ball Mountains lives the rare Mountain Nyala (*Tragelaphus buxtoni*), a magnificent but timid antelope which does not occur anywhere else in the world. In these mountains it either rains or hails every day for eight months of the year and waterbirds are plentiful. In the marshes live the Widgeon (*Anas penelope*), the Egyptian Goose (*Alopochen aegyptiacus*) and the timid Wattled Crane (*Bugeranus carunculatus*).

BABOONS

Mrs Aston, the owner of a farm in Namibia, had the idea of using the Black-footed Chacma Baboon (*Papio cynocephalus*) to look after her goats. She shut a few young females in an enclosure with the goats so that they could get used to one another. After a few days the baboons were accompanying the goats to pasture without any difficulty. They kept the herd of goats together and in the evening drove them into the enclosure in a close group. One morning Ahla, a female baboon, ran away from the pasture with a loud cry and returned to the enclosure. The person who milked the goats had in fact left two kids behind, and Ahla took them to the

In the south of the Ethiopian highlands, on the border between Kenya and Somalia, lives the Somali Lion (*Panthera leo somaliensis*). It has a sparse flaxen mane, changing colour to a collar of darker, even black hair. Lions living in the wild never have such large manes as those kept in zoos, since the hairs are regularly torn off as they hunt in dense bush country.

The Drill lives in dense forests. A tame young male guarded our camp better than a good dog. It would sit fastened by a small chain to the gates and pretend to be sleeping, but in fact watched everything out of the corner of its eye. If a stranger approached it would dash forwards unexpectedly, terrifying him.

The Mandrill is a favourite in zoos due to its beautiful colouring. Adult males punish lower-placed individuals harshly, even injuring them severely. For this reason they need a large run with hiding places for the subordinate animals.

The Gelada Baboon lives in the alpine belt around Lake Tana in Ethiopia. The social group consists of between 300 and 400 members in times of sufficient food, splitting in times of shortage into smaller groups led by one adult male.

others in the pasture. When the herd returned home in the evening, Ahla would select about 20 kids in a group, one after the other, carefully take them to their bleating and waiting mothers, and place them right by the udder. She knew exactly which kid belonged to which goat. The baboons managed all this without being taught, simply by working according to their own social troop instinct.

Baboons live in good numbers in the majority of African states, in savannah, bush and rocky mountainous country. In some places they can be a real menace to fields and plantations, but this is partly attributable to the fact that people have shot their natural enemies, mainly leopards.

Baboons spend the whole of their lives in troops of between 40 and 60, in which they feel safe. The troop is a strictly organized society of

The Anubis Baboon inhabits a large region from the upper waters of the River Senegal, in the west of Africa, as far as Ethiopia and the Great African Depression from Lake Victoria to Lake Tanganyika. The typical baboon eye ridges are lacking and the nostrils extend beyond the front edge of the nose. The tail looks as if it has been broken, hanging down at right angles.

What the Lion eats.

individuals with graded hierarchical positions. Baboons have exceptionally gregarious dispositions. When the troop is on the march weaker males form the vanguard; behind them go young adults and old females; females with young are in the centre, surrounded by strong males who have an important position in the troop. An enemy approaching from any side always meets adult males, who can defend the troop fiercely and in an organized fashion. Smaller families form within the baboon troop, consisting of a male and several females with young. The members of these families take great care of one another, the sign of this being mutual coat grooming.

Apart from pregnancy and suckling, female baboons can conceive during one week in each month. At first they mate with younger males, later moving on to stronger superior males. These 'loving couples' usually go to the edge of the troop, where they may spend a few hours together, or occasionally even several days. A male never claims a right over a female for long and does not pair with more than one female at a time. The daily timetable of the troop consists of feeding, games, mutual grooming, a doze at noon, courting and mating, occasional conflicts and squabbles, more feeding, and at dusk the return to a suitable rock or large tree where they all spend the night.

The Hamadryas Baboon (*Papio hamadryas*) used to be venerated by the ancient Egyptians as the guide of the god Thoth. It ranges from Port Sudan in Ethiopia to approximately 8° latitude north, and west as far as Lake Tana and the valley of the River Awash. It is distinguished from other baboon species by its red face and fair, nearly pearl grey coat. Of all baboons it has the longest and most conspicuous mane, on the front half of the body. It ranks among the smaller baboons, males reaching a weight of 20 to 30 kilogrammes. The Guinea Baboon (*Papio papio*) lives in West Africa. It has a black face and the coat is brown to reddish brown, males having a longish mane on the front half of the body — less conspicuous, however, than that of the Hamadryas Baboon. From the upper stream of the Senegal River as far as Ethiopia and Kenya, and along both sides of Lake Victoria as far as Lake Tanganika, lives the olive-coloured Anubis Baboon (*Papio anubis*). An adult male can weigh up to 45 kilogrammes. They differ from other baboons in their head profile, which lacks a noticeable protuberance on the forehead, and in their nostrils, which extend over the upper lip. South and east of the territory inhabited by the Anubis Baboon lives the Yellow Baboon (like the Chacma Baboon, a race of *Papio cynocephalus*). It is slender, does not have the typically 'broken' tail, and bears a yellowish brown coat on its back, the lower part of the body being whitish. It prefers bush country to open savannah, ranging from Angola across southern Zaire, Malawi, Tanzania and northern Mozambique, along the east coast of Africa and across Kenya as far as Somalia.

In mountainous regions as far as the alpine belt of Ethiopia lives the chocolate-brown Gelada Baboon (*Theropithecus gelada*). This has grey on the cheeks, males possessing long manes and a red patch of bald skin on the chest bordered by white, bead-shaped swellings which turn pink in the mating season.

In the West African forests dwells the Mandrill (*Mandrillus sphinx*), which differs from all other monkeys with its fantastically coloured face and colourful spots on the rump. The middle of the face and the nose are crimson, the lengthwise grooves along the sides of the muzzle are cobalt blue, the ears pink with whitish spots behind, and the orange beard on the face turns to white on the chin. The Mandrill's coat on the body is dark greenish brown, the lower part of the body being pale to white. Mandrills range from the Sanaga River in Cameroun south as far as Gabon. They are omnivorous, moving predominantly on the ground in forest areas and sleeping in tall trees at night. From the Sanaga River as far as the Cross River in

The Sacred or Hamadryas Baboons maintain a strict hierarchy even in captivity; in the confined space of the baboon house it is often intensified. When food is put down the males with the highest positions eat first, while the others take pieces of food surreptitiously and quickly stuff them into their cheek pouches. Only when the dominant animals finish eating do the others consume what is left. Then they move aside and eat the reserves in their cheek pouches.

The Anubis Baboon has a remarkable ability to seek out water, finding it in places where people would not think of looking. It is able to dig down to a spring very dexterously. The mother carries the smallest young under her abdomen, the older ones on her back.

39

A Hamadryas Baboon expresses threat by showing its teeth, baring its large canines.

Nigeria lives the Drill (*Mandrillus leucophaeus*). Somewhat smaller than the Mandrill, this monkey has a short black muzzle which is bordered by greyish white, the lower lip being edged by red. It has exceptionally coloured hind quarters. Drills live in a similar manner to Mandrills.

GAZELLES

Gazelles are among the most elegant animals in all Africa. Both males and females are horned in the African species, and most have a lengthwise dark stripe along the flanks which serves as camouflage at twilight and when on the move. This conspicuous contrasting pattern has additional significance for signalling and for mutual recognition of the same species. Gazelles often fall prey to lions, leopards, hyaenas, cheetahs and African wild dogs, their young being hunted by jackals, eagles and vultures. Apart from their protective colouring, however, gazelles are equipped with other defensive features: they are very fast, and have excellent senses of smell, hearing and sight which enable them to recognize moving objects at great distances.

Thomson's Gazelle (*Gazella thomsoni*) is smaller, darker and more thickset than Grant's Gazelle (*Gazella granti*). The males have sturdi-

Organization of a baboon troop on the march and during an attack by a predator.

Anubis Baboons gather food in strictly organized troops, which ensure their safety. Large males weighing 40 kilogrammes protect females and young.

er and longer horns than females. Both sexes of Thomson's Gazelle have the conspicuous black stripe along the flanks, whereas among the Grant's species only females have this stripe. Both species often graze together in the rainy season. In times of drought and scarcity, Grant's Gazelles have little difficulty in surviving as they need hardly any water and are content with dry grass and any foliage they can reach. Thomson's Gazelles have a lower tolerance to drought, needing water regularly and also being unable to make do without fresh grass. For this reason, every Thomson's male tries to obtain a patch of grassy pasture for itself, which it then guards as its territory. This is very important, since gazelle females will only mate with males who have successfully fought for and obtained their own territory. Males try to attract females to their territory and encourage them to stay. The owners of territories are in a minority, however, and the other, usually younger and weaker males form themselves into small all-male groups. Occasionally these also try to obtain females, but because they do not own territories where they could mate, this courting is not successful.

Males mark their territories with scent markers. They urinate or defecate in conspicuous places, or use their suborbital glands, which excrete a strong-smelling substance, marking out their territory by rubbing against trees and bushes at its boundaries. Other males are warned in this way that the territory is already occupied.

The savannah is divided into a whole network of 'wedding' territories. In fact the males hardly have time for anything apart from guarding their territories and females. They are constantly on the move, reminiscent of shepherd dogs guarding a grazing herd.

During a fight over territory Thomson's Gazelles approach each other cautiously with their heads lowered and their horns pointing forwards, each hoping to gain victory without a serious conflict. This manoeuvre, however, is generally ineffective. The adversaries then ram each other's heads and circle round, each trying to catch the other unawares and attack, thus forcing him to flee.

Grant's Gazelles prefer a demonstration of strength to a real fight, as males have usually been acquainted for a long time and know in

The Guereza or White-mantled Colobus is probably the most beautiful of all monkeys. It lives in undisturbed forest along rivers, from the western borders of Zaire across Uganda and Kenya, as far as Ethiopia. A family troop consists of between five and 20 individuals. During the last century Guerezas were massacred in large numbers for their fur. Even as late as 1961, 26,000 pelts were taken from Ethiopia. Today they are very rare, and are strictly protected almost everywhere.

Examples of co-existence in nature:

a) In the digestive system of termites, bacteria assist in breaking down cellulose;

b) An elephant sinks a water hollow into a dried-out river bed, from which other animals also drink;

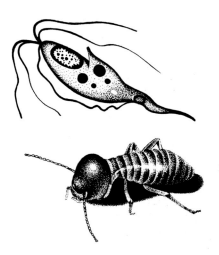

c) Acacias provide ants with accommodation, whilst the ants protect the acacias from too many browsing animals;

d) Oxpeckers attend to the hides of large animals, cleaning them and ridding them of parasites. By their sudden take-off and squawking they also signal the approach of danger;

advance which of them is stronger. They adopt fighting postures and stand a few paces apart, looking threateningly into each other's eyes and shaking their heads menacingly. If this behaviour fails, they move closer to each other and circle around, stopping from time to time to scratch their heads with their rear legs, snatch a tuft of grass, rush at a bush with their horns,

or urinate. All this is done to relieve the tension which has been created. If this tension continues to build, there is no alternative but to start a fight. The opponents move their heads up and down with their ears raised and lock their horns together, trying to twist the adversary's neck. The fight usually ends with the retreat of the weaker rival.

e) Antelope eat tree fruits and nuts. After the hard seed husks have passed through their digestive system they are slightly damaged and so able to germinate:

f) Herons hunt insects around large animals and, by means of sudden take-off, warn the animals of danger.

The Mountain Nyala is threatened with extinction. Only exceptionally has it been kept in zoos.

The Bushbuck is partial to the leaves of shrubs and low young trees. In order to ensure a year-round food supply in captivity we cut the shoots of leafy woody plants, press them into net bags and freeze them.

Grant's and Thomson's Gazelles have similar habits during courtship and mating. The female at first tries to flee, and adopts a posture which makes it impossible for a male to approach her. These overtures can last up to several days. Finally the female allows the male to sniff and lick her, although she retreats constantly, often kicking at the male with her hind legs. At last she stops, raises her tail, gently lowers her head and slightly arches her back, which is the signal for the male to start mating. A pregnant female remains in the herd almost until the time of delivery. Just before this takes place she leaves the herd, settles alone in a quiet corner and there gives birth to one, sometimes two, young. For the first couple of days the mother licks up the

Various herbivores graze on grass of differing heights. From the left: zebras, wildebeest, antelope, hartebeest.

Speke's Gazelle, the smallest African gazelle, ranges from the Sahara to Somalia.

The Dama Gazelle is almost snow-white in colour with a fine sandy tinge on the back and neck. When it lies down to rest on the Saharan sand it is almost invisible.

excrement of the young so as to remove traces of scent which could attract predators. The young are exposed to the greatest danger during the first few days of life because they have not yet developed their protective flight instinct, nor do they have the strength to run. Dama Gazelles live in deserts, being rare inhabitants of the Sahara. Of the five sub-species, two have already been hunted to extinction and the others are in the same danger. These gazelles can cover large distances, in the rainy season deep into the heart of the Sahara, in the dry season back to Sudan. They usually live in small groups of 10 to 30; in the rainy season they may form herds numbering several hundred.

Soemmering's Gazelles (*Gazella soemmeringi*) have so far survived in Sudan and Ethiopia. They live in grassy bush country in groups of between five and 15. Males form their own separate territories and are very aggressive during the mating season. Mating proceeds in the same way as with all other gazelles — while walking,

How plants withstand grazing. In the East African savannah, Couch Grass is a favourite food of many herbivores. This durable vegetation, often only 10 centimetres high, grows better after being bitten off close to the ground. Grazing animals eat everything except the leaves which are spread flat on the ground, these being enough to keep the plant alive until it quickly grows again. The buds bearing the new stalks and flower heads also lie on the ground, or even below the surface, where they are protected from animals.

Spotted Hyaenas live in large family clans of up to 20 animals. The coat colour is highly variable: some animals are almost brownish-black, while others are silver-grey or light yellow-brown.

The Brown Hyaena differs from other hyaenas on account of the abundant back mane which hangs down over its flanks. It is much rarer than the Spotted or Striped Hyaenas.

both partners hold their heads raised and the male grips his partner firmly with his front legs.

The Dorcas Gazelle has been known in Europe since ancient times. It was often praised by Oriental poets and even mentioned in Solomon's Song of Songs. Apart from predators its greatest enemy is the human. Closely related to the Dorcas Gazelle is Speke's Gazelle (*Gazella spekei*). On the ridge of the nose older males have transversely wrinkled skin. At a warning cry that resembles a shot from a pistol the upper part of the nose is inflated to the size of a tennis ball, serving as a sound amplifier.

The Laughing (Spotted) Hyaena covers the entrance to her lair with her own body; her young are within. We disturbed this female just as she was on the edge of the small crater around her lair, feeding her three cubs.

How snakes catch frogs: a striped African Emerald Snake (*Gastropyxis smaragdina*) has caught a large frog on the trail behind our camp. The frog's head was larger than its own.

With an enormous effort the snake began to swallow the frog; it took 22 minutes. Only when, with twisting movements, it had the frog in the upper third of its body did the snake slowly slink away into the grass.

HYAENAS

It was formerly believed that hyaenas fed only on carrion. In the course of constant study and observation, however, it has been discovered that they are superb hunters. Indeed, they are often driven away from their own prey by lions. The Spotted Hyaena (*Crocuta crocuta*) can run at speeds of up to 65 kilometres per hour. When hunting it usually catches the pursued animal by the leg and holds on until the animal falls, after which it immediately tears open the abdomen. It will hunt everything from small antelope to wildebeest and zebra, and sometimes even attacks young rhino calves. During the mating season the male hyaena bows in front of the female, nearly touching the ground with his head and pawing the air with his front legs. Mating is protracted and sometimes repeated several times. A number of males court each female. She is won by the strongest male, who then drives off his rivals. Hyaenas can live for

as long as 40 years and are relatively easy to tame.

The Striped Hyaena (*Hyaena hyaena*) occurs only in North Africa, apart from the Sahara, but also inhabits a considerable part of South Asia. It was once believed that its fat was an excellent remedy for rheumatism, and that anyone who ate the heart of a hyaena would become courageous and fearless. The images of hyaenas can be found in ancient Egyptian paintings, and it is likely that the Egyptians trained them for hunting.

The Brown Hyaena (*Hyaena brunnea*) lives in southern Africa, preying on hares, small antelope, grasshoppers, dead fish washed up by the sea, and even eggs. It is distinguished from other hyaenas by a long mane, which hangs down on both sides. It is persecuted mercilessly by local inhabitants under the pretext that it threatens cattle. Its numbers are dwindling rapidly and it is in danger of extinction in some areas.

The Greater Kudu is the largest representative of the bush-buck, nyala and kudu group. Females kept in zoos are usually docile. Full-grown males, however, are often very aggressive and dangerous to humans. When a keeper enters the run a male threatens him by turning to one side in order to show the full surface of his large body, and moves closer. If the keeper does not withdraw, the male will attack. Males and females are very timid in the wild.

BUSHBUCK

Bushbuck (Tragelaphinae) males have magnificent spiralled horns, the females being hornless. All species have large white spots of varying sizes between the eyes and on their cheeks; along the sides of the body they have white stripes. They graze on grass and also eat tree and shrub foliage, and regularly go to watering places.

The Greater Kudu (*Tragelaphus strepsiceros*) assembles in herds numbering up to 40 individuals, in hill country, foothills and plains covered with shrubs. Adult males live in small groups which approach the main herd during the mating season. They are able to jump obsta-

cles up to two and a half metres high! Kudus graze early in the morning, in the evening and at night and their enemies are the larger predators, African wild dogs and humans. The male begins his courtship by standing sideways in the way of the female with his head raised high. The female tries to run away but the male pursues her persistently, at the same time making quiet whining noises. When he catches up he places his neck against her nape, standing to one side of her. The female then runs away again and the whole pattern repeats itself several times until the point of real mating is reached. Males can weigh up to 270 kilogrammes and can stand 150 centimetres high at the shoulder. The spirally twisted horns have three twists and may be 170 centimetres in length.

The Lesser Kudu (*Tragelaphus imberbis*) frequents dry, thorny bush country on the upper plains of East Africa. Small family groups usually consist of one male and several females with young. When resting they lie down in a star formation with their hind quarters towards the centre, so that they can see in all directions and be ready for danger. They also like to lie with their backs protected by thick shrubs or large trees. Males weigh up to 90 kilogrammes, being 105 centimetres high; their slender horns, placed closer together than on the Greater Kudu, can be up to 90 centimetres in length.

The Mountain Nyala occurs only in mountain valleys and on the Arusi plains south of Addis Ababa. These creatures are very cautious and lie down in shallow hollows with only their heads visible above ground level. As soon as they sense danger they jump up and disappear

In the Lowland Nyala the males are very dark with long black fur growing under the abdomen; females have neither this fur nor horns.

behind a hillock. They are somewhat smaller than Greater Kudu males, weighing up to 230 kilogrammes and with a shoulder height of 130 centimetres. The horns form only one twist and can be up to 110 centimetres in length.

The Lowland Nyala (*Tragelaphus angasi*) can be found in the lowlands and hill country of southern Africa. It lives in bush or denser forests where there is an adequate water supply. On its way to the watering place the herd marches one behind the other, an old experienced female leading the way, the procession generally being completed by a male. In their appearance, males differ considerably from the inconspicuous greyish-brown females, being dark brown with a fleece-like long coat hanging from the abdomen and extending from the neck to the rump. They also have the most conspicuous mane of all bushbuck, running along the neck and down the back as far as the tail. The weight of a male can be 130 kilogrammes, the height at the shoulders 110 centimetres, and the horns up to 90 centimetres long.

Of all bushbuck the Situtunga (*Tragelaphus spekei*) is best adapted to life in marshy country and water. On hard ground these creatures move ponderously and with great effort, but their unusually elongated and splayable hooves carry them safely over swampy terrain. Situtungas are excellent swimmers: in the day they often rest in swamps or in water and always flee

Every evening a solitary old Egyptian Vulture would come and sit on a wooden pole near our camp by Lake Tana in Ethiopia. In the daytime he would take the leftovers that we tossed on the rubbish heap.

The Situtunga is a common zoo species. After a number of generations in captivity, this species begins to develop uncharacteristic white spots on various parts of the body — a sign of domestication. In order to prevent this it is necessary to bring new males into the herd, ideally from the wild.

to water in danger, diving so deep that only their nostrils are visible. During courtship the male lays his head and back on the back of the female from behind, forcefully pressing her down towards the ground. The female responds by shaking her head around, symbolically butting her head forwards where there is in fact nothing to attack.

The Bushbuck (*Tragelaphus scriptus*), known to the Afrikaaners as the Bosbok, lives in a variety of habitats — forest, shrubs and sparser bush country, both on the plains and in mountains up to 4,000 metres. It is the smallest of the bushbuck family, being 95 centimetres tall at the shoulders and weighing 75 kilogrammes.

THE ENDLESS STEPPE
The Sudanese savannah belt

The southern edge of the Sahara is not clearly defined. The desert slowly changes into steppe; the vegetation gradually changes from obvious desert species into Sudanese steppe plants. The dry, sandy or rocky desert becomes dotted with occasional grassy areas and shrubs, and the sand dunes become firmer due to the binding vegetation. This is semi-arid country in which rain, although still rare and irregular, is nevertheless sufficient for more plant species to be able to survive.

The Sudanese savannah is the first of several belts of vegetation which run across Africa from the Atlantic to the Nile valley, and in places as far as the coast of the Indian Ocean. These belts, however, do not have sharply defined borders. If one travels from the Sahara towards the south, the precipitation increases and the landscape gradually changes into grassy savannah, stretching far away beyond the horizon and interrupted only here and there by a small tree, bush or hill.

The Sudanese savannah lands are relatively densely populated by herdsmen, who mostly devastate it with their herds of goats, sheep and cattle. Farther south, acacias and thorny shrubs such as *Balanites aegyptiaca* begin to appear, along with the typical Sudanese Duma Tree (*Hyphaene thebaica*) which can only survive where there is a regular rainfall. The grassy areas increase in size: Aristida Grass, Millet and *Cenchrus biflorus* grow there. In these semi-arid steppes the pasture is good for about two months of the year, the grass being dry for the remainder. However, even dry grass, which is actually standing hay, is nutritious, which means that the savannah can feed incredible numbers of animals. Both trees and shrubs are deciduous, usually having corky or waxy bark which protects their valuable moisture from evaporation. Tree roots reach to great depths, as far as the lower water level, or have richly branching root systems.

On the steppe the plants go to seed in succes-

sion, so that there is a constant abundance of seeds for birds. The most numerous of these are weavers (*Ploceus*) and avadats (*Estrilda*), firefinches (*Lagonosticta*), the Cordon Bleu (*Uraeginthus bengalus*) and whydahs (*Vidua*) —

which, like cuckoos, lay their eggs in other birds' nests, usually those of weavers. The Red-billed Dioch or Quelea (*Quelea quelea*) can be as much of a disaster as locusts. Flocks numbering millions of these birds fly from place to place and destroy countless amounts of grain. They nest in gigantic colonies and their numbers are so great that birds of prey are unable to diminish them. Their colonies have been burnt out, even soldiers with flame-throwers coming to help, or sprayed with poisons. In spite of all this, however, they continue to increase. The largest bird in the world, the Ostrich (*Struthio camelus*), lives in the Sudanese savannah.

Animals on the steppes form herds and often group into larger mixed formations composed of various species, migrating together in search of better pasture. Near the dividing line between the savannah and the desert lives a magnificent race of the Gemsbok (*Oryx gazella gallarum*) and the Dama Gazelle. Antelope are hunted by cheetahs, and hares and birds are caught by caracals. Towards the south the tree and shrub acacias become more numerous, so that instead of oryxes the Western Giraffe (*Giraffa camelopardalis peralta*) and, even more common, the Red-fronted Gazelle (*Gazella rufifrons*) are found. From time to time animals from the

Not far from Lake Turkana, close to the Sudanese border, live the Turkana with their herds of cattle, goats and sheep. It is astonishing how many cattle and wild animals can find enough food in the almost dry Sudanese steppe.

The Comb Duck nests in hollow trees, an exception among ducks. It lives in Africa south of the Sahara, but also in the East and West Indies and in tropical parts of South America. At night it often sits in flocks on the crowns of trees.

as a table and where it floods over 15,000 square kilometres. Large swamps and marshes form suitable habitats for water birds, the Waterbuck (*Kobus ellipsiprymnus*) and Cape Buffalo (*Syncerus caffer caffer*), as well as Wart-hogs (*Phacochoerus aethiopicus*). Across the Sahara fly water birds which nest in Europe and Asia, mingling there with a number of tropical heron species, storks and pelicans to create a marvellous spectacle. The most common migratory birds living in the region are the Common

The African Ground Hornbill (*Bucorax abyssinicus*), known in Ethiopia as the 'abbagamba' and in Sudan as 'abugarn', is the best-known of all African hornbills. It is a large sturdy bird that feeds on insects, mice and lizards, and is not afraid of snakes. It is easy to tame.

damper savannah areas also stray there, such as the Korrigum (*Damaliscus lunatus korrigum*), which was once the most abundant antelope species of all; the Roan Antelope (*Hippotragus equinus*); and the African Elephant (*Loxodonta africana*).

A large swampy region is formed by Lake Chad, which has no outflow and into which flow the Sari, Kamadugu and Jobe Rivers. The area of the lake varies according to the amounts of recent precipitation. The abundant River Niger has its source in the mountains of Guinea, spilling widely over lowlands which are as flat

The Common Pintail nests in northern Europe, and also inhabits large parts of Asia and part of North America. From November until March it lives as a migratory bird as far as the River Niger, together with large numbers of other ducks, pelicans and storks. The female is very inconspicuous. The male is attractively coloured with a brown head and nape, a white neck from which a narrow white stripe extends to the head; the back and sides are grey, the abdomen white and the underside tail coverts are black.

Male Ostriches differ conspicuously in colour from females. The male's body is covered with black feathers, the females have grey plumage. Magnificent pure-white plumes, once a sought-after adornment, grow from the tail and wings. This bird swallows small stones, which assist in grinding up food in the stomach.

Pintail (*Anas acuta*) and the Garganey (*Anas querquedula*). Of native birds the most frequent are the White-faced Tree Duck (*Dendrocygna viduata*), the Comb Duck (*Sàrcidiornis melanotus*) and the Egyptian Goose.

The Ostrich is the largest living bird. It is not able to fly, probably as a result of increased weight, which in turn brought about the stunted flight muscles.

OSTRICHES

The Ostrich grows to two and a half metres tall and weighs 150 kilogrammes. People have been fascinated by this bird since time immemorial: paintings of it can be found in the caves of prehistoric hunters, and Chinese chroniclers wrote that the Emperors of the Heavenly Empire were given its eggs as a rarity, which they then placed in their jewellery boxes. The Assyrians considered the Ostrich to be sacred and the ancient Egyptians saw it as a symbol of justice, since they knew that this bird's feather was the only one in the world with identical vanes on either side of the shaft. The organizers of games in ancient Rome showed Ostriches as a marvel to the astonished citizens. Aelius Lampidus described a feast at the court of the Emperor Heliogabalus in the 3rd century AD, at which 600 of these birds' brains were served as a delicacy. Julius Capitolinus recorded a grand hunt convened by Emperor Gordian III at which 300 of the species, painted red, were released. The Egyptian ruler Firmius used to have Ostriches harnessed to his chariots; in the Middle Ages knights decorated their helmets with their feathers; and as late as the last century ladies still adorned their heads with them. There have been Ostrich races; the Arabs and Tuaregs used to hunt them on horseback; and lately large breeding farms have been established. Ostriches do not bury their heads in the sand as the old superstitions

claim — but during the nesting season they do lie their heads on the ground, doing the same in the case of approaching danger. Several females may lay eggs in a single nest. The grey female sits on the eggs in the daytime and in the evening the blacker coloured male comes to the nest to relieve her for the night. A nest is easily found, therefore, by following a particular male.

The numbers of these beautiful birds are decreasing in the wild, even though the species is superbly adapted for life on the open plains. It is a fast and enduring runner, using its wings like oars when changing direction. It will feed on insects, reptiles and small rodents but it prefers plant food, especially tough plants, which it tears up together with the roots and swallows whole. Ostriches also have excellent eyesight. In company with antelope, which have excellent hearing and smell, they form a perfect defensive community when feeding in open country.

Male birds can make honking and lowing noises, and roar almost like lions. During the pairing season birds of both sexes feed peacefully in a flock in the daytime, but as soon as night falls males begin to attract females loudly, chasing off other males by kicking. A gobbling male circles a female, crouching on his heels, waving and flapping his wings, rippling his plumage and spreading his fan-like white feathers. During this mating dance the male is effectively blind and deaf to his surroundings. The female stands in front of the male with her head lowered and wings spread. Suddenly the male jumps up abruptly, the female falls to the ground and the male mounts her, constantly flapping his wings. When building their nest the pair rake the soil and sand, stamping out and tearing up all the grass and roots within a three-metre circle. A mature male attracts between three and six females, but for the purposes of sitting on the common clutch and rearing the chicks, he chooses only one. A month-old chick can run at a speed of 45 kilometres per hour, and adults are capable of up to 70 kilometres per hour.

The Cheetah seldom breeds in captivity. The female gives birth to between two and four young. The young can be easily tamed provided they are taken away from the mother at the age of around two months and fed artificially from a bottle, as with dogs.

CHEETAHS

The Cheetah (*Acinonyx jubatus jubatus*) is a solitary animal for most of its life. Sometimes pairs form for a while, although this is exceptional out of the mating season. A group of these big cats is not a mixed gathering such as the pride formed by Lions, but a female with adult young. The size of a Cheetah territory varies between 60 and 130 square kilometres. These cats do not stick to their territory too rigidly, however,

and they tolerate one another. The period of pregnancy is 90 to 95 days, the female giving birth to between three and five cubs. The record holder is a female at Moscow Zoo which gave birth to 10 live and active cubs. In general, however, only one or two, or more than five, cubs in a single delivery are exceptional.

Cheetahs, unlike their relatives, do not have retractable claws, and do not roar, but mew in a manner similar to domestic cats. They are also the fastest runners on earth. I personally measured the speed of an escaping specimen, which reached 97 kilometres per hour. Some experts quote speeds of 112 kilometres per hour. The animal has enormously fast acceleration, being able to reach maximum speed only 18 metres after starting, but it can run at its top speed only for a maximum of 400 metres.

Cheetahs knock down their prey with a punch of the paw, killing it with a strong bite into the neck. They usually eat the prey on the spot, but when possible like to drag it away to the shade. After feeding this animal never returns to its kill, always consuming only fresh food.

In the past the Cheetah occurred in numbers roughly corresponding to those of Lions. They live from the Cape as far as North Africa, apart from the Atlas Mountains and tropical rain forests, dense forests and deserts. Outside Africa, the species also lives in Arabia, on the southern coast of the Caspian Sea, in Jordan, Syria, Iraq, Iran and Afghanistan. At one time it extended as far as Central Asia and farther east to India.

A half-grown young Cheetah is still unable to hunt by itself and usually follows its mother, concealed in an elevated spot. It begins to hunt by itself when physically almost full-grown and with a completely developed set of teeth. At first it preys on smaller antelope species.

Nowadays it occurs only rarely from East Africa to Namibia. Cheetahs used to be kept as hunting animals. The male can be 220 centimetres long, weighing 45 to 60 kilogrammes, the female being somewhat smaller.

ORYXES

The Roan Antelope is a well-built animal about the size of a stag. Males and females have their long, transversely-ridged horns curved into a backward arch. They live in dense bush or gallery forests, needing a regular water supply and drinking twice or three times daily. Apart from people only Lions can be a danger to these strong antelopes. They are very aggressive and

A herd of Beisa grazing with Boehm's Zebras and a small ▶ herd of domestic cattle, in northern Kenya. They were startled at the approach of our small two-seater plane. While the herd of cows continued to graze undisturbed, the Beisa and zebras took flight.

In mimicry, the colour and markings of the coat are essential for survival. They also serve as a reliable method of distinction between sub-species.

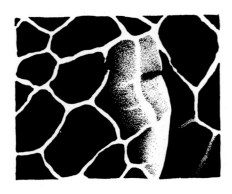

The Reticulated Giraffe (*Giraffa camelopardalis reticulata*) is somewhat smaller than other giraffes and has reddish-brown patches separated by brilliant-white, relatively narrow stripes.

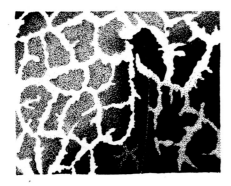

The Masai Giraffe (*G. c. tippelskirchi*) has a slender head without brow ridges, irregular patterning which looks as if it were frayed, and the colour is lighter than in the Reticulated Giraffe.

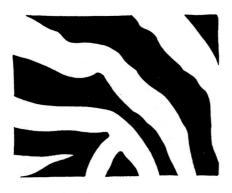

Boehm's Zebra is a sub-species of the Steppe Zebra. It has broad, brilliant-white and shiny black stripes. The striping is very eye-catching and without 'shadow stripes', finishing just above the hooves. Foals have light-brown stripes which gradually darken as they grow older. The stripes on the back retain their brownish tinge longest.

Grévy's Zebra has narrow stripes all over the body, the finest being on the head. The abdomen is white, and along the back extends one black stripe. It has large, round ears and is the biggest of all zebras.

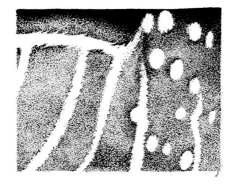

The Bushbuck has perfect protective colouring composed of white spots and stripes on an orange or dark-grey background. If it stands motionless in a thick tangle of bush it becomes virtually invisible.

The Okapi ranks among the rarest animals of Africa. It is coloured dark reddish-brown. On its back haunches it has brilliant-white tapering stripes running parallel with the back. There are white stripes on the upper parts of the front legs; the chest and neck have a darkish brown colour.

The Bongo is the largest forest antelope species, being light red in colour. It has between 11 and 13 white stripes on both flanks, running from the chest to the back haunches, a small white stripe on the base of the nose, and white spots on the sides of the head and on the legs.

will not give up even if knocked down to the ground, attacking with their horns, kicking and roaring threateningly. An adult weighs about 250 kilogrammes, the height at the shoulders being 150 centimetres. A Roan Antelope can badly injure a whole pack of dogs, and a case has been recorded in which a single male successfully faced a pride of Lions. The cats surrounded it, but the antelope fiercely attacked each one which attempted to approach. Finally it charged at one female, which was startled and began to flee. In this way the male broke successfully through the circle and saved itself.

The Sable Antelope (*Hippotragus niger*) is somewhat smaller than the Roan, weighing 220 kilogrammes and with a shoulder height of 135 centimetres. The males, however, have larger and longer horns than Roan Antelope. Their numbers in East Africa are decreasing dramatically. Another population lives in Mozambique and Zimbabwe. In central Angola there lives a sub-species called the Giant Sable (*H. n. variani*), the males of which are even larger and have even longer horns. These magnificent creatures, however, are in immediate danger of extinction.

The True Gemsbok (*Oryx gazella gazella*) can still be found relatively frequently in southern African savannahs and bush country. They are also often kept in the open on farms in Namibia. The Afrikaaners call it the Gemsbok, or

'Chamois goat', although it has nothing in common either with goats or chamois. In the Kalahari it likes to dig up melon-shaped fruits called *chama* with its front legs. The succulent roots of these fruits enable the Gemsbok to do without water for long periods. During the rainy season they live in small parties, but if these oryxes set off in search of water and fresh food they can group into herds several hundred strong. They are reminiscent of greatly enlarged gazelles and are light-footed, although the trot is heavier, with a fast gallop and great stamina. When grazing they mix well with Cape Eland and other ruminant species. They are shy but not timid. Africans used their horns for the points of their spears.

Addaxes (*Addax nasomaculatus*) used to be kept as domestic animals by the ancient Egyptians; several paintings have been preserved in which they can be seen standing in rows by mangers in stables. The Egyptians also kept the Scimitar-horned Oryx (*Oryx dammah*). They had a special way of protecting themselves from the sharp horns: they bent the horns of young animals when they were only just beginning to grow, fixing them into special clamps. Addaxes are now only rarely found, in small groups of between five and 15, as they migrate across the endless wilderness in the constant search for pasture. They can withstand lack of water for a couple of months. They are at their most lively

Roan Antelope: between 1970 and 1971 we brought from Uganda to our zoo two males and seven females. Within 12 years we have reared 147 young.

at night, shielding themselves in the daytime from the burning sun by digging pits into the ground with their front legs and then lying in them.

The Beisa (*Oryx gazella beisa*) also belongs to the *Oryx* genus. It ranges from Tanzania as far as Somalia and is lighter in colour than the True Gemsbok. Also from Tanzania, as far as the River Tana in Kenya, lives the Fringe-eared Oryx (*O. g. callotis*). This sub-species has longer, pointed ears, finished off with a small tassel of longer hair. It has a darker, reddish colouring.

The True Gemsbock (*Oryx gazella gazella*) has a fighting temperament, which shows even in captivity. In our zoo we placed them in a common run with Blue Wildebeest and Greater Kudu. The wildebeest male attacked the Gemsbok male and pierced its front leg with its horn. This injured male then chased all the wildebeest out of the run and would not allow them back in.

In Kenya, Sable Antelope now live only in the protected
Shimba Hills reservation close to the East African port of
Mombasa. The males of this East African race are a shiny
black, the females light red.

THE HORN ON THE BROW OF AFRICA
The Somalian promontory

Africa forms a horn at the point where the Red Sea meets the Indian Ocean, and if it were not for the Ethiopian mountains this horn would be connected to the semi-arid belt of Sudanese savannah. As it is, however, it forms a distinct natural region comprising Somalia, the eastern part of Ethiopia and part of Kenya as far as Lake Turkana. The region is bounded in the south by the mountainous massif of Kenya and the River Tana, which forms a significant watershed in spite of its small size. This whole area is almost completely arid. Extensive parts in Kenya are taken up by lava fields.

The Red Sea coast is one of the hottest regions in the world, and is also one of the places where the life of coral can be observed on a large scale. Small islands, devoid of either vegetation or drinking water, are scattered along the coastline, and in spite of the lack of water all the bird species from the entire northern Indian Ocean nest there.

On the Somali coast nests the little-known Crab Plover (*Dromas ardeola*), which excavates underground passages. Into these the females lay single chalk-white eggs, which are enormous in relation to the size of the birds. Dry savannah plains stretch from the coast towards the interior, interspersed with patches of sparse shrubs, to be replaced in the south near the River Juba by richer savannah. The desert region is hot and inhospitable, so that only a few hardy animals can live there. Among them is the rare Pelzeln's Gazelle (*Gazella pelzelni*), which can survive a long time without water.

The coastal plains, several hundred kilometres wide, are separated from the mountainous interior mainly by limestone slopes, ranging from gentle to steep, which ceased to be part of

The Migratory Locust has a large head bearing thick strong antennae and biting mouthparts. Enormous swarms of locusts can number several hundred million insects, eating all greenery over many hundreds of square kilometres.

The Desert Locust has a distinctive keel in the centre of its forehead, on which a small simple eye is situated. Two more of these eyes are sited close to the small depressions on the crown of the head. The front pair of wings are narrow and more strongly reinforced with chitin; the back pair are broader and softer.

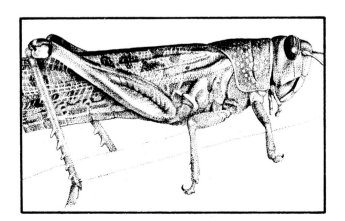

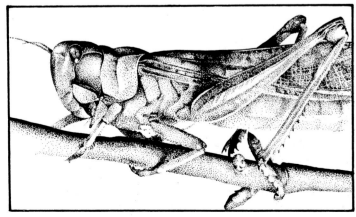

the sea bed 60 million years ago. The Golis Range, 2,400 metres high, extends parallel with the Red Sea to form the base of the triangle shape that makes the Horn of Africa. Towards the south the coastal lowlands become an upper plain, and the temperature falls as precipitation increases. By the time one reaches the Ogaden plain at 1,400 metres the hot dry coast is far behind. Here are pleasant pasture and acacia trees, and higher still the dwarf junipers begin to grow.

South of the Ethiopian highlands a dried-up area about 800 kilometres wide extends to the interior towards Lake Turkana, one of the largest alkaline lakes in the world. The terrain is lava fields, black to reddish in colour. Among the lava boulders drifts a fine dust which rises in whole clouds, forming a sticky substance when it is wet. Rainfall is irregular. Yet even on these inhospitable plains live Grant's Gazelles,

The Black Rhinoceros is (after the African Elephant, White Rhinoceros and Amphibious Hippopotamus) the fourth-largest land mammal in Africa. It is scarce in Somalia — indeed, almost everywhere their numbers are dwindling rapidly, for which reason it is a strictly protected species.

Grévy's Zebras and Beisas. In Somalia, Soemmering's Gazelle replaces Grant's Gazelle. On the high upper plateaux lives the small Speke's Gazelle, while Grévy's Zebras become fewer in number, this being the largest of all zebra species and sporting the finest striping and the largest rounded ears. It is remarkable that such animals remain in good condition even when the grass is dried up and extremely scarce. The Somali Wild Ass (*Equus africanus somaliensis*) lives in the worst semi-desert conditions.

In the south-eastern corner of the promontory the grazing Hirola Antelope (*Damaliscus hunteri*) can be found, often in the company of its close relative the Topi (*Damaliscus lunatus topi*). Here the rains come once a year, sometimes only once in several years. If the rainfall happens to be heavier than usual a gigantic reactivation of the whole natural environment takes place. The plants put on a spurt of growth, birds build their nests, the flowers shed their blossoms and go to seed and even the dry shrubs burst into leaf. This idyll does not last for long, however, and soon the wildlife returns to its original arid state. The umbrella acacias and acacia shrubs have large and deep root systems, so that often whole areas are vegetated only by them, and grass does not grow among them. For this reason animals there live by the rivers, feeding on the foliage which they bite off trees — Elephants, Giraffes, Rhinos, Gerenuks (*Litocranius walleri*), small dik-diks (*Madoqua*) and Waterbuck. In higher places the Greater Kudu and Lesser Kudu also browse on the shrubbery.

Deeper in the interior live two typical foliage-eating species, the Dibatag Gazelle (*Ammodorcas clarkei*) and the Beira Antelope (*Dorcatragus megalotis*). These mostly prefer myrrh (*Commiphora*) leaves, which are not fed on by many other herbivores. Raptors are abundant, and during the winter months thousands of guests from Europe and Asia add to their numbers. Eagles, falcons, kites and vultures hunt by sight. Owls, of which the Verreax's Eagle Owl (*Bubo lacteus*) is the largest, hunt at twilight by sight and in darkness by hearing, which is very sensitive and capable of localizing an object so that the owl can determine exactly where the prey is situated. They do not eat carrion, this being disposed of by hyaenas and jackals.

Lake Turkana (formerly named after Rudolf, successor to the Austrian throne) belongs to the Great Trench Depression lake system. It is 240 kilometres long and from 30 to 50 kilometres wide. Several rivers flow into it, the largest being the Omo, which has its source in the southern Ethiopian highlands. This lake was once much deeper and connected to the Nile by means of a pass which has since dried up. This former linking section is why Nile fish species now live in the lake, especially the Nile Perch (*Lates niloticus*). Enormous crocodiles in the lake have unusual protuberances on their bodies caused by the alkaline water; these reduce the value of their skins, which has luckily saved them from extermination. The area around

Lake Turkana is inhabited by the nomadic Turkana. The smallest 'nation' in Africa also lives there — the people of the Elmolo tribe. In a recent study, the tribe had 102 members living in three villages.

LOCUSTS

The Somali promontory is the main region producing innumerable quantities of Desert Locusts (*Schistocerca gregaria*), these being the most important of the three migratory locust species in Africa. Swarms of millions fly over as

Reticulated Giraffes are slightly smaller than the Masai or Rothschild's sub-species. They live from the banks of the River Tana in Kenya towards Somalia. Near the town of Nanyiuki, at the foot of Mount Kenya, hybrid Reticulated and Masai Giraffes are a common sight, as the ranges of these two sub-species overlap.

The Gerenuk lives in Somalia and Kenya as far as the River Tana, as well as around Uhuru (Kilimanjaro). It can survive in dense thorny bush, where apart from shrub and tree-type mimosas not even grass will grow; for this reason other antelope avoid the region.

African herbivores make thorough use of the vertical grazing possibilities of shrubby bush.

far as the Caspian Sea, the Bay of Bengal and south to Tanzania.

The Migratory Locust (*Locusta migratoria*) can be a catastrophe for people in tropical and sub-tropical regions. The earliest record of a disaster caused by locusts, which destroyed the whole of the flora of Egypt, can be found in the Bible, in the Book of Exodus. All locusts are herbivores, as distinct from grasshoppers which are predatory and feed on other insects. Locusts can completely destroy the vegetation of large areas. The largest observed swarms were 250 kilometres long and numbered 35,000,000,000 locusts, weighing over 50,000 tonnes. Locusts sometimes migrate at a low level, at others times high up, in a swarm that can be 30 metres deep. In windless weather they fly at a speed of 16 kilometres per hour; with a following wind they can cover greater distances.

When laying eggs the female locust seeks out a suitable place on the ground, digs a small hole with her short, cigar-shaped ovipositor,

The Gerenuk has a diet restricted to fine, small acacia leaves, which made it difficult to feed. Only after a long period did these antelope learn to eat alfalfa dried in the shade, and granulated food. Later I discovered that when they are not given water they thrive well on cooked macaroni.

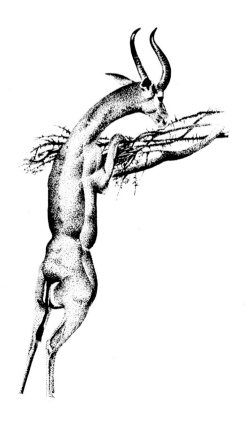

Male Gerenuk have lyre-shaped, striped horns, the females being hornless. These antelope are able to walk on their hind legs, lightly resting on small branches while they feed on delicate acacia foliage up to a height of two and a half metres.

The Dibatag lives in small groups in the sandy steppes of eastern and central Somalia. It feeds mostly on the small fine leaves of shrub-type thorny acacias. The males have forward-curving, transversely-ridged horns which grow to 30 centimetres long. The females are hornless.

Female Impala with newborn young returns to the herd, which ensures their safety.

and lays between 300 and 500 eggs in the hole, spraying them with a foamy glandular secretion. This foam hardens and together with adhered particles of earth it forms a compact egg container. The eggs remain in the ground through the winter. Under suitable conditions, several locust generations can mature in one season. In such circumstances the hatched young literally rub against one another. These densely concentrated 'hoppers' move in great multitudes in the same direction — towards food. When they reach their mature form and their wings have grown, throngs numbering millions take to the air and their great migration begins. When we take into account that one young locust eats approximately 10 times the weight of an adult before its first take-off, and that adults still eat at least twice their own weight, we can calculate that an average-sized cloud of locusts consumes approximately 30,000 tonnes of plant foodstuffs during its development and migration.

The Desert Locust also carries out regular migrations, hatching twice a year. After the winter hatching season there follows a southwards mi-

Lesser Kudu live on the border between Somalia and Kenya, together with Gerenuk. They are most frequently among the dense riverside vegetation of the River Tana. The male has no breast mane, but possesses two white spots and at least twelve transverse stripes.

The Grey Rhebuck can withstand severe cold. In winter it grows a thick, long, soft coat. The zoo at Dvůr Králové is the only one that has successfully managed to breed it. The species lives in the mountains of southern Africa.

gration in spring. South of the Sahara occurs the so-called monsoon hatching season, after which follows the migration back to the north, to the winter region. In 1955 southern Morocco was attacked by a giant swarm of locusts 250 kilometres long and 20 kilometres wide. Within five days they had consumed 70,000 tonnes of oranges in an area of 5,000 square kilometres — more than the annual consumption of oranges in the whole of France. In 1966 trains and cars in the Republic of South Africa were unable to operate for an entire day, as the rails and roads were covered with locusts.

The Egyptian Locusts (*Anacridium aegypticum*) do not move from place to place, and so are less dangerous than the migratory species. Even so they can do great harm, since they eat tree and shrub foliage in large quantities, especially those of cotton plants, as well as vegetables and legumes.

On the inner side of the thigh of its rear leg a locust has a ridge with a lengthwise row of little teeth: by rubbing this against the raised vein on its wing the insect produces a high or low chirping, creaking or rattling sound.

ANTELOPE

Impalas (*Aepiceros melampus*) are slender, elegant antelope which can jump three metres in height and as far as 10 metres. They are good-natured, go daily to watering places and live in typical 'harem herds' in which a single strong male rules over a large number of females. The male has much work keeping the herd together and chasing off other males. Even maturing males of about one year are driven off, these

The Springbuck, of which the rare white and black forms were caught in south-west Africa, is kept in our zoo at Dvůr Králové.

then forming small male groups. Strong males sometimes fight fiercely among themselves. During mating the male at first watches the female for some time from a distance of about 20 metres, then he suddenly rushes towards her and pursues her. They both gradually decrease speed until they are walking. The male follows the female with his neck extended, occasionally licking her rear, before actual mating starts. Mothers give birth to young in solitude and then often group together to form special maternal herds, only later returning to the original herd.

The Grey Rhebuck (*Pelea capreolus*) is a beautiful grey antelope about the same size as

Grévy's Zebra inhabits northern Kenya, Somalia and southern Ethiopia. This picture was taken at the time of capture. According to the jeep's speedometer, zebras can run at a speed of 62 kilometres per hour.

a roebuck. Only males have the straight narrow horns, about 20 to 30 centimetres long. They live in small groups of up to a dozen in the mountainous areas of southern Africa. During the mating season males often fight fiercely among themselves. Otherwise they are timid animals and descend into valleys to the watering places mainly at night. They are superb climbers of steep hills and are also excellent jumpers.

The Dibatag (*Ammodorcas clarkei*) lives in a small area of Somalia, on plains vegetated with thorny trees and bushes, feeding on their foliage. The horns are curved forwards. Like the Gerenuk, the Dibatag stands on its hind legs and

Grant's Gazelle lives in the region from Lake Turkana towards Uganda. The males have the strongest and largest horns of all gazelle species. According to the size of the body, shape of the horns and the colouring, it is possible to distinguish three geographical sub-species: Bright's, Peter's and Roberts'.

rests its front legs on branches when feeding on leaves, so as to reach as high as possible. Both species live in small groups of about 10 individuals. When the Gerenuk is startled it stands motionless in a thick bush with its head raised high, staring to see what is happening, itself hardly visible. Sometimes it manages to outwit the foe by creeping silently away from the bush with its neck stretched out horizontally. Males have lyre-shaped, transversely ridged horns, with the points turned slightly forwards.

The Gerenuk (*Litocranius walleri*) lives in East Africa. It never drinks water, not even in captivity. During the mating season males mark their females on the chest and rump with the secretion from their scent glands to warn other males that the female is already spoken for. When mating the male approaches the female, raising his front legs rigidly to an almost horizontal position and lightly tapping the female's hind leg in a symbolic manner. Such behaviour — light tapping with the front leg on the hind leg of the female — is, with a number of variations, typical of many antelope species during the mating season.

The Springbuck or Springbok (*Antidorcas marsupialis*) is a South African antelope, the males having lyre-shaped, inwardly curved horns up to 40 centimetres long. Females have thin, much shorter horns. During the last century these antelopes made up enormous, almost innumerable herds. They migrated in millions from one area to another in search of water and pasture. They are superb jumpers: when jumping they keep all four legs fully extended and close together, with their heads lowered and

Sanseviera (*Sanseviera cylindrica*) has succulent, rod-shaped leaves with thorns at the tips. These are eaten only by elephants, which chew the leaves, and spit out the hard indigestible fibres. Areas densely vegetated with Sanseviera resemble sisal plantations.

backs arched like cats. While in the air a white stripe on the coat, extending from the root of the tail to the middle of the back, opens out. They use this as a signal to flee, indicating that something unusual or suspicious is happening and generally expressing disturbance and unease. The jumping moves like a wave through the whole herd. Nowadays there are few Springbuck in southern Africa: they are more frequent on farms in Namibia and on some reservations.

In the great family Bovidae there are 16 subfamilies with 128 genera. Apart from antelope the family contains chamois, goats, sheep, oxen, domestic cattle and many other hoofed animals. 'Antelopes' do not in fact form a true single group: this unscientific, popular term is nevertheless commonly used for certain species of horned artiodactyls (even-toed hoofed animals). Bovidae vary from small antelopes the size of a hare to that of a bison. Their build may be either slender and elegant or massive and large. The eyes are usually large and give a tender im-

Beyond the River Tana in Kenya and Somalia grows an unusual dry-country plant *Adenium obesum* known in Swahili as 'mdagu' (the desert rose). It looks like a miniature Baobab. The sap from the cut bark is highly poisonous and the local people extract arrow poison from the seeds and venom for catching fish from the roots.

pression. Nearly all members have two horns on their heads, apart from four-horned antelopes. In some species both sexes have horns, in others only males.

Bovidae are mainly herbivorous, only exceptionally feeding on other animals. They have slender legs, always equipped with two main toes and hooves adapted for running on a hard surface. They are ruminants, the stomach having four chambers which enable them to eat large amounts of food quickly and then digest it at leisure. This is an important protective device, as these animals are constantly threatened by the greatest danger from predators and people.

73

THE LAND BURNED BY FIRE
The Guinea savannah

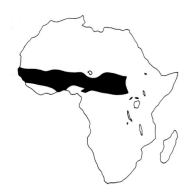

The broad belt of land stretching across Africa from the Atlantic coast of Senegal to southern Sudan is known as the Guinea savannah. It is about 5,000 kilometres long and only 400 kilometres wide; an almost uninterrupted belt of forested country which one can walk along from one end to the other and still be surrounded by the same species of trees, shrubs and grasses. From the north to the south the trees become more numerous and taller, until they finally form a kind of wall which marks the southern boundary of the savannah. In the north the belt changes imperceptibly into grassy savannah, the Sudanese steppe belt.

The difference in rainfall between the grass and tree savannah belts can be as much as 500 millimetres in a year. The dry season in the south is about two months shorter than in the north. In the Guinea savannah region the heavy rains last for about six months and it rains every second or third day in this season. The dry period lasts approximately six months, with infrequent rain. Both trees and shrubs there are deciduous, with dense shrubs and evergreen trees existing only along rivers. This belt produces an enormous amount of plant matter, sometimes even more than tropical rain forests, for which reason it can support an incredible number of animals. Fires break out easily in the dry season.

The northern Guinea savannah consists of thinly wooded country in which two *Isoberlinia* species predominate among trees, these being the Mutobo and Munhundo (*I. doka* and *I. dalzielli*); they can always be found together with beard-grass (*Andropogon*). Farther to the south the woodland is more varied, with lophyras, bauhinias, daniellias and terminalias being typical. In the northern savannah the yearly cycle begins with the first rains in March or April. Within a short time the arid savannah turns emerald green and the trees are covered with leaves. The air is clear and humidity increases, the grass growing to heights of almost two metres. Birds begin to lay their eggs immediately after these first rains. Magnificent weavers are abundant everywhere, as well as multicoloured rollers, hoopoes and pigeons. Most birds complete their breeding in the rainy season. By the end of September and October the heavy rains cease, and the onset of the dry season is heralded by a harmattan — a dry wind from the desert that lasts for several days and carries with it a fine dust, restricting vision to less than 200 metres. This dust makes the whole country look as if it were covered in a pink haze. The air becomes drier and the nights grow cooler. With each wave of harmattan another wave of migrating birds flies from the north, among them the Kingfisher (*Halcyon leucocephala*) and the

How plants resist fire. The majority of grasses on the savannah and in the bush are able to regrow after having been burnt. Some species are able to survive by boring their caryopsis (type of seed) under the layer of charred soil (upper dotted part). A spiralled awn (bristle-like projection) expands and contracts due to warmth and moisture, and in this way a caryopsis bores into the ground. In the top right of the picture is an enlargement of an awn thread. On the bottom right are the bristles on the sharp point, which help the caryopsis to grip the soil and to grow out of it again.

Grey Hornbill (*Tockus nasutus*). The migration of birds within Africa has much in common with that of European species flying to spend the winter in the south, however, this has not yet been thoroughly researched. A major proportion of the West African migrations is in fact only a shuttle movement of birds from the northern drier regions to the savannah and back. Abdim's Stork (*Sphenorhynchus abdimii*), for instance, breeds in the rainy season in the northern Guinea savannahs and in the southern part of the Sudanese savannahs. When it is dry in the north it flies to the plains between Tanzania and the Transvaal where the rainy season is just starting, returning to the north as the rains begin there.

Even large animals and birds flee from the danger of fire. Small animals and insects are most affected by fire, mostly grasshoppers, of which millions perish. A number of birds that feed on lizards, insects and small rodents will fly straight through spreading fire to obtain food. Only those small animals which hide in holes, underground passages, cracks and hollows can save themselves.

In the monkey group, the Anubis Baboon, the rusty coloured Hussar Monkey (*Erythrocebus patas*) and, along rivers, the Green Monkey (*Cercopithecus aethiops*) commonly live in the Guinea savannah. Farmers do not like monkeys, however, as they plunder their fields. Of the herbivores, the Roan Antelope, the Common Hartebeest (*Alcelaphus buselaphus*) and the Cape Buffalo can be found on the savannah. In

The River Benue flows through the national park of the same name in Cameroun. In this river live hippopotami, and in the gallery forests and on the grassy savannahs roam African Elephants, Black Rhinos, Giraffes, Giant Eland, various hartebeest species, Lions, Leopards and Cheetahs.

the vicinity of water live Buffon's Kob (*Kobus kob*), the Defassa Waterbuck (*Kobus ellipsiprymnus defassa*) and the Bohor Reedbuck (*Redunca redunca*). Oribis (*Ourebia ourebi*) live on the open savannah, as well as Bushbuck, and several duiker species (Cephalophinae) frequent shrubs along streams. Elephants also occur, along with the largest antelope in the world, the magnificent Giant Eland (*Taurotragus derbianus*), the males of which are up to 190 centimetres tall at the shoulder and can weigh 1,200 kilogrammes. Farmers hunt down and push back these wild animals towards regions infested with Tsetse Fly.

Several large rivers flow through the Guinea savannah: the Senegal, the Niger, the Benue, the Volta, the Chari and the Kamadugu Jobe. The greatest of these is the Niger, which is the third-largest river in Africa. All of them flood their banks in the rainy season, and floods are common. The Blackhead Plover (*Sarciophorus*

The Korrigum in the Manda National Park in Chad. It lives in the savannah bush with elephants, hippopotami, Roan Antelope, Lelwel Hartebeest and large predators. It is the largest sub-species of the *Damaliscus* genus.

The Tsessebe is one of the largest hartebeest species. The males can weigh up to 180 kilogrammes. They have relatively short and widely spread horns.

76

The rare Red Hartebeest (*Alcelaphus buselaphus caama*) has only been kept in zoos in large numbers in recent years. It was brought from south-west Africa.

The Hirola is one of the rarest animals kept in zoos. All captured animals come from the Garissa region of Kenya where they live in only one small territory. Part of the Hirola population also lives in neighbouring Somalia.

tectus), the Wattled Plover (*Afribyx senegallus*) and the Gull-billed Tern (*Gelochelidon nilotica*), as well as the Lesser Black-backed Gull (*Larus fuscus*), can be found along the rivers. The banks are usually full of holes in which nest the European Bee-eater (*Merops*

The Topi in smaller than the Korrigum, and has more contrasting colours with bluish patches on the shoulders and rump. In the southern part of the Ruwenzori National Park in Uganda, over one thousand of these animals live on the plains by the River Ishasha.

Near Lake Chad, in the Waza National Park in Cameroun, lives the most northerly sub-species of African Giraffe, the Nubian Giraffe. It has an inconspicuous yellow-brown colouring. The northern sub-species have almost white legs without coloured spots, whereas in the southern sub-species the spots are more numerous. The Cape Giraffe has legs spotted to the hooves.

apiaster), the Carmine Bee-eater (*Merops nubicus*), great colonies of insect-eating birds, several swallow species and many water birds.

HARTEBEEST

Hartebeest are remarkable among antelope in having their hind quarters lower than the shoulders. Both sexes have transversely-ridged horns that are curved into various shapes and usually beautifully coloured. The old Boers called them *Hartebeest* because this means 'enduring

	Body length in cm	Shoulder height in cm	Weight in kg	Max. horn length in cm
Genus: *Damaliscus*				
Species:				
Sassaby				
(*Damaliscus lunatus*)				
Sub-species:				
Tsessebe				
(*Damaliscus l. lunatus*)	180	120	140	47
Topi				
(*Damaliscus l. topi*)	180	110	100	60
Jimela				
(*D. l. jimela*)	180	110	105	62
Tiang				
(*D. l. tiang*)	185	120	125	67
Korrigum				
(*D. l. korrigum*)	190	125	135	72
Species:				
Hirola				
(*Damaliscus hunteri*)	160	105	80	72
Species:				
Bontebok				
(*Damaliscus dorcas*)				
Sub-species:				
Bontebok (*D. d. dorcas*)	150	100	90	43
Blesbok (*D. d. phillipsi*)	145	95	80	51
Genus: *Alcelaphus*				
Species:				
Lichtenstein's Hartebeest				
(*Alcelaphus lichtensteini*)	185	125	135	60
Species:				
Bubal Hartebeest				
(*Alcelaphus buselaphus*)				
Sub-species:				
North African Hartebeest extinct				
(*A. b. buselaphus*)				
West African Hartebeest				
(*A. b. major*)	210	135	190	70
Lelwel Hartebeest				
(*A. b. lelwel*)	200	130	175	68
Tora Hartebeest				
(*A. b. tora*)	180	115	130	50
Swayne's Hartebeest				
(*A. b. swaynei*)	180	120	135	52
Jackson's Hartebeest				
(*A. b. jacksoni*)	195	130	160	67
Coke's Hartebeest				
(*A. b. cokii*)	185	120	145	60
Cape Hartebeest				
(*A. b. caama*)	200	130	170	66

animal'. Hartebeest are indeed enduring, excellent runners and can change course unexpectedly at full gallop, for which reason they are less vulnerable than wildebeest or zebra. Their strong horns are highly effective weapons when the need arises. They are hunted by the Lion, Leopard, Cheetah, various hyaenas and African Wild Dogs, and also fall prey to the native inhabitants. They have first-rate meat, their coats can be used to make blankets, their processed hides make clothes and belts, and their horns can be worked into decorative objects.

Hartebeest mark their territories with the secretion from their suborbital glands, rubbing this against leaves or grass stems. The scent becomes impregnated with sand and warns rivals not to approach. Females do not remain permanently in one territory, although they may stay with one male for several days. If a female comes into a territory, the male runs to her with tail raised and neck stretched, squatting several times in front of her; if the female advances towards him he understands this as consent to mating. If the female is not interested she simply leaves and the male does not bother her further.

At present the most widespread hartebeest species are Lichtenstein's living in the woodland terrain of southern Tanzania and Mozambique, and the Bubal Hartebeest (*Alcelaphus buselaphus*) which prefers open plains covered by low grass. The most beautifully-coloured hartebeest is the Bontebok (*Damaliscus dorcas*), which lives in southern Africa. The Sassaby is widespread throughout almost the whole of Africa, having conspicuous bluish spots on its chest and rump. These live in small herds of 10 to 30 animals, although they occasionally form herds of several hundreds or even thousands.

THE TSETSE FLY

The *Glossina* genus of flies has 20 species in Africa, of which the Tsetse Fly (*Glossina palpalis*) is easily recognizable by the axe-shaped mark in its wings, the blades of the axe facing the front. Both males and females suck blood; the tip of the stinging proboscis pierces both the skin and the fatty tissue beneath until it encounters a small blood vessel. The fly then injects saliva into the small wound to prevent the blood from coagulating. Along with the saliva, microscopic animals called flagellata enter the wound, each being only 0.05 millimetres long. These are the organisms which cause sleeping sickness. They reproduce in the digestive tract of the fly.

The Tsetse Fly: cars must stop at the road blocks marked 'Tsetse Control'. Guards then check the cars to ensure they are not carrying Tsetse Flies. They spray the bottom of the car with chemicals and catch any flies inside with nets.

Someone who catches this illness at first feels pains in the body, then becomes feverish; the neck glands swell, confusion occurs and the sick person loses weight, possibly even dying. Domestic animals brought to Africa perish from 'nagana', another sleeping sickness which is also caused by flagellata carried by several blood-sucking fly species. For this reason it is not possible to keep cattle or to work farms in regions where the flies occur.

Sometimes Tsetse Flies can copulate for as long as five hours, but after this the female is fertilized for the whole of her life. During the subsequent 200 days she lays larvae in loose soil. The larvae have hatched from eggs in the body of the female, being nourished by means of special glands and shedding their skin three times in succession — also in the body of the mother. She is unable to suck blood before delivery as there is not sufficient room inside her — a larva can be up to 10 millimetres long. During delivery the mother assists with her legs.

In the struggle against the Tsetse Fly, J. K. Chorley became notorious by having nearly one million large animals shot in East Africa in the 1930s. Of course the hunt was without success. Scientific research has revealed that the flies feed mainly on the blood of wart-hogs and less on the blood of other animals. Modern research is being carried out to combat this dreaded insect biologically, with chemical sprays and traps.

VERVET MONKEYS

Vervet Monkeys have rounded heads with flat faces, slender limbs, long thumbs, long tails, spacious cheek pouches and (for monkeys) average-sized bald patches on the rump. They are among the most gregarious monkeys. Vervet troops cannot be missed in the forest: even if you do not hear the call of the leader, plenty of noise is caused by them running through the tree-tops. When not on the march they play, sit around and sunbathe. With the exception of the Hussar Monkey, vervets are only seen on the ground when there is something there to eat. They run along branches, jumping with agility and not minding at all if the branches are thorny.

Troop leaders play an important role in the life of vervets. They always go ahead of the troop, being first to descend to a watering place and warning or calling to the others. When the troop is resting the leader usually takes the highest position in the tree, leading them to feed and guarding them against danger. If the

The largest living stork, the Saddle-billed Stork, lives in pairs. It builds strong flat nests in trees in inaccessible marshy places. The eggs are similar in both shape and colour to the eggs of the White Stork, measuring on average 76 by 57 millimetres.

In the swamps and ponds around Lake Kainji in Nigeria we startled a large flock of Tree Ducks. These birds are 50 centimetres long and look very slender due to their long feet. In spite of having the foremost part of the head white, from a distance they look completely black against the sky. They are common in northern, central and, in places, even East Africa. They make a high-pitched 'sip sip sien' sound.

leader is killed the other members are seized by panic and confusion, fleeing wildly in all directions.

When a troop sets off for the grain fields of the local farmers the leader proceeds with constant caution, and the rest follow over the same trees and branches. He surveys the situation several times from the top of a tree, and if he is satisfied he calms the troop by means of guttural sounds; if not, he gives a warning signal. Close to the field the whole troop climbs down a tree and bounds towards the grain with long leaps. Each then quickly tears off several ears of grain and stuffs them into its cheek pouches. Only when the pouches are completely full do they begin to feed more slowly. They sniff each ear they tear off, and if they do not like it they throw it away: out of ten ears they might throw away nine and eat only one. Farmers hate them because of this devastation of their crops. From time to time the leader raises himself on his hind legs and, standing erect, looks around. If the troop feels safe in the field the mothers will let their young down from clinging to their bellies and they play. In the event of danger the leader calls in a tremulous tone and the mothers sieze their young, and they all quickly flee, every monkey still trying to tear off as many ears as it can. When the leader stops and the troop is out of danger the important task of grooming each other's coats begins. After this they return once again to the fields. Eventually they move off to sleep, settling in branch forks close to a tree trunk, huddling together for warmth.

Vervets are hunted by the Leopards, Crowned Eagles and occasionally by pythons. Every vervet species has its favourite habitat. Four geographical sub-species of the Green Monkey prefer open savannah: the Grivet (*Cercopithecus aethiops aethiops*), the Tantalus (*C. a. tantalus*), the Callitrix (*C. a. sabaeus*) and the Vervet itself (*C. a. pygerythrus*). Allen's Monkey, the Talapoin and the Greater White-nosed Monkey, and sometimes also Brazza's Monkey, mostly prefer swampy places where

The Blue Monkey is greyish-green with a black back, black arms and legs, and black on the top of the head with a conspicuous light diadem shape. The most beautiful sub-species has a golden-red back and lives in the forests around Lake Kivu as far as Uganda.

they can feed on foliage, young plant shoots and fruit. Vervets are most active in the afternoon and morning, resting in the shade in the noonday heat. The various species can be readily distinguished by the way they carry their tails when running. The Hussar Monkey is the fastest runner of all, being an inhabitant of sparsely vegetated savannahs. It does not take refuge in trees even when in danger, as do the other species, but escapes by galloping over the ground. Nevertheless the Hussar Monkey can climb very well and usually spends the night in trees.

The Hussar Monkey is the fastest runner of all monkeys. Although it can climb trees, it prefers to run from danger along the ground.

	Body length in cm	Tail length in cm
Allen's Monkey (*Allenopithecus nigroviridis*)	46	50
Talapoin (*Miopithecus talapoin*)	35	40
Owl-faced Monkey (*Cercopithecus hamlyni*)	55	58
Brazza's Monkey (*Cercopithecus neglectus*)	52	62
L'Hoest's Monkey (*Cercopithecus lhoesti*)	58	70
Blue Monkey (*Cercopithecus mitis)*	65	80
Greater White-nosed Monkey (*Cercopithecus nictitans*)	50	90
Diana Monkey (*Cercopithecus diana*)	55	80
Green Monkey (*Cercopithecus aethiops*)	50	65
Moustached Monkey (*Cercopithecus cephus*)	52	72
Mona Monkey (*Cercopithecus mona*)	50	70
Hussar Monkey (*Erythrocebus patas*)	75	65

WHERE THE WHITE NILE FLOWS
The Upper Nile basin

About 35 million years ago, what is now the eastern bank of Lake Victoria was a watershed from which rivers flowed westwards. Volcanic activity and shifts in the earth's crust stemmed the natural flow of the rivers and created several lakes. The shallow Lake Victoria gradually formed with its main tributary, the Kagera, which has its source in Rwanda. In Uganda the lake waters flow out as the Victoria Nile, which enters Lake Kyoga, forming the Kabalega Waterfalls, and then flowing into Lake Albert. The waters reach Sudan as the Albert Nile, subsequently bearing the name of Bahr-al-Djabal (the Mountain Nile) from the Nimule Pass. Downstream from the junction with the Bahr-al-Ghazal it is known as Bahr-al-Abyad — the White Nile.

The varied topography of the Upper Nile basin, the number of rivers, the flat swamps and the remarkable wildlife constitute a natural region in its own right. The typical swamps of northern Uganda and the vast swamps known as 'Sud' in Sudan are the result of heavy rainfall, during which water collects in shallow valleys and is not able to drain out quickly. Suitable conditions, with warmth and bright sunlight, enable a rich growth of floating plants which spread outwards and downwards to form an almost continuous floating carpet. This can support quite large animals but renders it impossible for larger vessels to navigate the Nile.

The swamps are the home of the *Anopheles* Mosquito, the females of which are malaria carriers. Using her piercing mouthparts the female penetrates the skin, puncturing a blood vessel and squirting a drop of saliva into the wound so that the blood cannot coagulate. She then drinks her fill. The area which has been bitten itches unpleasantly and becomes very swollen. Microscopic organisms (Haemosporidia) enter the host's blood via her saliva. They attack the red blood cells and reproduce rapidly, bringing about, after three or four days, heavy and recurring attacks of fever. If not treated the disease may result in death.

The largest flat swamp, the Sud, has an area of thousands of square kilometres. It lies at the point where the White Nile turns eastwards towards the town of Malakal, being swelled by water from several other rivers. These swamps form an almost impassable obstacle through which even Roman legions could not penetrate. Only in the 1870s did the explorer Speke manage to cross this region and discover the sources

The Bichir is over a metre in length, greenish on the back and a dirty white colour on the abdomen. The dorsal fin consists of a row of smaller fins one behind the other. Each of these is supported on the forward edge by a bony ray. A number of soft rays point towards the back and a membrane is stretched between them.

The Electric Catfish differs from other catfish species in that it does not have a dorsal fin and the side fins do not have spines. It has a plain, slimy, indistinctly grey skin, covered with irregular black spots concentrated along the sides and fins.

of the Nile. Around the permanent swamps are vast areas which are wet only in the rainy season, whilst in the dry season they have rich pasture on which thousands of domestic and wild animals graze. Some animals, such as the Nile Lechwe (*Kobus megaceros*), live even among the marches and floating islands. This remarkable waterbuck has enlarged hooves and loose skin on its feet, so that it does not sink into the swamp. The undersides of the feet are naked, so

The Nile flows through the East African lake system, which maintains the river's water level with its tributaries. The waterfall in the Elgon Mountains drops by 52 metres. In the dry season it is only a small stream. With the arrival of the rains it becomes a large river, flowing together with the Nile into Lake Kyoga.

Pygmy Hippos, in contrast to the larger Amphibious Hippo, often fight each other in captivity and may cause serious injury. For this reason the pairs must be kept apart.

that when running it can grip the slippery surface like a car tyre without slipping. In the swamps Nile Lechwe is well protected from predatory big cats. It escapes from its enemies by submerging as far as the head. Buffon's Kob lives with it in the swamps.

The most conspicuous plant of this region is Papyrus (*Cyperus papyrus*). It grows as high as five metres, forming whole forests with its three-sided, leafless, hard stems that carry a single bunch of long, thin leaves at the top. The roots, together with dead plant matter, form a carpet half a metre or more thick, a growth so dense that people have to cut their way through it. Nothing, apart from a few fern and creeper species, grows among papyrus. On the open water, Water Cabbage (*Pistia stratioides*) grows. Neither this nor Papyrus is eaten by animals. In some places Saw-grass (*Cladium jamaicense*), Club-rush (*Typha australis*) and Bog-reed (*Phragmites mauritianus*) may replace Papyrus, although these flourish better in drier regions. The water on which these plant carpets float is almost lifeless, as all the oxygen and nutrients are used by the upper plant layer. Peat is formed at the bottom from the remains of dead plants.

Situtungas and hippopotami (*Hippopotamus amphibius*) — the third largest African mammals — live in the swamps and in the undergrowth on riverbanks and lake shores. The latter serves an important function in this habitat, by eating low quality foods which are almost indigestible for other herbivores. It also bores tunnels and trails through the dense undergrowth of bulrushes, making the swamps accessible to other animals. Its abundant excrement helps to fertilize the water, encouraging growth of minute algae and plankton which in turn serve as food for fish. In some places there are still sufficient Nile Crocodiles (*Crocodilus niloticus*) to keep a balance among the various animal species. Where crocodiles have been exterminated, however, predatory fish such as the Nile Catfish (*Clarias mozambicus*) eat so many other fish species that fishing has run into serious difficulties in some places. For this reason attempts are being made to re-introduce crocodiles.

Many African Pythons (*Python sebae*), which can be up to seven metres long, live in this region. Around the swamps and on small islands dwell large numbers of various birds, feeding predominantly on fish. Among these are two cormorant species, the Cormorant itself (*Phalacrocorax carbo*) and the Long-tailed Shag (*Phalacrocorax africanus*), the Anhinga (*Anhinga rufa*), many herons, the Sacred Ibis (*Threskiornis aethiopicus*), the Open-billed Stork (*Pelecanus rufescens*) and a remarkable bird, the Shoebill Stork (*Balaeniceps rex*), known in Arabic as Abu Markub, or 'Father shoe'.

Among the many remarkable fish species is the Bichir (*Polypterus bichir*), which moves from

swamps to rivers in the dry season and hunts small fish at night. Various species of elephant-trunk fish (Mormiridae family) can produce weak electric shocks of up to two volts by means of a special organ situated near the tail. Using their downward-turned snouts they stir up the mud in search of food. The Nile Perch ranks among the largest freshwater fish, growing to 180 centimetres in length. The Electric Catfish (*Malapterurus electricus*) can measure up to 120 centimetres long and has a smooth, scaleless body. Its enormous electric organ lies under the skin, extending from the head as far as the beginning of the anal fin and accounting for a quarter of the total body weight. It produces electric shocks as strong as 350 volts.

Along both banks of the Nile, including the Semliki tributary, the abundance of plants and animals is one of the greatest in the world. In the Kabalega and Ruwenzori National Parks, elephants have become too numerous and have devastated whole areas of woodland savannah, slowly transforming it into grassland. The natural balance has been disturbed in many places in this region, often due to human interference, and this is harming both the vegetation and the animals. Herbivores which would normally browse on tree and shrub foliage are now virtually absent, whereas animals which graze on grass are becoming more prominent.

HIPPOPOTAMI

The Amphibious Hippopotamus (*Hippopotamus amphibius*), usually called the 'hippo', was well known to ancient peoples. From the wall paintings of the ancient Egyptians we know that, at that time, they inhabited the whole Nile basin and hunting them was a favourite amusement of the powerful. It is also evident from the Bible that hippopotami lived on the banks of the

In the early evening, before sunset, hundreds of African Elephants living in the Kabalega National Park in Uganda go to drink and bathe in Lake Albert. Adult females drink between 80 and 100 litres of water at once, but go to water only every two days. Old large males will drink between 100 and 150 litres, travelling to the watering places every two or three days.

Jordan. The Romans were bringing live hippopotami from the Nile Delta and showing them in the arena during gladiatorial games as early as the first century BC.

The hippo is an amphibious animal, spending over half its life in water. It prefers depths of up to one and a half metres in places where there is no strong current. It has nostrils, eyes and ears lying high on the head and which are frequently all that is visible of a submerged hippopotamus. The nostrils close automatically under water. Newborn young can stay under water for perhaps 30 seconds, and an adult for as long as five minutes. The creature has an enormous mouth which it can open unbelievably wide, revealing its strong lower canines, when it wants to frighten an opponent; it can remain in this posture for quite some time. The co-existence of hippopotami with Mud-fish (*Labeo velifer*) is an interesting phenomenon: these fish, about half a metre long, swim around the hippo and by means of their specially adapted mouths rid it of leeches.

The White Stork builds a substantial nest of strong sticks, clumps of soil, grass and leaves. It extends the nest every year. Each spring wild storks visit nests at our zoo on their way north. They circle above, clap their bills, and only after a few days do they continue on their way.

East African Elephants (*Loxodonta africana knochenhaueri*) after bathing, feeding on the bank of the Nile at the edge of the Kabalega National Park in Uganda; they are accompanied by Cattle Egrets.

Grass is the staple diet of hippopotami. They have stomachs consisting of three parts and the intestinal tract is over 50 metres long. They have an unusual habit of swinging their tails when defecating, both on dry land and in water, thus

scattering the excrement far from the body and over shrubs and grass. In this way they mark their territory and pasture areas, informing other hippos that the territory is already occupied. The habit is described in an old African tale: when God created the hippo, He ordered it to cut grass for the other animals. However, when the hippo arrived in Africa and discovered how hot it was there, it begged God for permission to be allowed to stay in water during the day and to cut grass at night. God, however, did not want to permit this, as He was afraid that the hippo would eat the fish in the water. Finally He did give permission, but from that time the hippo had to scatter its excrement with its tail, so that God could see that it does not contain fish bones.

When undisturbed, the hippopotamus moves slowly in water. When aroused it rushes at its rival or enemy, charging forward with large leaps

An unconventional meeting on the bank of the Ishasha River, on the border between Uganda and Zaire. On a narrow trail two large males came face to face — an elephant and a hippo. They stopped, looked at each other for a moment, and then the hippo slowly and calmly stepped aside from the trail, leaving the elephant to continue walking undisturbed.

and stirring up the surface of the water far and wide. If hippopotami are disturbed suddenly while resting peacefully on a bank, they can run to water quickly and jump in with agility, down to depths of six metres. The voice of a hippo is impossible to imitate, being a longish, powerful bass roar, usually finished off with three short shrieks that sound as if they come from a giant drum.

In the basin of the White Nile a short heavy rainstorm sometimes breaks unexpectedly over a small area in the period before the main rainy season, while only a short distance away the sun is shining.

Abdim's Stork is similar to the Black Stork, but considerably smaller. It prefers to nest close to villages or even among the buildings. There can be as many as 30 nests in one large tree. The eye is greyish-brown, the bare patches round the eyes blue, the bare face and throat red, the bill yellowish-green with a red tip. The grey-brown legs are light red at the joints.

▶

In the Ishasha River in the daytime, several thousand hippopotami of various ages lie in the rushing water. If disturbed they form a group and disappear surprisingly quickly into the dense undergrowth on the shore, where tunnels and trails have been trodden by elephants, hippos and Forest Hogs.

The majority of disputes among males are over females. Hippopotami slowly approach each other in the shallow muddy water on the shore of Lake Edward, and when they are close rush at each other with mouths open wide. They do not collide, however, but stop close together. The weaker of the two usually retreats.

The African Fish Eagle in its adult dress. It lives near lakes, sizeable rivers and coastal areas. This eagle occurs in large numbers around Lake Victoria and the whole White Nile basin. The head, neck, nape, upper part of the breast and tail are a brilliant white, the back plumage and wings bluish-black, the wing coverts and underside brown-red, the iris, cere and legs bright yellow, and the beak blue-black.

In the swampy regions of the White Nile where there is an abundance of plants, hippopotami leave the water only rarely and feed on the vegetation even in the daytime. Lotus forms their staple diet, although water reeds and sedge make welcome supplements. When eating, the enormous head is submerged under water for a while as it wrestles with plants and stirs up the mud. It then surfaces with its head full of torn-off plants, laying the bunch on the surface of the water and eating slowly. Plant stalks hang from the corners of its mouth and green juice mixed with saliva flows from its bloated lips as it spits out half-chewed clumps and swallows them again.

In places where the hippo has to climb a bank to feed, however, it behaves differently. About an hour after sunset it leaves the water,

listening carefully and sniffing in all directions. Near human settlements it can devastate a field of crops in a single night, as although its appetite is enormous it tramples down more than it can eat. The hippo also threatens the lives of domestic animals and people on its grazing rounds. A case has been recorded in which a hippo bit to death four donkeys which were standing peacefully in harness. On another occasion two women were passing a grazing hippopotamus in the evening, talking to each other loudly. The hippopotamus suddenly attacked them and bit them so badly that they both died.

Most hippopotami are a steel-grey colour with a pinkish abdomen, although the colour of the almost completely bald skin is quite variable. The animals mate in shallow water and copulation is prolonged. During mating the female is almost completely submerged and has to raise her head for air quite frequently. After copulation the pair jump up several times, dive under the water and after a while attempt mating again.

I once observed two males fighting for a female on heat. She wallowed in the mud, showing her pinkish abdomen to a large male lying nearby. Another sturdy male approached, cruising through the water like a submarine. The first male became alert, raised himself and sat on his hind quarters like a dog. When they were about four metres apart they both stood on all fours, watching each other for a while. Suddenly they

The Hammerhead has a stunted cylindrical body, a short strong neck, a relatively large head and a tall bill which is longer than the head. The bill together with the crest creates the impression of a hammer placed on the neck. The broad wings are rounded, the tail being formed from twelve plumes. The colouring is an even brown, somewhat lighter on the abdomen. It has a deeply-cut web between the toes.

A young adult African Fish Eagle is still unable to hunt, although it can fly. It remains close to the nest and the parents bring fish several times a day, placing it on a rocky outcrop or dropping it from a height of several metres onto a flat rock. The parents announce their approach with fluttering wings and a loud screeching.

charged at each other with their mouths opened wide, their tusks gleaming menacingly in the sun. I was expecting a terrible collision, but they suddenly stopped with their mouths only a few centimetres apart, swaying their heads from side to side as they slowly retreated. After a few seconds the charge was repeated. The first male did not retreat from his position, however; on the contrary, he moved forwards until the second dashed round in a curve to make his escape. The first pursued him fiercely for a short way, stopped after a few paces, snorted and then returned to the female.

Struggles between males are not always so peaceful. Sometimes they can fight for as long as two hours, digging their canines into each other's bodies with powerful blows of the head,

The Shoebill makes a large nest between three and four metres in diameter, low down and close to water, either on strong bushes or stunted trees. It is a beautiful ash-grey in colour, the edges of the larger plumes being light grey and the flight and tail feathers greyish-brown. The young are a dirty rusty-grey.

The Squacco Heron has a strong bill and a crest of rusty yellowish-white bordered by reddish-brown feathers. The sides of the head and neck are a light rusty-yellow. The wing coverts and the very fine cloak are a crimson-flaxen colour, while the remaining parts of the body are white.

In the swamps near the White Nile gleams the snow-white plumage of the Great White Heron (*Casmerodius albus*). At nesting time one of these birds may have as many as 50 decorative plumes, each up to 50 centimetres long, on its back. At this time the bill is coloured grey-black. Outside the nesting season it lives alone in small flocks.

causing deep wounds which bleed heavily. Once it happened that one hippo's canine pierced straight to the opponent's heart, although such serious wounds are rare.

The female hippo usually gives birth in water, forming a dam between the bank and deeper water with her body. Immediately after birth the calf begins to tread water so as to reach the surface quickly and take in air, making these swimming movements even when the female gives birth on dry land. During the first few days of life the young sometimes fall prey to crocodiles, hyaenas and other large predators. Adult hippopotami, however, have nothing to fear except humans.

The Pygmy Hippopotamus (*Choeropsis liberiensis*) lives in a relatively small region in the tropical marshy forests of West Africa. For a long time little was known about it. In 1912 the hunter Schomburg managed to send to

The Cattle Egret can be kept in the open air in zoos without clipping its wings provided they can be with elephants, rhinos, hippos or Cape Buffalo. These birds fly after the animals in the outside runs and return with them at night to the houses.

The Purple Heron passes the winter in Africa. It is relatively timid and has excellent eyesight. It lays between four and six eggs which are blue — unlike the eggs of other heron species.

Hamburg five live specimens, causing a sensation. So far we know little about these animals from observation in nature: what we do know comes from keeping them in zoos.

The body of the Pygmy Hippo is cylindrical in shape and covered with a smooth blackish-brown skin which excretes a slimy mucus on dry land, although to a lesser extent than the larger species. It also needs water, but lives much more among waterside shrubs; indeed it flees to dense shrubs in case of danger, rather than to water, in contrast to the amphibious hippo. It does not live in groups but is a solitary animal, coming out to feed at night on various plants. During the day it sleeps in hollows washed out of waterside banks or in puddles by the shore. This animal extends its waterside hollow in such a way as to make exits both to land and water.

The male Pygmy Hippo lives with the female for a short time during the mating season. He approaches a female on heat from behind, placing his head on her back. As a result of rubbing against each other they often become almost completely covered with white foamy mucus from the skin glands. The female runs away a few paces several times, finally stopping and allowing the male to press her down onto her abdomen, and they copulate in this position. Young are born at the beginning of the dry season, staying with their mother until their third

The largest African heron species, the Goliath Heron (*Ardea goliath*), has a wingspan of up to two metres. It has a white throat; the head, crest and wing curves are chestnut brown; the upper body is ash-grey to blue. The upper part of the bill and the legs are black; the lower part of the bill is violet at the root and greenish-yellow at the tip. It can catch fish weighing over a kilogramme. It inhabits an enormous area from Ethiopia to southern Africa.

year. As with elephants, rhinos and the amphibious hippo species, the mother usually walks with them in front of her or by her side.

On the White Nile, on the lakes of the Great African Depression and smaller ponds and swamps, the African Wood Ibis is a common bird. It is about the same size as the White Stork and nests in flocks in high trees, building a nest of up to two metres in diameter and laying up to three eggs.

HERONS, SHOEBILLS AND HAMMERHEADS

Herons (Ardeidae) number 62 species and are widespread all over the world. Like almost all waders they have long legs, slender necks and long bills. They can place themselves in the most extraordinary postures as they hunt by stealth, remaining motionless for hours at a time on the lookout for prey. Their gait is cautious; their flight is not without agility but monotonous, except for the nuptial flight, which is beautiful. During this they fly in extraordinary curves and loops, turning over in the air like pigeons. In the air they do not keep their necks extended like storks or flamingoes, but hold them in an S-shaped curve. They are agile in running to and fro among the reeds and are also good swimmers. The heron's voice is an unpleasant screech; its eyesight and hearing are excellent. The beautiful, predominantly light-coloured eyes are somewhat reminiscent of a snake.

Herons nest in colonies but they cannot be called gregarious birds: even among themselves they can be intolerant. They are strictly monogamous and build untidy nests among reeds. Avoiding larger animals, they feed on smaller ones such as fish and frogs. Smaller heron species are also insectivores and indeed will not turn down anything they can catch; many search through the sand and mud below the water in the same way as hens peck in dry soil. When hunting they release their sinuous necks like coiled springs, plunging the bill or even the whole head into the water. They either gulp down the captured prey immediately or first straighten it in their bills. When in difficulty, herons protect themselves fiercely, often attacking the eyes of their opponent with their awl-shaped bills.

The Purple Heron (*Ardea purpurea*) has a body 80 centimetres in length and a wingspan of 140 centimetres. Its range includes the southern part of Europe, South Asia and the whole of Africa. This heron likes to nest in colonies among reeds in deeper water. In the vicinity of the nests they construct 'resting places' from broken club-rush or reed stems. As nesting continues the number of these resting places increases until they join together, forming bridges and paths over which the nestlings make their first trips.

The Squacco Heron (*Ardea ralloides*) is a smaller bird, its body measuring up to 50 centimetres and its wingspan 80 centimetres. It has a long yellow crest on its head. In Europe it nests south of the Danube, from where it flies to spend the winter mainly in the Nile basin. When hunting it generally remains in one place all day, having a nap and resting at noon, hunting again in the afternoon and in the evening flying to roost among the densest shrubs or reeds. It lives mainly on fish, catching only small species in shallow water.

The Cattle Egret (*Bubulcus ibis*) has a wingspan only 10 centimetres greater than that of the Squacco Heron. In the breeding season it has a rusty-coloured crest and the elongated plumes on its back and throat are also rust-coloured: otherwise it is completely white. In contrast to the other species it is not so dependent on water, often hunting in fields or on savannah where it moves among cattle and other large animals. Its range extends from the Mediterranean across the whole of Africa and Madagascar as far as Western Asia, and it also lives in Central and North America. Once it was even spotted in England. During locust migrations thousands of these egrets appear on the savannah, spending the night at the edge of the forest and returning in the morning to the herds. They live in harmony with humans and are venerated in Madagascar.

The Shoebill Stork (*Balaeniceps rex*) is a rare bird in zoological gardens. Its natural home is the upper part of the White Nile and areas of Uganda and Zaire. It settles in inaccessible swamps near lakes and rivers, preferring places where reeds alternate with shallow water. This species stands about one metre high and has long toes, so as not to sink too deeply in the mud. Its magnificent plumage is grey and the

The Sacred Ibis has a bald head and neck in adulthood which is coloured greyish-black. Up to the age of two years, however, the head and neck are covered by blackish feathers indented with white. After the first moulting the young grow split spatula-shaped feathers, which they retain until adulthood. Local hunters like to decorate themselves with these feathers.

bill is an unusual boat shape. It usually hunts alone, walking slowly and cautiously through shallow places with its head lowered to water level, watching out for prey. This stork catches mainly fish but will also eat frogs, turtles and even small crocodiles and mammals. In their nests, constructed from reeds and twigs in the swamps, Shoebill Storks greet one another by clapping their bills like storks whilst lowering their heads towards the nest and making extraordinary movements, as if vomiting — this is how they demonstrate their friendship.

The Hammerhead (*Scopus umbretta*) is a striking bird that habitually sits with its neck completely withdrawn, making it look as if the head were situated directly on the shoulders. It sometimes raises and lowers its crest, otherwise it can remain motionless for minutes at a time. This bird is at its most lively in the morning and at dusk, and is usually found only on the banks of forest brooks or rivers. It lives on fish, frogs, various larvae and insects and almost anything else that lives in and around water.

Hammerheads are skilful builders of enormous nests interwoven with sticks, reeds, grass and clay. Inside a nest are three compartments: an antechamber, a store and a sleeping area, connected by corridors so that the bird can crawl through them. The rear chamber, the sleeping area, is the largest and is higher than the other two. The nest can take as long as five months to build. The male and female take turns at sitting on the eggs and one of them often keeps watch in the antechamber. Other birds nest on the edges of these gigantic constructions, so that some people believed the Hammerheads did not build their nests alone.

There are many superstitions connected with Hammerheads. In Angola it is thought that whoever bathes in water through which this bird has waded will fall ill with skin eruptions. In Madagascar there is a widespread superstition that whoever destroys its nest will encounter bad luck. When it crosses someone's path, the person prefers to turn back rather than go on. In some places people will even move their dwelling somewhere else if a Hammerhead appears nearby, since it is believed that the bird attracts bad luck.

STORKS AND IBISES

The White Stork (*Ciconia ciconia*) is well known and nests throughout the whole of Europe. It also nests in North Africa, and migrates to its African winter quarters by two routes. West European birds fly across France, Gibraltar, Morocco and Tunisia or Algeria in a broad front across the Sahara towards the south. East European members fly across Hungary, the Balkans, Asia Minor and Israel to the interior of Africa. Their route to the south takes them over the Nile, the lakes of the Great Trench Depression and down the coast of Africa. Storks can cover up to 250 kilometres a day.

The Black Stork *(Ciconia nigra)* differs little from the above species in size, but is white only on the abdomen. Its range is a broad belt across Eurasia and it nests mainly in forest areas, in Asia ascending to heights of 2,200 metres. It also returns to winter in Africa by two routes.

The largest species, the Saddle-billed Stork (*Ephippiorhynchus senegalensis*) is up to 150 centimetres long with a wingspan of 240 centimetres. It builds its nest in tall trees on river banks and prefers to feed on locusts and grasshoppers, which it can catch even on the wing. If it tackles larger prey it first smashes the victim, throws it into the air and then skilfully catches and swallows it.

The Open-billed Stork is smaller than the White Stork. Before dawn in thick fog it strides slowly to the riverbanks or swamps for food. Africans regard the young of this stork as a delicacy, and in Madagascar even the adult birds are hunted.

The Marabou Stork, together with vultures, feeds on the remains of large animals. It lives near towns where it will eat leftovers on rubbish heaps. It can be easily tamed in captivity. The Arabs call this bird 'Abu Sein', or 'Father of the Pouch', on account of the bald pouch, thinly covered with short hair-like feathers, which swings with each step it takes.

The Marabou Stork (*Leptoptilos crumeniferus*) lives near human settlements, although it can also be found on savannahs. It often accompanies predators, with which it shares prey. It rests either in high, often solitary, trees or on rocks. When these storks fly to their nests they greet one another with hissing noises and by clapping their bills, bowing low and spreading their white undertail plumage. There is no more greedy bird than the Marabou: it can gulp down a calf's leg, a lizard, an insect or a snake, and even rags soaked with blood.

The Open-billed Stork (*Anastomus lamelligerus*) lives in Africa and Madagascar. It is a strange-looking black bird, with the vanes of the feathers on its neck, abdomen and thighs elongated into long, narrow, horny plates which shine greenish-purple. It also has a striking bill on which the ridges of the upper and lower mandible do not meet in the centre. This stork feeds mainly on snails, frogs, grasshoppers and worms. It builds a nest in trees or among reeds; as many as 60 nests were recorded in one tree.

The Yellow-billed Stork (*Ibis ibis*) has a bald red face, a long downward-curving bill, yellow legs and white plumage with a pink tinge. The wing coverts are conspicuously pink, the wing tips and tail greenish-black, and the bird is very

stork-like both in gait and flight. In the morning and evening it hunts small mammals, young birds and also fish, lizards and worms. It never strays far from water.

The Sacred Ibis (*Threskiornis aethiopicus*) lives in swamps, marshes and forests. It walks with a measured pace, never at a trot, and is a good swimmer. It nests in trees and shrubs. The ancient Egyptians greatly revered this species: thousands of mummified ibises have lasted to this day. According to Roman writers, the god Mercury took the form of a Sacred Ibis. Plineus mentions that the Egyptians invoked this bird as a protector against poisonous snakes and that they also venerated it as a bringer of rain. Aelianus relates that the Ibis was dedicated to the Moon because it needs exactly as many days to hatch its clutch of eggs as the 'Star of Isida' takes for one orbit.

The Hadada Ibis (*Hagedashia hagedash*), which lives in East Africa, is possibly the most beautifully coloured of all ibises. Predators dislike this bird, however, as it announces every approaching danger with its hoarse call (especially if the danger is human) and so warns the hunted animals. It has a greyish-brown head with a white band above the eyes. The wings and back are a striking glistening blue-green, the tail plumage being black and the bill black with a red ridge.

The Hermit Ibis (*Geronticus eremita*) inhabits North Africa, Ethiopia and the coast of the Red Sea. It flies from its rocky hiding place to nearby savannahs, lakes and river banks for food. As late as the 16th century this bird was still living in Austria and Switzerland, although it has gradually disappeared. One reason for this

The majority of large Nile Crocodiles live beneath the Kabalega waterfall in Uganda. They often sun themselves on little sandy islands or climb out onto the banks. The females lay between 30 and 90 eggs into dug-out pits. After laying the eggs they carefully cover them and watch over them with great vigilance.

Adult crocodiles often rest in the open sun with their mouths wide open. In the mouth the leathery fold which completely closes the gullet can be seen.

was the fact that it was greatly hunted by humans; its retreat to the south was also influenced by fundamental climatic changes. It was described for the first time to science by Konrad Gessner in the 16th century, although few took his description seriously. This interesting bird was described in 1758 by Linné (Linnaeus) as *Upupa eremita* — that is, a relative of the hoopoe with Switzerland as its original home. It was subsequently put into the *Geronticus* genus by the naturalist Wagner (1835). Today, its habits are little known and it is very rare.

CROCODILES

It would be possible to write several volumes on crocodiles, with one fascinating story after another. Such an account could extend from the early culture of the ancient Egyptians to the present time. Some of the stories would be fables, but a good half would certainly be true. Even as early as the writings of Herodotus, we find that crocodiles were considered to be sacred in ancient Egypt. The inhabitants around Thebes and Lake Moiris tamed a chosen crocodile, hanging earrings made of melted glass and gold from its earlobes and putting gold bracelets round its legs. After its death they embalmed it and buried it in a sacred coffin. It was believed in ancient Egypt that it was necessary to pacify the god of the River Nile by sacrificing a beautiful maiden to the crocodile every year.

On the Sesee Islands in Lake Victoria, the natives considered crocodiles to be the high priests of a god and brought them human sacrifices. The ancient writer Strabo wrote that in the town of Arsinoe, in Egypt, the priests had a tame crocodile. They would approach it, one of them would open its mouth, another would place a cake and a piece of roast meat into it and wash these down with wine. When the animal had gulped this down it would dive into the water of the lake and swim to the other bank.

Konrad Gessner, in his book *Historia animalium* of 1551, wrote that people suffering from fever should anoint themselves with crocodile fat, which is completely white, and that crocodile blood was a recognized remedy for eye ailments. The famous tale about crying 'crocodile tears' was known to a Franciscan monk, Bartholomew Anglicus, who taught natural sciences in Paris around 1225. He taught his students that when a crocodile kills a human it first cries over the body, only then eating it. Mandeville's travelogue, published in Liège in 1357, also describes how crocodiles hypocritically shed tears over their victims. This was believed by Shakespeare, and the supposition was even given credence by scholars of the 18th century. A healthy crocodile, however, does not produce any tears. A 'crying crocodile' may occur if it is kept in unsuitable conditions, when it may catch an eye infection and really weep.

Any behaviour resulting from the simple biological needs of animals, but which differs from the needs of humans, tends to be explained by attributing to it a magical importance. In addition to this, strong individuals of a tribe such as chiefs or witchdoctors need secret, frightening rituals to reinforce their power and control their subjects easily. Apart from leopard-men, lion-men and snake-men, the crocodile-men came into existence in river basins and around lakes. During their rituals they place crocodile masks on their heads; at initiation ceremonies people have been killed in order to obtain their hearts, lungs and brains, which were eaten for magical purposes.

After the first rains small ponds form and the dry bush begins to turn green. Large numbers of migrating animals, sometimes numbering tens of thousands, begin to break up into family herds and disperse on the steppes of the Serengeti in Tanzania and the Mara Masai in Kenya.

The Nile Crocodile (*Crocodylus niloticus*) lays eggs in excavated holes on riverbanks, under shrubs, in reeds and under trees, in the shaded damp soil. The eggs are always placed in layers, the top layer being well covered by wet humus and sand mixed with mouldy leaves. The nest is superbly camouflaged and may contain up to 90 eggs. The female often stays in the vicinity, partly to guard the nest and partly because as soon as she can hear the croaking of the young hatching she scrapes off the cover and helps them into the world. Immediately after hatching, the young hurry to water by the shortest route in order to escape from enemies, or their mother takes them down to water in her mouth. Their nests are often plundered by monitors, Marabou Storks and vultures. I have watched a Marabou hunting hatched crocodiles: even the mother could not hold it off. Although from time to time the bird had to leap away from her, nevertheless within a short time 11 little crocodiles had disappeared down its gullet.

Crocodiles have conical, pointed teeth which are slightly curved backwards. A spare tooth grows beneath each exposed one, completing its growth only if the first is broken off. Crocodiles have an immobile tongue attached to the lower part of the mouth cavity. They can breathe through their noses even with their mouth open in water, because a broad membranous valve in the rear part of the mouth cavity firmly closes the windpipe and gullet. The nasal passages, which protrude above the water, can be safely closed when diving. The eyes, with their upper and lower lids, also protrude from the top of the head, so that the crocodile can lie almost submerged in water, yet breathe comfortably through its nose and observe its surroundings. The reptile swims with the aid of its large tail, its limbs pressed close to its body.

Crocodiles are essentially waterbound animals. The dry season may be the exception, when the rivers and swamps disappear and crocodiles can be seen lumbering across country in search of a river or lake. Instances have been known where crocodiles have dug themselves into the mud during the dry season, showing no signs of life until the first rains. During mating, males raise their heads high and open their mouths wide, giving out a prolonged roar which sounds like a roll on a large drum. Courtship takes place in water. In Lake Turkana, crocodiles most often mate between 9 and 11 in the morning, having previously warmed

The Shiluks, belonging to the Nilotic group and living in southern Sudan, build round huts with a roof skilfully thatched with papyrus stalks. Beside each hut there is a raised verandah on stilts, under which they sit in the noonday heat of the dry season. On the floor they store their supplies. The various Shiluk tribes together number about 250,000 people.

themselves up on the bank. As soon as a male, swimming to and fro within his territory along the bank, encounters a female he raises his tail, curving it over in such a way that the tip stays in the water. He lifts his head and roars so loudly that he stirs up the water. At first he swims after the female, then alongside her, then he overtakes her and forces her to swim in a circle. The female either flees or allows him to place one paw on her shoulder and mount her. Their tails intertwine and beat against each other, the male holding onto the female with his paws and both partners continuing to swim even during actual copulation, which lasts up to two minutes.

Very young crocodiles spend much of the time close to the bank in shallow water, feeding on insects, frogs and other small animals until they are about 150 centimetres long. Then they are ready to start catching fish, which remain their staple diet for the rest of their lives. Large crocodiles often keep watch at watering places, trying to hunt a larger animal by seizing its head or leg, pulling it under the water and keeping it there until it drowns. In this way they can occasionally catch an antelope, zebra, cow or even a human.

From a freshly-killed animal a crocodile can only tear off the ears or the tail; crocodile teeth are not able to rip away or chew large pieces. For this reason it usually drags its prey to a quiet spot near a bank and waits until the skin softens. The crocodile then tears off a piece of meat from the body by biting firmly and twisting and turning in the water. When a lump is detached by this wrenching movement, the crocodile lifts its head half out of the water and lets the meat go deeper into its gullet. After each

gulp it remains on the surface for several minutes, breathing heavily, and then dives again to tear off another piece. Crocodiles probably manage to hunt down and eat a large prey like this only once or twice a year.

In 1974 we set up our camp for captured animals on the left bank of the River Tana in Kenya. Our hunters and assistants were from the Pokomo tribe and lived on the nearby islands, the river flowing around them. In the mornings they would wade across the Tana, which was full of large, dangerous crocodiles. Stripped naked, carrying their clothes and tools on a pack on their heads, they waded across one following close upon the other; one hand held the pack while the other splashed the water. Nothing unpleasant ever happened during their crossing, although they never entered the water alone. At other times they would drive cattle or camels just ahead or close by their sides, as protection against the crocodiles.

The African Slender-snouted Crocodile (*Crocodylus cataphractus*) can grow to a length of five metres. It inhabits areas of West and Central Africa, from Senegal as far as Angola, and is also abundant in the Congo. This species has extended narrow jaws and large bony plates behind its head. The colour is ochre, more olive on the back and yellowish-white on the abdomen. It attacks humans only rarely; on the other hand the flesh of the young crocodile is said to be full of flavour. The even smaller Broadnosed Crocodile (*Osteolaemus tetraspis*), of the tropical gallery forests of Central Africa, grows to a length of just under one metre. It has remarkable bony plates both on its back and sides.

101

THE INHOSPITABLE WILDERNESS
The East African bush

Crossing the sandy dunes behind Mombasa, the traveller ascends a gentle slope for some time until the humid coastal belt is left behind and the eastern part of Kenya and Tanzania is reached. This is the country the natives call 'Nyika', covered by dense thorny shrubs and trees. During the short rainy season the landscape turns green and bursts into flower, and the atmosphere is sultry and oppressive. The dried-up gulleys fill with thundering water carrying with it trees, dead animals and much soil. During the dry season the heat is tremendous and what little water there is often undrinkable, being either salty or contaminated by other animals. Two short rainy seasons alternate with longer dry seasons.

In Nyika the plant cover is the result of particularly complex relations between climate, soil and water. A remarkable tree called the Baobab (*Adansonia digitata*) grows there. When it sheds its leaves it looks as if it has been planted upside down, with roots at the top. Some of these trees are over 2,000 years old, ranking among the oldest plants in the world. They are perfectly adapted to their environment. Standing around six or seven metres high, their rounded greyish trunks contain a soft pulpy marrow. The thick smooth bark prevents loss of water. During the rainy season the Baobab clothes itself in leaves, from which Africans prepare a tasty salad. The large waxy flowers blossom for only one day; the oval fruit contains a sweetish edible pulp as well as seeds.

The ecological balance among the trees, shrubs and grass is intriguing in Nyika plant cover. The only trees and shrubs that can survive are those with a moisture reserve or those able to reach the lower water level with their deep roots. The grass grows sparsely there, for which reason fires are uncommon. The balance in the Nyika is, however, occasionally disturbed by large animals. At shrub and tree level the main browsers are Elephants, the various hooked-lipped rhinos and Giraffes. Lesser Kudus and Gerenuks also crop the leaves. Grazing impala and Waterbuck herds live around permanent sources of water, and small antelope live in the dense shrubs. Lions and other big cats frequent more plentiful sources of water.

There are termites everywhere. They dispose of plant remains and are themselves food for the Aardwolf (*Proteles cristatus*), which has small teeth and does not feed on flesh but which can consume as many as a thousand termites in an hour. Aardvarks (*Orycteropus afer*), also known as Takarus, also feed on termites. They have strong paws for breaking into the termite mounds and they also excavate large underground burrows for themselves with as many as 30 exits. Among the heaps of boulders near foothills live hyraxes and Klipspringers (*Oreotragus oreotragus*). Large numbers of birds nest

The Royal Antelope (*Neotragus pygmaeus*) lives in the forests of Liberia as far as the Ashanti region. It has a bright reddish-brown coat with a darker blaze and back. The lower part of the body, including the lower neck, is lighter in colour.

Bate's Dwarf Antelope (*Neotragus batesi*) is one of the smallest ruminants, measuring 25 centimetres at the shoulder, and lives in equatorial forests. The head sits on a very short neck and seems disproportionately large compared with the body. The ears are smallish and distinctly rounded.

Jentink's Duiker (*Cephalophus jentinki*) lives in Liberia and is larger than a Roe Deer. It has a grey body, a lighter abdomen, and the head and neck are sharply defined by its dark coat. It is very timid, usually being glimpsed as it makes its escape.

on the hills, especially kites, vultures and eagles. The tops and slopes are usually bare, and only bearded lichen (*Usnea*) will grow there. Other plants can take root only where there is level ground or a hollow with fertile soil.

Umbrella acacias are typical trees in the region. One acacia species, *Acacia drepanolobium,* protects itself against animal browsers by forming an empty wooden blister where the thorns grow from the stem. When this blister dries and hardens it becomes the home of small black ants. The tree offers the ants a home and safety.

The Gabon Duiker (*Cephalophus leucogaster*), like other duiker species, has a large bald muzzle and bald rings around the eyes. It is named in Latin after its brilliant-white abdomen, which is unmistakable even when viewed from the side.

Great lava fields between three and four centuries old are spread over the Tsavo National Park, along the road to Lake Turkana and around the Marsabit Reservation in Kenya. Over time they have become covered with a thin growth of grass, and here and there by bushes. In this inhospitable, apparently dead landscape live Grant's Gazelles, hyraxes, small antelope species, Ostriches and African Elephants.

A solitary adult male crosses the almost completely dried-up Galana stream in Tsavo, in order to cool itself in the noonday heat and drink the warm muddy water.

In return, as soon as an animal starts to chew the acacia's leaves the ants swarm out and bite it on the muzzle. The ants bore a small entrance hole into their blister on the lower side and, when the wind blows through the Nyika, these millions of holes produce a mournful wailing.

The ants' defence is only partially successful. Impalas are driven away but Giraffes mind the ants as little as the thorns. Elephants and rhinos even chew up whole branches, thorns and ants and all. Baboons do not mind the ants: on the contrary, they tear off the blisters and chew them up together with the ants, as a source of animal food, and then spit out the husks.

Large acacias are also the home of the only African rat species, which lives in trees. These rats build nests in tree crowns, feeding on the pods, seeds and the resin which flows out of the tree. Fruit bats nest in solitary large acacias, hanging head down. Among them are the Epauletted Fruit Bat (*Epomophorus wahlbergi*) and the Straw-coloured Fruit Bat (*Eidolon helvum*).

DUIKERS AND OTHER DWARF ANTELOPE

Duikers are small antelope with a crest of longer fur on the nape, a large bald muzzle and a medium length tail. Their horns are straight, or sometimes gently curved, and small. The 17 species live south of the Sahara in tropical rain forests and in the bush. These are distinctly territorial animals, marking the boundaries of their

The Beira is light reddish-grey, with a markedly lighter abdomen. The small horns, possessed only by males, are thin, curved forwards and widely spaced. It lives in the mountainous regions of northern Somalia.

The Bay Duiker (*Cephalophus dorsalis*) belongs among the larger duiker species. Its basic colouring is reddish-brown. A black band extends along the back, widening towards the rump. The Bay Duiker is widespread throughout almost all African forests.

104

The Oribi is a small antelope, just a little smaller than a Roe Deer. It is a light yellowish-brown. The spots above the eyes are white, as are the lips, chin and insides of the ears. The edges of the ears are reddish-brown. Only males have the small horns, which are thin, almost straight and have transverse rings at the base. The females give birth to a single young.

territory with the secretion from their suborbital glands, which they rub against small twigs and grass stems. They are mainly herbivorous, although given the opportunity they will also kill and eat birds.

The largest and most striking species is the Yellow-backed Duiker (*Cephalophus silvicultor*). It has a blackish-brown body, light grey cheeks, a rusty-brown crest and a progressively widening yellow band extending from the middle of the back towards the rump. It inhabits forests from Sierra Leone as far as Angola and northern Zambia.

Grimm's Duikers (*Silvicapra grimmia*) live mostly in the bush, fleeing from danger by zigzagging and occasionally leaping high. They browse mainly at night and if their food is sufficiently juicy these mammals can survive without water for long periods. The Red Duiker (*Cephalophus natalensis*) is a medium-sized species and is the only duiker which lives as far south as the Cape.

There are 14 species of dwarf antelope. The smallest members of the Bovidae have long ears, a large head in relation to the body, and the males have short horns. The Suni (*Neotragus moschatus*) gives off a strong musky scent from its suborbital glands. It is active in the early evening, during the night and early morning. It makes weak barking and whistling sounds.

The Dik-diks (*Madoqua*), of which there are some seven species, have long muzzles and red

A small herd of mother elephants goes in the early evening to feed in the open shrubby bush. Too many elephants in Tsavo have had catastrophic effects. The tree and shrub vegetation has been destroyed in vast areas, and the bush has begun to change into open savannah. From 1971 to 1974, when a heavy drought hit East Africa, several thousand elephants in Tsavo died of starvation.

On the rocks in the foot-hills of Uhuru (Kilimanjaro) a Syrian Hyrax (*Heterohyrax syriacus*) and a Klipspringer unexpectedly encountered each other on a boulder. They sniffed at each other cautiously; the hyrax remained and the Klipspringer ran off into the bush.

crests which stand on end when the animals are agitated. They live in pairs in small territories, the boundaries of which they mark with small piles of dung and the secretions of their suborbital glands. The young live with their parents for up to 12 months, but then the father drives his son off the territory and the mother does the same to the daughter. They inhabit the area from Ethiopia to the Cape.

Swayne's Dik-dik (*Madoqua saltiana)* lives in pairs on small territories in thorny bushland. It is frequently content with a thick cluster of bushes only a few metres across. Short, black, transversely-ridged horns are carried only by the males. The muzzle is completely covered with fur apart from the nasal partition, which is bald.

The Klipspringer (*Oreotragus oreotragus*) is an excellent runner and can leap across even the steepest rocks; it can also stand motionless for a long while on large boulders. This dwarf antelope lives among the hills and mountains of East Africa, up to heights of 2,500 metres. In fine weather it climbs the mountains, in rain descending to the valleys. Oribis (*Ourebia ourebi*) live in pairs or small groups on open savannah and on the edge of sparse bush country. During the dry season they can survive a lengthy drought.

ROCK HYRAXES (ROCK-BADGERS)

Rock hyraxes *(Procavia)* are not rodents, as was formerly believed, but miniature relations of elephants. They are superb rock climbers, the balls of their feet being soft and roughened to enable them to use their soles as suction pads on smooth rock faces. They run with agility in all directions and jump down as much as five metres without hesitation.

Tree hyraxes (*Dendrohyrax*) live mainly in groups, in trees. They are cautious and will post guards while they rest and warm themselves in the sun. As soon as a guard spots anything suspicious it whistles and the whole group becomes alert. If the danger approaches the guard whistles more strongly and all the hyraxes disappear into their rocky burrows. When these animals are upset they grind their teeth, stamp their feet — which (like elephants) have small hooves — and the hair on their backs stands on end. Although they do not look capable, tree hyraxes can bite painfully. They are hunted by eagles, vultures and genets.

POISONOUS SNAKES

There are about 2,700 snake species living in the world, reproducing either by laying eggs or by giving birth to live young which develop from eggs inside the mother's body. Snakes feed exclusively on other animals and their teeth are not adapted for biting food, so they have to

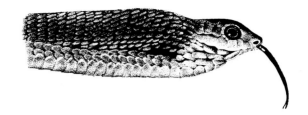

The Tree Snake is a much-feared poisonous snake. There is no antidote to the venom. My African assistants were terrified of this snake, and before they began to cut the twigs we needed as animal food they would search every tree carefully.

Lesser Kudu males have twisted narrow horns, the females being hornless. It is difficult to rear their young in captivity. Keepers feed each newborn calf with artificial milk similar to mother's milk, in order to see them over the critical first two months of life.

swallow their prey whole. Out of the total number of snake species, only one tenth are poisonous. These snakes have a number of enlarged teeth in their upper jaw which are equipped with a small canal or groove on the front: these so-called venom teeth are connected to the duct of the venom gland.

When biting, the snake presses or squirts out into the wound a venom which has several components. One is a neurotoxin, which affects the victim's brain and nervous system. A vein-affecting poison breaks down the walls of blood vessels, while blood cells named platelets cause blood to clot in the veins. Also in the venom are haemolysins, which break up red blood cells and cytolysins, which break up white blood cells. Some venoms contain chemicals which slow down blood clotting so that the venom can be distributed more quickly throughout the blood. In addition there are antibacterial substances, which diminish the defences of the victim's blood, and zymoma, which the snake requires for its digestion.

The venom supply renews itself regularly and the venom teeth are replaced by new ones every few weeks. A poisonous snake can bite in any position, even under water. Even the severed head of a snake is capable of giving a deadly bite. Poisonous snakes do not, however, attack 'with the speed of lightning'. A rattlesnake attacks with a strike of two to seven metres per second; a cobra is six times slower. Most snakes can strike over a distance of half their own body length. African snake species which spit venom are able to hit the eye of their opponent precisely from a distance of three metres.

The Tree Snake (*Dispholidus typus*), called the Boomslang by the Afrikaaners, lives in East and southern Africa in trees and shrubs, especially in thorny acacias. An effective serum against its venom has not yet been discovered, for which reason its bite is dangerous to humans and sometimes even fatal. After the bite heavy internal bleeding occurs, so that the victim must be

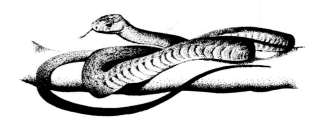

The Black Mamba is the most feared and the largest venomous snake in Africa. It is timid, however, and will usually retreat by disappearing into the crown of its tree at lightning speed. It will not attack without reason, but if it bites then the venom takes effect very quickly.

given several litres of new blood. This species hunts lizards and birds, and plunders birds' nests.

Cobras are highly poisonous and some are capable of spitting venom. The smallest species is the Black-necked Spitting Cobra (*Naja nigricollis*), which reaches a length of 160 centimetres. Larger is the well-known Egyptian Cobra. It was probably this snake which Queen Cleopatra used to commit suicide. This cobra can measure up to two metres. The largest cobra, which can be up to two and a half metres long, is *Naja melanoleuca*.

The Black Mamba (*Dendroaspis polylepis*) is deadly poisonous and the largest African poisonous snake. Mambas are famous for their rapid movements in tree branches. They are timid, however, and do not attack people without reason. When they do bite, the venom takes effect very quickly, and without the use of serum, a bite usually ends in death.

The River Jack (*Bitis nasicornis*) lives in west equatorial Africa, usually on lake and river banks. It is a good swimmer and much feared by the local people. It is distinguished from other vipers by the double small horns on its nose. The Puff Adder (*Bitis arietans*) lives on savannahs throughout almost the whole of Africa. When provoked it hisses fiercely, inflating its body to as much as twice its normal size, raising its head and closely following every movement

The River Jack is a close relation of the Puff Adder and the Gabon Viper. It lives in western equatorial Africa.

of the approaching enemy. In the daytime it lies quietly in shrubs or grass, being active at twilight and at night.

The Gabon Viper (*Bitis gabonica*), which can grow to 180 centimetres in length, has venom teeth up to 5 centimetres long. Its body is covered with regular geometric patterns in all shades of white, yellow, reds, browns and velvety black. It is a slow-moving snake and not easily aroused, although its bite can be deadly.

In snake-infested areas, to avoid being bitten when walking it is best to move slowly, stepping on the full sole of the foot. Although snakes have poor hearing they are enormously sensitive to vibrations in the ground. In the eyes of

A gigantic Baobab in the middle of the Tsavo Park in Kenya (not quite a kilometre from the main road from Nairobi to Mombasa). It measures 586 centimetres in diameter. The Baobab is a striking tree of East and central Africa, the low trunk attaining the greatest width of all trees — up to nine metres. It sheds its leaves in the dry season. Cucumber-shaped fruits with an edible pulp grow on long stalks.

a snake, a human is a large animal and is not potential food. Nevertheless, he represents danger for the snake. If a snake recognizes this in time, it prefers to move out of the way. So firm, steady steps give a snake maximum advance warning.

THE PLAINS FULL OF ANIMALS
The East African grasslands

Travelling westwards from the East African coast through the thorny Nyika, gradually you reach the more benevolent interior. The heat is not so intense and the nights are cooler, and small brooks and rivers have water all year round. Here you are greeted by the majestic outline of Mount Kilimanjaro, the summit covered by glistening glaciers and snow. Ahead stretch the endless grassy plains, on which live immense numbers of animals.

In places the transition from thorny bush to open plain is sudden, elsewhere it is more gradual. This rapid transition cannot be explained merely by the change in climate, different amounts of rainfall, the composition of the soil or volcanic activity. The grassy plains of East Africa are probably the result of human activity: for years a steady destruction of forests has been taking place, and there are regular fires, as well as the burning of tree trunks for charcoal. Erosion has removed the fertile upper layer of soil, and in the soil that remains, tall trees will not grow. So it seems that the grassy plains are the result of a combination of the effects of fire,

soil erosion and the over-grazing of the vegetation by domestic and wild animals — especially elephants, which destroy trees and clear the way for fires.

Some plains came into existence on the sites of swamps and lakes, while others are of volcanic origin and have only a little top soil. At the bottom of the Great Trench Depression, however, the soil is rich and good quality grass grows there. Most common is Redgrass (*Themeda triandra*), which in places forms vast reddish-brown areas. Couchgrass (*Cynodon*) is most valuable for grazing, and small clover flowers also grow at the bottom of the Ngorongoro Crater. This grazing is sweet and nutritious, even during the dry season.

As late as World War II there were so many animals living on these plains that their numbers seemed infinite. During the war, however, thousands of animals were killed, and this extermination continues in order to make room for the growing herds of domestic cattle. The Masai and other pastoralist peoples are currently experiencing a population explosion, with

The Colony Agama (*Agama colonorum*) is up to 35 centimetres long and attractively coloured. In the heat of the noonday sun its metallic bluish-green body shines brightly, and the head is a fiery orange-red. Its habitat extends from Senegambia across the Ivory Coast, the Central African Republic and Sudan to the borders of Ethiopia.

the result that they and their herds are pushing into other territories. There is a danger that they may move into protected areas and reservations.

The most common large animals there are the Blue Wildebeest (*Connochaetes taurinus*), Boehm's Zebra (*Equus burchelli boehmi*) and Coke's Hartebeest. These animals do not compete seriously for pasture. First zebras pluck off the tallest grass shoots, then the wildebeest, hartebeest and gazelles eat lower layers of herbage. No single species completely consumes the grass by its grazing and when each has grazed

Ngorongoro in Tanzania is the largest crater in the world, having a diameter of 16 kilometres; the bed measures 270 square kilometres and is from 600 to 800 metres deep. In 1959 the Ngorongoro Crater, together with its surrounding territory, was proclaimed a state reservation with strictly protected wildlife. Apart from larger animals and various species of hoofed mammals the crater is also famous as a bird reservation, thanks to its lakes.

On the plains of the Serengeti National Park a small herd of Thomson's Gazelles grazes in the noonday heat, in the shade of tree-type umbrella acacias.

The Manioc (*Manihot utilissima*) was introduced to Africa from South America. It is grown for its root tubers, these being several kilogrammes in weight and up to 40 per cent starch. In the raw state these tubers are slightly poisonous, but baked or boiled they are edible. Bread, various cakes and pancakes can be made from manioc.

on the grass at its favourite height, it moves on. Other species, for example the Korrigum, Waterbuck and Impala, like to graze on marshes.

The local people are filling the pastures with ever greater numbers of cattle, goats and sheep, which is disastrous for grassy areas. Domestic animals are more selective than wild animals, preferring only certain grass species and not touching others, for example *Pennisetum*. For this reason the sweet, good quality grass species are rapidly disappearing in those areas where domestic cattle graze and *Pennisetum* is beginning to predominate, making the pasture worthless. In addition, domestic cattle move across pasture in compact herds, trampling down the grass and soil. Mixed zebra, wildebeest and gazelle herds, besides grazing on *Pennisetum*, are scattered over great areas and constantly on the move, so they do less damage.

The most important predators on the plains are the big cats, hyaenas and wild dogs. A great number of jackals, birds of prey and snakes also live there, so that nothing killed on the plains goes to waste. Only when periods of severe drought strike or the animals are hit by disease epidemics, during which many of them perish, are predators unable to consume the numbers of dead. During such catastrophes, many animals which have perished lie decomposing.

Ants and other insects also take part in the final elimination of carrion.

On the plains there are enormous numbers of birds, ranging from the great Ostrich to tiny little seed-eaters. Among the predatory birds the Secretary Bird (*Sagittarius serpentarius*) takes pride of place; also the Jackal Buzzard (*Buteo rufofuscus*), the Black-shouldered Kite (*Elanus caeruleus*), the Bateleur Eagle and the African Marsh Owl (*Asio capensis*) hunt here.

In winter the plains swarm with kestrels and eagles, which fly from Europe to spend the winter. Several vulture species also live there. They do not kill their prey, but feed on carrion; the most common are the White-backed Vulture (*Gyps africanus*) and Rueppell's Griffon (*Gyps rueppelli*), which live in large colonies — the former in trees, the latter on rocky cliffs. The Bat-eared Fox (*Otocyon megalotis*), which lives in a lair, hunts small mammals and birds and also feeds on insects, eggs and plant foodstuffs. The local people prize both its meat and fur. At dusk and at night the Springhare (*Pedetes capensis*) comes slowly out of its burrow to collect

The Bateleur Eagle is an excellent flier. Fast loops, spins and unexpected turns are unique to this species of eagle.

The Masai, called 'Il-Masai' in their own language, is a large tribe inhabiting south-west Kenya and northern Tanzania. The three dialects, belonging to the eastern Nilotic group of languages, are spoken by about 380,000 people. Fundamental to their religion is a cult of nature spirits and an ancestor cult, although they believe in one main god.

Wildebeest became too numerous for their environment in the Serengeti region in the years 1960 to 1975. Every expansion of the population is nevertheless subject to regulation by nature. During these years the populations of Lions, hyaenas and African Wild Dogs also doubled in size, so that predators began to reduce the numbers of wildebeest. The leader of a pack of dogs usually chooses the weakest member of the herd — a sick or ageing animal — which the pack then hunts down.

seeds and eat foliage and roots, putting the food into its mouth with its short front paws. It moves slowly on all fours but regularly jumps two to three metres on its hind legs. During these leaps the front legs stay crossed over the chest. If pursued it can jump as far as ten metres.

When I first came to the African savannah I was surprised at the peace that reigns there. Lions laze about here and there in the shade, a Leopard rests in the crown of a tree, zebras and antelope graze unhurriedly hardly a hundred metres from a resting pride. There is nothing to indicate that events could be heading towards a tragedy. In fact statistics show that the risk of a zebra being eaten by a big cat is the same as that of a person being knocked down by a car in the city. Just as people walk along city streets unworried, zebras and antelope do not become frantic with fear when grazing near

After a short chase, during which the dogs surround the chosen animal in a jointly organized effort, they go in for the kill.

a resting predator. The energy of living creatures is limited, and a constant state of tension between hunter and prey would be an enormous drain on their strength. As long as predators do not feel hunger they do not perform a single unnecessary action. Nor do they hunt out of a pure desire to kill.

The animals being hunted can sense the intentions of their predators so well that they can afford to raise the alarm at the last possible moment before the attack. Then the peaceful situation changes in a flash. A wildebeest herd, which only a few seconds earlier was scattered and grazing peacefully, quickly forms a semicircle. With their heads raised they watch the place where hunters could be hiding. At such moments even the smallest movement is enough to cause panic among the herd, reaching its peak in a wild flight — which predators use to advantage.

Few places in the world can compare with the beauty of the Ngorongoro Crater or the Serengeti plains in Tanzania. Sometimes it seems unjust to us that beautiful zebras, noble antelope or delicate gazelles are killed by predators, and that they can be taken by a Lion in such a terrible and cruel way, with their remains becoming the prey of squabbling jackals and vultures. However this represents an indispensible link in the natural food chain.

The food chain in fact begins with the sun. Its light is trapped by green plants, which are eaten by herbivores, and then predators which feed on herbivores. In this way all species preserve the balance of nature, as well as maintaining evolution by the selection of the fittest individuals for continued life. The fate of every animal is to eat or be eaten, so that the energy cycle can be completed and renewed.

AFRICAN WILD DOGS

African Wild Dogs (*Lycaon pictus*) have variegated coats, in which white, black and ochre

Skeleton of a male adult Rothschild's Giraffe, probably killed by Lions, in the protected hunting region of Debasian at the foot of the Kadam Mountains in Uganda. The skull has a noticeable third horn on the brow and two small horns on the nape of the neck, besides the main two, for which reason it is sometimes called the Five-horned Giraffe.

spots predominate. They have excellent senses of sight, hearing and smell. When hunting they produce unusual sounds which could be likened to bells ringing in the distance or the shriek of a bird. They bark only in fear or anger. Wild Dogs live in packs numbering approximately 20, each pack having its own strictly-guarded territory. The members maintain a hierarchy which they fight out among themselves. They inhabit extensive areas of savannah south of the Sahara.

A bitch gives birth to pups, or 'whelps' in a dug-out hollow. She does not leave them, and other pack members also care for them. The hunting method of these dogs is to us appalling: they do not even kill their victims, but eat them alive. They are not able to bite their prey to death as their 42 teeth are small, being designed for tearing off small pieces of meat.

One day late in the afternoon I came across a resting pack of dogs comprising eight adults, eleven pups and four maturing young. Two adult dogs suddenly began to push the others with their muzzles, until all the adults were crowding round the pups and playing with them. They rolled and jumped over one another, whining in a strange way. According to the American zoologist G. Schaller, this behaviour is a kind of war dance prior to hunting.

After a while the two leaders set off purposefully, with the others running after them and the pups last. They extended into a long line and trotted along; our vehicle followed at a speed of 25 kilometres per hour. Gradually the leaders went faster until the pups were no longer able to keep up; then they slowed down abruptly. Close by a swamp, a herd of wildebeest were grazing. The two leaders remained standing,

Lions have their favourite trees, which the park-keepers number. A large male rests in tree number 17 by the River Ishasha in Uganda.

while the other adults began to run round the wildebeest in a semi-circle. The wildebeest raised their heads and watched the dogs, and the latter suddenly speeded up and drove the herd straight towards the two leaders, hidden in the grass. When the rushing wildebeest were about 20 paces away, the dogs dashed out of the grass, both rushing at a weak young wildebeest. It turned and fled from the herd in an arched curve. The first dog intercepted it and snapped at its head several times until it caught the wildebeest's lower jaw. The second dog tore at its abdomen. The wildebeest fell and the dog once again tore at its abdomen. When the first dog let go of the animal's head, the wildebeest jumped up and tried to escape but that moment the other adults arrived. They began to tear pieces of hide and meat off it. As soon as the young dogs reached it, however, the adults fell back and allowed them to eat. For almost an hour the pups gorged themselves and not one adult dog took so much as a morsel.

Lioness has climbed up for a rest in the cleft of a tree, four metres above ground. She has placed her three cubs, which are not yet able to follow her up, at the foot of the tree in a hollow under a thick bush.

LIONS

Although we tend to regard the Lion (*Panthera leo*) as a typically African predator, in times long past it also lived in Europe, as witnessed by cave paintings in Spain and excavations in Greece. Lions were hunted to extinction there around 200 BC. At one time the Persian Lion (*Panthera leo persica*) was also widespread in parts of western Asia, Arabia and India. In the Gir reservation in western India live the last 250 Indian or Asiatic Lions (*Panthera leo goojratensis*).

Compared with these, the situation of African Lions is much better, although two sub-species have been exterminated: the Berber Lion (*Panthera leo leo*) and the Cape Lion (*Panthera*

The Spring Hare lives in mountains and plains, inhabiting relatively poor country. It often lives in large colonies. It digs underground burrows with long branching corridors leading to a deep cauldron-shaped chamber. These complex burrows are often inhabited by several families.

Lioness resting on an uprooted tree in the Amboseli region at the foot of Uhuru (Kilimanjaro) in Kenya. This was evidently a favourite spot for this family, as they returned there often.

leo melanochaita). Today in Africa the majority live in large national parks.

The social life of the Lion's family group is fascinating. The leading male is attentive and tolerant of the young, which are allowed to do almost anything. They are the first to eat, along with several of the highest-placed members in the hierarchy, while the more mature young and lower-placed members must wait. The young jump on the adult males, pull their ears, lie on their backs and particularly enjoy playing with their parent's tails.

On the bank of the River Uaso Nyiro in Kenya I saw a killed, half-eaten male Degassa waterbuck, with a large male resting nearby. Two cubs were trying to tear meat from the prey, snarling at each other, and occasionally squabbles broke out. On several occasions one of the cubs bit the old male in the heat of the fight. The latter merely looked round, once even licking the cub on its side and head. Eventually his patience ran out and he got up, moved a little to

one side and lay down again. When feeding time began, all the cubs in the group tried to suck at once, alternating between one mother and another. After a while it was no longer possible to tell which cub belonged to which mother.

In the mating season, lionesses give off a particular scent which indicates their condition to males. The dominant male usually accompanies the lioness to a quiet spot close to water, where they remain for several days. Throughout this period they do not hunt and eat almost nothing, only drinking, exchanging caresses and mating up to 30 times a day. During intercourse the male bites the nape of the female and she roars excitedly. It sometimes happens that males from neighbouring territories stray into the nuptial territory, which can lead to fierce fighting.

Schaller once observed, on the Serengeti, a family with two powerful males. One lioness showed signs of being on heat and both males made a move for her. She chose one; the other left resignedly, lay down and slept. The female, during a period of two and a half days, then mated regularly both day and night, a total of

Lions — a pair of adults with cubs — cross the small open plain in the Kidepo National Park, Uganda.

170 times — once every 20 minutes. Finally the male quietly disappeared into the bush. Then the second male arrived, and, as the lioness was evidently still on heat, he began to mate with her as well.

The Lion is not really the 'King of Beasts'. Its mighty, deep roar in the quiet of the night is not intended to terrify those around it, but rather to inform other males that the hunting ground belongs only to him and his family. The beast is not even particularly majestic. When walking it carries its head low, and when in difficulties holds its head deep between the shoulders with its mouth wide open. They are quite timid:

The Black-shouldered Kite is ash to greyish-blue on the upper part of the body, the forehead and lower part being white. The wings and shoulders are black, the iris brilliant red. It has black spots around the eyes extending to the temples. The two central tail feathers are grey, the other tail feathers white with greyish borders, the outer feathers pure white. It lives in pairs, its staple diet consisting of mice, grasshoppers and other small animals.

Boys and young warriors of the Samburu tribe daily drive
their cattle and donkeys to the watering place on the River
Uaso-Nyiro in Kenya.

encountered in the daytime, they usually run away. If provoked, however, they may well attack.

Lions kill quickly. In the course of the 10 years I worked in Africa, I saw a great number of animals hunted by them. The big cat adapts its technique according to whether the hunted animal is large or small and whether it is likely to fight back (such as the Roan Antelope or African Buffalo). Lions may also co-operate in hunting according to necessity. Most often they strangle the prey, sometimes breaking its neck, or killing smaller animals with a blow of the paw. They can have difficult struggles with larger animals, and on rare occasions they themselves may be killed. In general, hunting is carried out by lionesses; the main task of the males is ensuring the safety of his family.

WILDEBEEST

What the Afrikaaners call the Black Wildebeest (*Connochaetes gnou*), or White-tailed Gnu, once lived in great numbers in South Africa, although it was almost hunted to extinction in the 19th century. Today it lives only on a number of nature reservations and private farms. It is smaller than the Blue Wildebeest, with a body length of 190 centimetres, a shoulder height of 115 centimetres and weighing 160 kilogrammes. Its appearance has a touch of the diabolical, an impression reinforced by its wild, abrupt movements, a mane which stands on end and its powerful forward-curved horns.

The Blue Wildebeest (*Connochaetes taurinus*), or Brindled Gnu, has a characteristic and unique greyish-blue colour and zebra-like dark stripes on its flanks. Its habitat ranges across vast regions of Africa from Kenya and Tanzania to southern Africa and Botswana, and it extends as far as Namibia and Angola. Some groups number a dozen, but there are also vast herds numbering tens of thousands. Most wildebeest live in the Serengeti region as well as in the Ngorongoro Crater and adjacent areas, where their numbers are increasing steadily. According to a 1983 census their total number is estimated at just over one million.

At present there are five sub-species:
the Southern Blue Wildebeest
(*Connochaetes taurinus taurinus*),
Cookson's Wildebeest
(*Connochaetes taurinus cooksoni*),
Johnston's Wildebeest
(*Connochaetes taurinus johnstoni*),

the White-bearded Wildebeest
    (*Connochaetes taurinus albojubatus*),
and Mearnce's Wildebeest
    (*Connochaetes taurinus mearnsi*).
These differ from one other in the colouring of the beard, flanks and brow, and in the intensity of the striping. Adult males look proudly across the endless plains with slightly lowered heads, their dark horns gleaming and their manes hanging down both sides of the neck and chest. They stand as still as statues, but will suddenly snort, drumming their hooves on the hard, dried-up earth and swinging their long, horse-like tails through the air. In a moment two males can be fighting over territory, and the clash of their horns can be heard hundreds of metres away.

Territorial males usually comprise about 15 per cent of a herd, but their influence over the rest of the community is disproportionately great. Weak and solitary males which have not managed to gain their own territory often challenge the owners to a duel. These fights are often cruel, but seldom result in death. When a male gains his own territory he has access to females, as the latter will only mate with the ruler of a territory. In this way only the fittest

The Mara Masai Reservation in Kenya has an area of 1,800 square kilometres, and is only separated from the Serengeti National Park in Tanzania by the state border. It has the same composition of wildlife species as the Serengeti. The reservation was formed primarily so that the enormous zebra herds, wildebeest and elephants migrating along Lake Victoria, and from Tanzania to Kenya, would be protected from extinction by hunting. Male wildebeest young hurry after their herd.

122

According to Professor Grzimek in 1958, there were at that time in the Serengeti National Park and its environs, approximately 450,000 Serengeti wildebeest. An aerial count by Dr. Murray Watson in 1970/1 put the number at 650,000. According to our calculations of 1974/5 there were almost 900,000 wildebeest living in Serengeti, Ngorongoro and Mara Masai, including the area around the parks. The three parks together have an area of 23,800 square kilometres, the surrounding areas 12,600 square kilometres. This means 24 wildebeest per kilometre, together with hundreds of thousands of other animals.

individuals may reproduce. The mating season usually coincides with the beginning of the migration to summer pastures, and males which have secured their own territory must also maintain it during the hard conditions of the march. They are in constant conflict with other males as they are continually obliged to demonstrate their superior strength, whilst at the same time guarding their harems to make sure that their females do not disperse. In the middle of this general noise and confusion mating occurs from time to time. The act itself is brief, as the male has used up almost all his energy in fighting and guarding the females.

During migration a vast army of wildebeest marches hour after hour, ever onwards towards the north-west with an unaltered pace. Clouds of dust rise above the herd and the air trembles with the voices of the animals and the thunder of thousands of hooves. The young are born on the Serengeti, usually from December to February. Many are lost by their mothers during sudden flights of the herd from predators. When the herd calms down it is usual to see several young wandering here and there in search of their mothers. Some succeed in finding them. Others bleat insistently and try to join strange mothers, which do not usually accept them. On the second and third days the youngsters' calls diminish and they die or attract the attention of predators.

The White-tailed Wildebeest. We keep two herds at our zoo. During the summer they live in a large run. They are aggressive and the keepers tend them in pairs, one keeping watch while the other cleans and prepares food. In winter we keep them in separate stalls, as in the limited space of the winter house they would attack one another.

WHERE THE SUN NEVER PENETRATES
The tropical rain forest

The forests in Africa extend for almost 5,000 kilometres from east to west, and approximately 1,600 kilometres from north to south. With the exception of South America, Africa has the largest continuous rain forest in the world. Mainly evergreen, its mainstay is the enormous region in the basin of the River Congo. The Cameroun highlands, of volcanic origin, divide the western Guinea forest from the eastern areas of Zaire and Gabon. In times long past, during wet periods which corresponded to the ice ages in the north, these forests extended both south and north, overflowing across the Great Trench Depression and even to the East African coast; they also grew much farther up the mountain slopes than they do today.

The boundaries between the forest and the savannah are clearly visible, being formed by a shrub belt no wider than ten metres. Its outer edge, composed of small shrubs and luxuriant grass, can usually hold back fire, while the larger shrubs and small trees are generally not affected by it. The narrow boundary strip forms a sharp dividing line between two distinct habitats. Its shrubs are a favourite haunt of wild animals, and while forest creatures make use of the savannah, the reverse is rare. The balance is upset only by the elephant, which can destroy the protective screen of bushes so that fire can creep right to the edge of the forest.

In the tropical forest it is gloomy, the temperature is fairly constant, the soil damp and the air humid. The soil is not covered with grass or small plants, except for occasional ferns and mosses, but with fallen leaves that decompose quickly and so do not form deep layers. All

The Forest Elephant is much smaller than the Bush Elephant. On the edges of the forest in Cameroun, along the borders of equatorial Guinea, this sub-species grows to a maximum height of 220 centimetres, has rounded ears and nearly straight tusks. It feeds on the edges of the forest, individually or in small groups.

around there are shrubs and trees intertwined with liana creepers. It is seldom possible to see farther than 50 metres, and even an expert can easily lose his way after a hundred paces.

It is always quiet in the forest. In the crowns of the giant trees, the wind moans quietly. Occasionally a branch cracks, and the shriek of a monkey or the calls of birds may break the silence. You have the feeling that you should tread softly, and many people are gripped by strange fear and wonder.

African forest plants number something like 25,000 species. Large mahogany trees (*Khaya* and *Entandophragma*) usually form the upper level, while Oil Palms (*Elaeis guineensis*) are typical in the lower level. Few larger animals live in the forest, compared to the savannah. They include the Long-tailed Pangolin (*Manis tetradactyla*), Potto (*Perodicticus potto*), and scaly-tailed or flying squirrels (Anomaluroidea); reptiles, amphibians, ants, butterflies and other

Beyond Lake Kivu, 144 kilometres south of the equator, is a region of active volcanoes in the Kivu National Park, Zaire. The equatorial rain forests with evergreen trees begin at the foot of these volcanoes, looking from the air like a vast green sea.

insect species are also well represented. In the tree-tops live many more bird species than in any other habitat in Africa, although they are seldom seen.

Animals living in the forest feed on tree, shrub and creeper foliage, as well as fruits and roots. They include the Bushbuck, elephant, African Buffalo, Okapi, Bongo, various duikers, many monkey species and two hogs — the Giant Forest Hog (*Hylochoerus meinertzhageni*) and the River Hog (*Potamochoerus porcus*). Two ape species are forest inhabitants: the Gorilla and the Chimpanzee. Vervets are also common

In the Kivu National Park in Zaire and the Ruwenzori National Park in Uganda, hybrids of the Cape and Forest Buffalo are quite common. The head of the horned female resembles that of the Cape sub-species, while the orange-brown colouring of the body, coat and rust-coloured tufts in the ears are typical of the Forest Buffalo.

as well as mangabeys (*Cercocebus*) and the Guereza or White-mantled Colobus (*Colobus guereza*), which live predominantly on fruits and foliage. Baboons generally live on the savannah, but two species of their group, the Mandrill and the Drill, have adapted to life in

Pygmy Hippopotami are captured in carefully camouflaged pits dug in the trails they tread to the water. This type of capture is successful only on bright, fully moonlit nights.

the rain forest. The only large predator is the Leopard. Forests are inhabited by dwarf forms of many animal species: small elephants and Buffalo, dwarf antelopes, the Pygmy Hippopotamus and the Bonobo (Pygmy) Chimpanzee. And there are the Pygmies — races of our own species.

Small rivers and brooks flow through the tropical forests, often forming pools and small lakes. On sandy soil in the dry season surface water is rare however. The Benin Sands in Nigeria, for example, are so porous that even after a heavy tropical shower the water quickly drains away and after a few minutes the ground is dry again. Where there is sufficient water, in the region from Sierra Leone to Zaire, lives a primitive ruminant with three stomachs known as the Water Chevrotain (*Hyemoschus aquaticus*).

A significant proportion of tropical rain forests are situated on uplands. The rivers rush down through narrow passes, flowing mostly into the Congo. There are swampy regions in the Congo in which a kind of 'water forest' has evolved. Here grows a confusion of Raffia Palms (*Raphia vinifera*) and wild cane that is practically impossible to penetrate. The swamps can be navigated in boats, although one has to bend under the low branches every few seconds. Travelling this way, through a tunnel of growth, you often arrive at a quiet and utterly beautiful forest lake surrounded by tall trees. Hippopotami may live there, or the Shining-blue Kingfisher (*Alcedo quadribrachys*), and sometimes even the large Southern Kingfisher (*Ceryle rudis*) may be catching fish. The main fish hunter, however, is the African Fish Eagle. Crabs form the staple diet of the Cape Clawless Otter (*Aonyx capensis*). Hornbills, particularly the Black-casqued Hornbill (*Ceratogymna atrata*), and turacos such as the Great Crested Turaco (*Corythaeola cristata*) fly from tree to tree, the latter being relatives of the cuckoo. In the evening thousands of bats fly over the rivers, being fed on by Bat Hawks (*Machaerhamphus alcinus*). Armies of large ants on the move arouse terror in all living creatures. They are most active at night and in the rainy season. Anything that does not flee from their path is killed and carried off or eaten on the spot. Numerous snakes also inhabit the rain forest. The most feared are the poisonous mambas and superb climbing boigas; on the ground are the slower Gabon Viper and the River Jack.

Many forest areas are cut for lumber and to make way for fields. But reafforestation of these exploited areas is rare. As the rain forests diminish there wil be a fall in atmospheric humidity also, so that Africa may become even more arid.

HOGS

All hog species are similar in body structure to the European Wild Boar. The snout is used for foraging, and the mouth has large triangular fangs which are curved forwards. Roots, tubers, fruits, berries, mushrooms, insects, larvae, slugs and snails, reptiles, young birds, mice, dead fish and animal carcasses form their diet. They have keen senses, are agile and are not afraid of water.

River Hogs (*Potamochoerus porcus*) are distributed widely over almost the whole of Africa south of the Sahara. Their bodies are covered with short, soft, rather dense bristles lying close to the skin, which form a short mane along the spine. They also have long bristles on the tips of the ears. The young are striped. Hogs mostly move in quite large communities, living mainly in damp undergrowth and swamps, being fond of water. They can cause great damage in fields; they also have excellent meat.

The Wart-hog (*Phacochoerus aethiopicus*) has four warts on its cheeks. Its unusually large fangs, similar to tusks, can fatally wound natural predators and people. When in danger this hog tries to hide itself in an underground burrow, crawling in backwards and waiting for its attacker with tusks prepared. Wart-hog families stay in one area, roaming it constantly and eating mainly plants and roots that they dig up with their tusks.

The Wart-hog has a very sparse coat on the sides and lower part of the body. On the forehead and back it has long blackish bristles with brown ends, which extend down the sides as far as the upper abdomen. Thick bristles surround the eyes, which have thick brows, and form noticeable whiskers on the lower jaw. The tail is finished off with a brush.

The Giant Forest Hog (*Hylochoerus meinertzhageni*) is the largest African hog species, weighing up to 300 kilogrammes. Its body length is up to 180 centimetres and shoulder height 110 centimetres. It has a large head and a large broad snout with smallish tusks. Adult males have large warts under the eyes. This species does not forage as much as other hogs, living on plant food. It browses both in the day and at night, but only at night does it go out to the fields, where it can cause great damage. These animals live in small groups across the entire African forest region. They like to rest in shallow hollows and in river beds with mud and

The River Hog is brownish-yellow to red; the forehead, crown of the head, ears and limbs are black; the mouth and lower part of the body greyish-black. The narrow stripes on the back, face and top of the snout are white. This creature is most frequently hunted by the Leopard.

The Giant Forest Hog lives in remote regions and grows a thick black coat of even length, which on the chest and sides is tinged with silver.

The Goliath Beetle (*Goliathus druryi*) is one of the largest beetles in the world. It flies among the tree-tops in tropical rain forests. Males have a fork-like projection on the head which is absent in females. The wing-cases of the Goliath have a piece cut out at the root on both sides, through which the beetle extends its wings and lifts itself into the air.

water, where they cool themselves. In dense undergrowth they have their own trampled tunnels, and their main enemies are lions, leopards and humans.

OKAPIS

The first reports and hides of the Okapi (*Okapia johnstoni*) were sent to London by the British Governor of Uganda, Harry Johnston, in 1899. It was thought that the creature was a species of forest horse, but even by 1900 it became clear that the Okapi had nothing to do with horses. It is in fact related to the giraffe. Only in 1918 was a young specimen successfully captured and reared on artificial milk. It was sent to Antwerp Zoo, where it lived for only 50 days.

Okapis have a velvet-brown coat and conspicuous white stripes on the front legs and rear haunches. They live in the densest forest areas in higher, dry places. They avoid damp undergrowth, mud and soft soil, nor do they like dense undergrowth. Their patterning provides excellent camouflage. For grazing they come out to lighter forest areas in the mornings and evenings; during the day and at night they rest under large trees. They have excellent hearing and a superb sense of smell. These animals live alone and feed on foliage and the young shoots of forest plants with their unusually long tongues.

The Long-tailed Pangolin has a thick, cylindrical body. Broad scales, in places jutting out in a keel-shaped point, cover the whole body and the very long tail — even on the underside. The upper jaw hangs over the lower, the mouth opening is tiny. The eyes are small, the ears scarcely visible. Its legs are short, its fingers and toes not very flexible, and the digging claws on the front limbs are much larger than the nails on the rear toes.

The Giant Pangolin has an acute sense of smell. Females have mammary glands on the chest but the nipples are situated in the armpits. The jaws are completely toothless, so that the skull is without cheekbones. The rear part of the skull is rounded and smooth. To roll into a ball the pangolin, like a hedgehog, uses a special band of muscles under the skin on both sides of the spine.

PANGOLINS

Pangolins (scaly anteaters) form their own mammal order, Manidae, and have a distinctive appearance. Their horny scales make them look like large fir cones. The scales overlap one another like roof tiles and cover the entire body, including the long tail, with the exception of the abdomen, tip of the snout and inner sides of the limbs. The number of scales on each pangolin species is always the same, as it is with fish species, and a newborn pangolin has exactly the same number as its parents. Some species have hairs between the scales. The animal defends itself by spraying a pungent secretion from its anal glands. Using the strong claws on its front feet, it digs out ant nests and termite mounds, shovelling out the inhabitants with its long tongue. The jaws are toothless and the mouth is only just large enough for the long tongue, which is covered by sticky saliva so that the prey adheres to it.

Pangolins are nocturnal animals, sleeping during the day curled into a ball in dug-out burrows or hollow trees. They inhabit dense vegetation, walking slowly with a rocking gait. Some species are good tree-climbers and they are also able to walk on their hind legs. They tread on the ridges of their toes with the claws bent inwards.

The Bongo is a rare zoo animal. The zoo at Dvůr Králové keeps 14 Bongos, which come from the bamboo forests of the Aberdare Mountains in Kenya.

The impenetrable evergreen rain forests of the River Congo basin have vegetation in successive layers. Giant trees over 60 metres high form the pillars of the forest and stand about 100 to 200 metres apart. The layer of herbs, shrubs and lower trees forms the dense main body of the forest. From the branches of the larger trees hang an enormous number of intertwining lianas.

The Tree Pangolin (*Manis tricuspis*) is up to 95 centimetres long, with a tail that measures between 45 and 50 centimetres. The Long-tailed Pangolin (*Manis tetradactyla*) is only 40 centimetres long in the body, although its tail can measure up to 70 centimetres. The Giant Pangolin (*Manis gigantea*) is a massive animal, its body being 80 centimetres long and the tail up to 65 centimetres.

CHIMPANZEES

The Chimpanzee (*Pan troglodytes*), often called simply the 'chimp', is at home both in trees and on the ground. It usually walks on all fours, resting its front limbs on its knuckles and its rear limbs on the soles. When carrying something it can walk erect. It weighs 40 to 70 kilogrammes and lives mostly on plant food, although it also eats insects and small mammals. Some chimps have been seen to break off a stalk or thin twig and rummage in termite nests, using it as a tool, taking out and eating the termites that bite the twig. Chimps even hunt down larger animals such as young antelope, wild hogs or monkeys. They spend six to eight hours a day feeding.

The Chimpanzee's sex life dispenses with courtship and intimacy; mating takes place

The Water Chevrotain is dark brown with light spots on its back. On the front of the cheeks, sides and part of the neck it has lengthwise white bands. It belongs to a group of very ancient animals which lack upper incisor teeth. The molar teeth have short crowns and the upper canines are fangs which protrude out of the mouth.

The Moraceae plant family comprises over one thousand species. The most varied *Ficus* genus numbers over 600 species, ranging from slender climbing lianas to enormous trees. The aerial roots twist round the trunks of the host trees, spreading and growing into a trellis which completely destroys the tree. This type of liana is called a strangler.

without any sign (to us) of affection. They do help one another, however, and a strict hierarchy prevails in the troop. Dominant males try to make an impression by vaunting themselves and menacingly waving a branch, club or tree trunk torn out of the ground. Subordinate members usually scatter in all directions. A special form of impressive behaviour is the 'rain dance', carried out when a shower breaks. The males leave the nest, swing round the tree on one arm, climb up to the top and jump down. During their fall they break off branches and wave them about wildly. Chimpanzees live in an extensive area ranging from Senegal across Guinea, the Ivory Coast, Cameroun and Zaire as far as western Uganda and Tanzania.

The Western Chimpanzee (*Pan troglodytes verus*) has a light lower facial area. With increasing age the bald patch on the head grows larger, and males have a distinctly longer coat on the face than females, forming a beard. The Chego (*Pan troglodytes troglodytes*) has a light face when young; this grows darker with age. The head balds early. This subspecies occupies a range from Cameroun across Zaire to the River Ubangi. Schweinfurth's Chimpanzee (*Pan troglodytes schweinfurthi*) lives from the Ubangi towards the south-east as far as Uganda and Tanzania. It has a dark face, its bald patch forms late, and the whole of its body is covered with a thick coat.

The Pygmy Chimpanzee (*Pan paniscus*) is a species in its own right. It is half the weight of other chimpanzees. The face is elongated and the limbs long and slender. Both the skin and coat are nearly black. This chimp species inhabits evergreen rain forests south of the curve of the River Congo, where the dry season never penetrates.

GORILLAS

The Gorilla's homelands are the forests from the River Cross in southern Nigeria to the estuary of the Congo, then eastwards across Zaire as far as the volcanoes of the Kahuzi and Virun-

ga Ranges and the Ruwenzori. A small, isolated population also lives in southern Uganda. The zoologist and palaeontologist Professor Brentjes states that a silver vase depicting a hunt for these apes was discovered in an Etruscan grave of the 7th century BC. In 460 BC the Carthaginian admiral Hanno described in his account *Periplus Hannonis* how he saw large hairy animals resembling humans on his voyage along the African coast, probably near present-day Gabon. The first European to see a specimen, in

131

The Western Black-and-White Colobus Monkey (*Colobus polykomos*) has magnificent black skin and lank white fur which covers the shoulders and sides and forms a remarkable cloak. Native kings and chiefs have decorated themselves with this fur since time immemorial, which has been a cause of this species' rapid disappearance.

Chimpanzees we obtained in southern Cameroun from the forest region near the river Dja. We separated the young with white faces and white hands from those with dark faces. However, when they grew up their white faces, with the exception of one female, darkened and it was impossible to distinguish them.

1598, was the English officer Andrew Battel, who was captured by the Portuguese. Only in 1847 did the missionaries Savage and Wyman actually describe the Gorilla for science. In 1921 the American naturalist Carl Akeby obtained five individuals of the mountain race from the Virunga volcanic range. They were studied in detail only in 1959 by the American zoologist G. B. Schaller.

In the western part of the species' range lives the smallest of the three sub-species, the Western Gorilla or Western Lowland Gorilla (*Gorilla gorilla gorilla*). This weighs about 155 kilogrammes, has a short coat which turns from black to dark brown with age, and often has a chestnut patch on its head. In males the back and parts of the thighs are silver-grey.

In the Bufumbiro, Kahuzi and Virunga Ranges dwells the Mountain Gorilla (*G. g. beringei*). It attains a height of 170 centimetres and a weight of 180 kilogrammes. It has a long, thick, almost black coat, which protects it from the mountain climate. It lives at heights ranging from 2,600 to 4,200 metres. Old males have silver grey backs and a high crest on the head.

From Lakes Edward and Kivu towards the west, to the banks of the Congo, lives the largest gorilla — the Lowland or Eastern Lowland Gorilla (*G. g. graueri*), described only in 1914. Adult males measure up to 180 centimetres and

The Lowland Gorillas kept by Dvůr Králové Zoo were obtained from Cameroun at a breeding station in Sangmélima.

weigh around 190 kilogrammes. The Ugandan population in the Kayonza forest also belongs to this sub-species. They have short black coats, and old males have silver-grey backs. The face is narrow and the skull tall, due to a crest of bone.

Gorillas live in well-organized troops of up to 30 members. The group defends its large territory courageously. Every troop has at least one old 'silver-back' male ranking above all the others, and there may be additional experienced males in the troop. There is a strict hierarchy: subordinates always moving out of the way of higher individuals. Fighting is rare. Females also have a ranking system among themselves, a female with young having priority over others and usually also ranking above males with black backs. All adults rank above the young.

The close relationships between the young and their mothers last up to six years, and social relationships continue to adulthood. From time to time a large troop will split into two smaller ones. When moving through the forest these apes communicate by means of calls and can produce over 20 various sounds, although they generally use only about eight. They often drum their palms against their chests as a kind of emotional release. A staring look is to impress;

and lianas, while still higher grow giant trees which raise their branches skywards. There is a profusion of animal and bird life. Here live the smallest people in the world, the Pygmies of the Bambuti tribe. Early Egyptian reliefs depict these small people; Homer and Herodotus also mention them, and Aristotle locates their territory in the swamps and sources of the Nile. The term 'pygmy' derives from the Greek word *pygmaios*, which describes the measurement from the knuckles to the elbow.

The origins of these people are not clear. The men are seldom more than 145 centimetres tall, the women 135 centimetres. They have long arms, short legs, the nose is flat on the relatively large head, and the skin is yellowish-brown. Their speech differs from all other African languages and even their customs are not well known, although many scientists and hunters have lived with them and studied their lifestyle. They do not live in villages, but as forest hunters and gatherers they move from place to place. Their huts are simply constructed: they gather branches, bend them into a semi-circle, reinforce and bind them with lianas, and then cover the construction with leaves. They sleep on the bare ground. Possessions are few: wooden plates and a few pots and pans; bows, spears and small hatchets as weapons.

For catching antelope and fish, Pygmies use nets of various sizes. They make bowstrings from the fibres of fig trees, using a hitherto unknown method which makes them almost as strong as metal. Clothes are also made from the fibres and bark of the fig tree, softened between two stones. Each man takes one wife, which is

In the forests of northern Gabon and southern Cameroun grows the Raffia Palm. It has a short wide trunk and an enormous tail of leaves with stalks from 10 to 18 metres long; individual leaves are between one and two metres long. From the stalks which are as strong as clubs, we built huts in the western forests. From the leaves, folded in half and tied up with slender lianas, we fashioned a perfect roof cover.

an averted glance denotes reconciliation.

Gorillas are active during the day. They rise between 6 and 8 am and spend roughly two hours eating. They rest and sun themselves from 10 am until 1 pm, and then they become active again. They are exclusively herbivorous, living mostly on bamboo and liana shoots, wild celery, leaves, fruits and bark. Towards evening they build a nest low in a bush or tree and sleep in this. Oddly, it seems that these huge animals hardly ever drink in the wild.

PYGMIES

The forest on the River Ituri extends for approximately 150,000 square kilometres. It is perhaps the wildest forest in Africa. Above the shrubs and ferns rises a confusion of small trees

Poachers use an ingenious and treacherous crossbow placed in the vicinity of animal trails. The animals brush against a liana or string set as a snare, and the mechanism releases the bow-string which fires the arrow. This weapon is dangerous for passers-by or curious children.

Well-camouflaged suspended snares are placed by poachers along narrow trails, most frequently near watering places.

inhabitants of the camp abstain from sex. The morning of a hunting day is unusually quiet in the camp. The hunters breakfast in haste and take a small amount of food with them, siezing their spears and disappearing into the forest. As soon as they find tracks and fresh Elephant dung, they smear themselves with it so that their own scent will not give them away.

When they find their prey resting, one of the hunters creeps up to it quietly, throws his spear

Pygmies are diminutive inhabitants of the forest regions of equatorial Africa. They are related to Bushmen and Hottentots. They live in many tribes across the territory of Gabon, Cameroun, Rwanda, Congo and Zaire, as far as the Semliki Valley in Uganda, numbering up to 200,000. A young pygmy from the River Dja in Cameroun plays a primitive stringed instrument he made himself.

a rarity in much of Africa, and they believe in a single omnipotent god. A timid people, the Pygmies are essentially goodhearted and very honest. In one of their customs, if they pick a bunch of bananas from a cultivated plantation, or cut down a few pineapples, they place a piece of meat at the foot of the tree as compensation.

Some of the hunters will attack Elephants using short, strong spears. This is dangerous and demands great courage and skill. On the eve of a hunt the women perform magical dances during which they spray water out of their mouths, which is supposed to bring luck to the hunters. From this moment until the end of the hunt the

Poachers make a continuous row of snares of wire, sisal rope and (in recent times) synthetic fibres, in a clearing among inaccessible shrubby bush. The animals that walk this way, or are driven into the snares, become stuck in them and choke, although often they are caught only by a leg or horn and die in great distress.

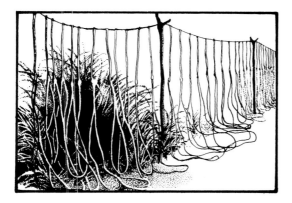

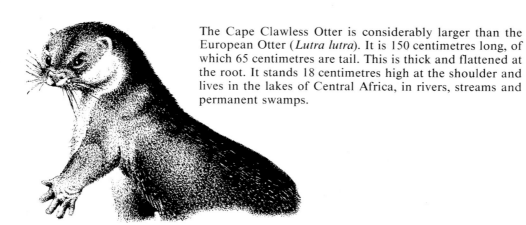

The Cape Clawless Otter is considerably larger than the European Otter (*Lutra lutra*). It is 150 centimetres long, of which 65 centimetres are tail. This is thick and flattened at the root. It stands 18 centimetres high at the shoulder and lives in the lakes of Central Africa, in rivers, streams and permanent swamps.

The forest on the River Ngounie extends to the water's edge. This river flows into the Ogone a little distance upstream from Lambarini, in Gabon.

with both hands into its hind leg and leaps back into the undergrowth. Tortured with pain, the victim breaks into shrill trumpeting and turns after its fleeing attacker. At that moment, a second hunter attacks it, thrusting his spear into another leg. If their throws are accurate, the animal soon collapses to the ground with severed tendons. The hunters then approach it carefully and cut off its trunk, so that it bleeds to death.

An African Elephant weighs as much as: two White Rhinos, or four Black Rhinos, or 17 Boehm's Zebras, or 38 Coke's Hartebeest. The sum of the weight of all organisms living in a given area is called the biomass.

THE LAND CALLED MIOMBO
The great southern savannah

South of the Congolese forest, and from the East African plains, extends an uninterrupted belt of woodland savannah over 2,500 kilometres long from east to west and varying between 1,200 and 2,000 kilometres from north to south. A narrow strip of desert separates this belt from the western coast, and a narrow strip of coastal plateaux and forest from the eastern coast. The southern savannah embraces the whole of southern Tanzania, most of southern Zaire, Angola, Zambia, Zimbabwe and Malawi. Uniform country extends endlessly, known in Tanzania as 'Miombo'. It is mostly rocky landscape, and through the ages the rocks have been disintegrating into a sandy soil which is washed away by the heavy tropical rains. These can last for up to half a year, sweeping through and leaching away its life, so that in places the soil is greyish-white and completely barren. Some trees grow on the ridges of the hills and highlands, while in the valleys acacias and acid grass are dotted about; hibiscus flourishes near flowing water. Upland sandy plateaux alternate with wet acid swamps.

Termites, or white ants, live anywhere where there are trees, bushes and grass since they feed on dead plants. Some people like to open the mounds and eat the termites without any preparation. They smell of almonds and taste reasonable. The body of a termite is composed almost entirely of proteins, which makes it a nutritious food.

Miombo is woodland savannah where trees predominate. The climate is similar to that of the northern savannah, except that the rain cycle is shifted by six months. Before the coming of the rains, Miombo undergoes a miraculous change. The main tree species, *Brachystegia* and *Julbernardia*, are vividly clothed in red, purple and copper-coloured leaves which gradually change to a burnished bronze, then to olive and finally to a bright green. Although the colours seem autumnal, they nevertheless signify new life. The rains last from November to May, during which period birds fly in from the northern savannahs where the dry season is beginning. Miombo is the last almost untouched region of Africa: it cannot support many people, and the Tsetse Fly makes livestock farming impossible.

On protruding rocky cones called inselbergs live hyraxes, birds of prey, night herons and baboons. More animal species inhabit Miombo than the northern savannahs, and some are peculiar to the region. Lichtenstein's Hartebeest, the Puku (*Kobus vardoni*), the African Buffalo (*Syncerus caffer*) and the Common Reedbuck (*Redunca arundium*) are all present and the Roan Antelope is abundant. The Greater Kudu ranks as one of the most beautiful animals of the Miombo, as does the Sable Antelope. There have never been the vast herds of animals seen in East Africa. Many animals were killed in the fight against the Tsetse Fly, as well as by intensive hunting using modern weapons. In this poor region it might be more helpful to give up vain attempts at intensive cattle rearing and concentrate instead on rearing large wild animals.

Most of the water in the region is drained by the many rivers and brooks into the famous Zambezi. In the rainy season the Wattled Crane inhabits temporary swamps, and it also lives in the Ethiopian highlands. The Zambezi swells and turns brown during the rains, but in the dry season its water is as pure and as blue as the sky, and full of fish. On the banks live vast numbers of herons, stalks, waders, kingfishers and

Termites (Isoptera) live in vast colonies and build remarkable fortress structures. The sexually active generation consists of the winged males and females, which have the task of reproducing. Wingless males and females function as workers and soldiers. Over 1,800 species of termite are known; they do the important job of consuming superfluous wood and plant matter.

139

When it drinks, this large, dark male Angolan Giraffe (*Giraffa camelopardalis angolensis*) must either spread its legs wide or dramatically bend its front legs.

the striking purple-coloured Carmine Bee-eater. There are numerous crocodiles. The rocks around the Victoria Falls are a paradise for hyraxes, safe from predators. Along the Rivers Zambezi, Kafue and Luangwa are fertile flooded regions in which a large number of animals live. This flooded area is bordered by

In the Luangwa Valley National Park live the brownish-yellow Zambian Giraffe *(Giraffa camelopardalis thornicrofti),* elephants, a large population of White Rhinos, hippos, Boehm's Zebra, Greater Kudu, Cape Buffalo, Cape Eland, Impalas, Waterbuck, Lions, Leopards and crocodiles.

The Masai Giraffe does not have a conspicuous horn on the brow of its long, pike-like head.

The Rothschild's Giraffe (*Giraffa camelopardalis rothschildi*) is also called the Five-horned Giraffe. Behind its normal horns it has two larger protuberances on the rear part of the skull, and a distinct horn on the brow. A sick giraffe is hardly ever found in the wild, since as soon as an animal becomes weak due to illness, injury or age, it is killed by one of the carnivores.

Unusual shot of Masai Giraffes taken on the edge of Lake Manyara in Tanzania. The conspicuously dark-coloured female standing in the foreground, with almost black head and white insides of the ears, has a relatively rare colouration.

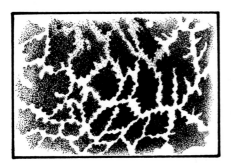

The Masai Giraffe has an unusual marbled pattern.

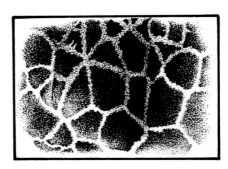

The pattern on a Reticulated Giraffe is formed by fine white stripes, the patches being a bright brownish-red.

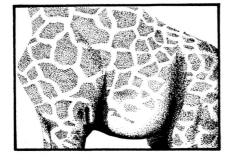

Pattern on the body of an Angolan Giraffe. The coloured patches of the majority of this sub-species have an inconspicuous yellowish-brown colour.

West African Giraffe: pattern on the body.

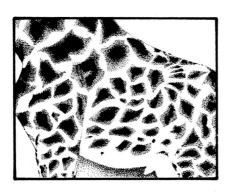

Pattern of the now-rare Cape Giraffe.

Colophosphernious forests (*Colophosphermum mopane*), or Miombo with poor quality grass.

Many swamps persist even in the dry season, and here one can encounter Hippopotami, hundreds of Waterbuck, African Jacanas (*Actophilornis africanus*), African Pygmy Geese (*Nettapus auritus*), Open-billed Storks, African Wood Ibis (*Ibis ibis*), several heron species and the great Saddle-billed Stork. Even 50 years ago a quarter of a million Red Waterbuck were living on the plains near the Kafue River, and a further 150,000 by Lake Bangweul. Enormous herds, however, have been hunted down and today only about 60,000 remain. In drier places the Sassaby can be found — said to be the fastest antelope in the world. Miombo is also swarming with insects, attracting insectivorous birds from Europe and Asia to spend the winter. The Hobby (*Falco subbuteo*) and the Red-footed Falcon (*Falco verspertinus*) are seen, as well as small birds and the tiny animals which also hunt termites when they are swarming.

GIRAFFES

Accounts of the Giraffe have always borne a strange air. The ancient Greek scholar Agatarchides, around the year 104 BC, wrote a book on the animals living west of the Red Sea. He described a creature briefly but succinctly: 'Among the Troglodytes (the wild peoples living on the North African coast) lives an animal which the Greeks call *Camelopardalis*, which is a compound name precisely describing the dual nature of this animal. Its coat is spotted like that of a leopard, its form resembles that of a camel, and its size is immense. It has a long neck, with which it can bite off leaves as high as the tops of trees'.

Giraffes are the tallest of all mammals, their legs and neck contributing most to their height. Along the back the body slants downwards abruptly and is relatively short, measuring only about two metres from the tail to the chest. The tail is around one metre long and is finished with a tassel of black hair. The coat is short and lies close to the skin and there is a short dark mane along the back and neck. These animals live south of the Sahara as far as Cape Town, in herds of about five to a dozen. They like to browse in the company of other species. They have excellent eyesight, hearing and smell. Apart from humans and the Lion they have few enemies; a Giraffe will occasionally even defend itself against the big cat, being able to smash its head with a single kick.

Giraffes live peaceably among themselves, and their ranking system is difficult to discern. A higher-placed individual holds its chin raised, as if it were looking down on lower-ranking animals, and walks at a more energetic pace, swinging its tail. Subordinate animals may not step in the way of higher-ranking ones. The herd is led by an experienced female, with a male accompanying and young of up to one year running around. Females over a certain

A Giraffe sleeps deeply in this position only for a few minutes each day.

age do not occupy leading positions but hand their place to a younger, but still experienced, female who is at the height of her physical strength.

Strong males fight among themselves for a female on heat. Such fights are highly ritualized. The two approach each other until they are several paces apart, observe each other with their chins held high, and occasionally stamp a front foot impatiently or shift from one foot to the other. Then they move closer and begin to circle. Finally they move so close that their chests are touching, and as if by command they swing their heads back and give blows into the side, chest or rump with their horns. As soon as it becomes clear which of the two is the weaker the duel ends, the defeated participant leaves unhurriedly and the victor accompanies him in a dignified manner. He follows the female with his head bent down to the root of her tail, and

The supply of blood to the brain of a Giraffe. The powerful heart (1) pumps blood to an artery (4), and from there to the sponge-like network of small blood vessels (3), which is situated at the base of the brain (2). The brain cannot be damaged by high blood pressure when the head is in this position, as the pressure is decreased by gravity on its way through the neck artery (4). The blood returns by way of the neck vein (5), which is equipped with closing valves (6).

Reticulated Giraffe.

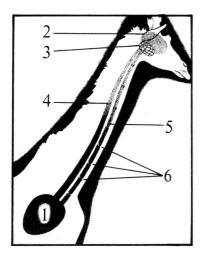

In Tanzania and Zambia bee-keepers suspend in the strong lianas hollow boxes closed at both ends, with one opening. These are gradually occupied by swarms of wild bees. As soon as the interior of the hive is equipped with honeycombs full of larvae and honey, the bee-keepers take the hives down from the trees, smoke out the bees and eat the honeycomb as a delicacy.

occasionally taps her hind legs gently with his front legs. The female usually moves away, and this ritual repeats itself until the female finally stands still. Only then does mating take place.

SECRETARY BIRDS

The Secretary Bird (*Sagittarius serpentarius*) is a curious creature. Ranging between 90 and 120 centimetres in height, it is called 'secretary' on account of the long crest of plumes on its head, which look like an old-fashioned quill pen be-

hind the ear. The Afrikaaners call it 'slangvreters' — snake-eater. It flies much less than other raptors (predatory birds), except in the mating season. Then the male flies round the female, the latter sometimes allowing herself to be led on into a spiral flight which goes far into the sky.

Early in spring Secretary Birds build their nests in the tops of large acacias. The female usually lays two eggs, these being slightly smaller than duck eggs. The young do not leave the nest for at least six months. These birds are excellent snake hunters, and unlike other birds they hunt their prey while running along the ground. When fighting with a cobra this bird is reminiscent of a swordsman, capable of making a lightning hit with its claws. It attacks with half-raised wings, cutting the air with its beak, and sometimes flapping into the air to attack again immediately. It feeds on lizards, snakes, steppe tortoises and small rodents.

The Wart-hog is widespread over the whole of Africa, apart from rain forests and deserts. Old males are solitary. While running they hold their thin tails and brush upright, like an antenna. Wart-hogs live on open plains, savannahs, shrubby and wooded bush country close to water, and on the edges of swamps.

A Wart-hog female suckles her maturing young in a standing position, keeping a close watch all around. The tusks of females are much smaller than those of males, although still well developed.

REEDBUCK AND WATERBUCK

Reedbuck, Waterbuck and their relatives (Reduncinae) are medium-sized to large antelopes. The males are horned, the females hornless, and they usually live in herds of up to 30. Some species form herds of tens of thousands on relatively small areas near swamps, lakes or rivers.

	Body length in cm	Shoulder height in cm	Weight in kg
Bohor Reedbuck (*Redunca redunca*)	115—145	65—90	35—65
Mountain Reedbuck (*R. fulvorufula*)	110—125	60—75	20—30
Southern Reedbuck (*R. arundium*)	120—150	80—100	55—90
Waterbuck (*Kobus ellipsiprymnus*)	180—220	115—135	170—250
Nile Lechwe (*Kobus megaceros*)	135—160	85—100	70—110
Lechwe (*Kobus leche*)	145—170	85—105	75—125
Kob (*Kobus kob*)	125—155	90—110	60—90
Puku (*Kobus vardoni*)	120—155	80—100	65—90

In the Semliki Valley, in western Uganda, about 15,000 Kob live in a small area. This number is composed of small groups of 10 to 12, each controlled by one adult male. As females are constantly on the move, the males would have to fight among themselves continually for shifting territories. In Semliki, however, every adult male fights for his own patch of a few square metres in size. He defends this, only leaving to graze or drink. In his absence another male occupies it and so, on returning, the first must either drive off the intruder or wait until another patch becomes available elsewhere.

The Bohor Reedbuck lives in pairs or small groups near swamps and water, among shrub or reed vegetation. When disturbed it jumps up, runs a small distance and then stops and watches its pursuer, whilst calling out with its distinctive voice. This species likes to graze on young corn in local fields.

In the backwaters and ponds around Lake Bangweulu in Zambia live about 60,000 Lechwe. Their general health has deteriorated considerably in recent years. Over half of the population are suffering from a strain of bovine tuberculosis which can affect all tissues and organs. The chief carriers of tuberculosis are domestic cattle.

The Defassa Waterbuck is recognized by the large white patch on the rump, and is much larger than either the Lechwe or the Puku. It is often prey to Lions. Once I was present when three of the cats organized a perfect hunt. The lioness hid herself in a small dip; the two young males stalked the buck and then chased it straight to her. She jumped out in one leap, brought the Waterbuck to the ground and killed it with a blow from her paw. Although the antelope is as large as a doe, the lioness carried it into the shade of the bushes like a dog carries a hare.

The Puku is plentiful in the Luangwa Valley National Park, Zambia. It is similar to Buffon's Kob but has slightly shorter horns and forelegs and a black stripe on the front legs; the shoulders are about 10 centimetres higher and the earlobes have black tips. This antelope is limited to woodland savannah and water, living in small herds.

Waterbuck lives in Ethiopia and eastern, southern and southwest Africa. It is the largest and strongest of its group. Six geographical sub-species differ from one another in their colouring and horn size, but hardly at all in body size. They live predominantly in thick bush country and among tall grass near water. The herds are never large, perhaps six to 15 individuals. They are not particularly timid, although if one of the herd smells danger and begins to flee, the whole herd can instantly be put to flight. This species is less prone than its cousins to taking refuge in water.

TERMITES

There are about 1,500 termite species throughout the world, of which over 600 are in Africa. In the termite society or 'state' there is usually one queen — a fertile female having the sole task of laying eggs. She does this with rigid regularity every two or three seconds, thirty to forty thousand per day, 12 million per year, and this over several decades! From time to time the queen is fertilized by a male. She lives in a special strong chamber, accessed by small corridors through which sterile, wingless female and male workers go to feed her, take care of her and carry away the eggs. Apart from males and females there are extra castes of males and females with their wings reduced to various stages of development. Their time comes only if the queen dies and they ensure the colony's continued existence. Both the reproductive females and males lose their wings after fertilization.

The workers feed the other termites and build and repair the nest's structure. The other important caste consists of soldiers. These blind males and females have strong heads and powerful mandibles, or they grow hollow pointed projections inside which are small glands producing a sticky substance. This can be squirted from a distance to fend off much larger insects in a fight.

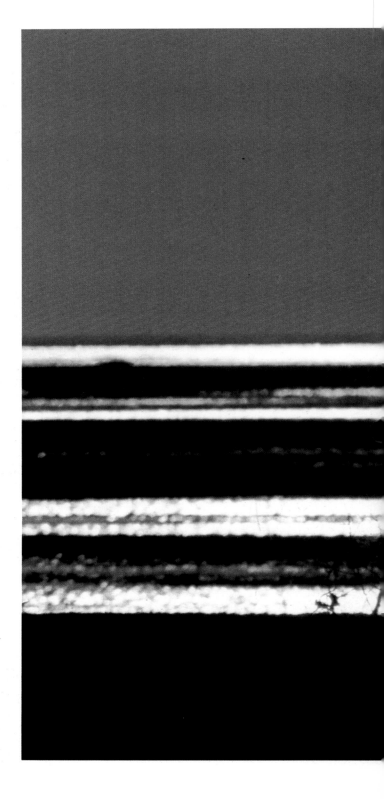

Even after sunset and during the night Lechwe stay close to swamps and patches of water, to which they escape if danger threatens. On the plains near the River Kafua in Zambia there were hundreds of thousands of these animals about 50 years ago.

GLACIERS ON THE EQUATOR
The East African mountains

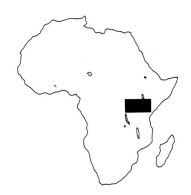

For centuries the local inhabitants have regarded Mount Uhuru (Kilimanjaro) with religious awe and have animated it with evil spirits and demons. The legend says that, as they had little idea what snow and ice were, they presumed it was silver sparkling on the summit. Long ago the chief of the Dzhaga tribe longed for this silver and sent several men up the high mountain with instructions to bring a little back. The men managed to climb to the summit and tried to bring down a little of the cold silver as quickly as possible. The gleaming 'metal', however, turned to water before their very eyes. They assumed that this magical change had been brought about by mountain spirits, and from that time the sky-touching summit was called 'Kilimanjaro' — mountain of demons.

An elephant skull has a small brain cavity containing a finely-wrinkled brain weighing about 5 kilogrammes. The skull cavities are filled with fine, shell-like structures which strengthen the structure and make it lighter.

The East African mountains do not form an unbroken chain, as in Ethiopia. Solitary peaks tower above the vast grassy plains; Uhuru, the highest mountain in Africa, is among them, being renamed from a Swahili word meaning 'freedom'. Along with Kenya and Ruwenzori, these are the only African peaks where snow and ice can be found all year round, and where small glaciers form. (Although snow covers the Atlas and occasionally the Ethiopian mountains, it never stays all year.) During the last ice age there was permanent snow on the equator. The glaciers extended much lower than now and were more widespread. Mount Kenya, for instance, was completely covered with ice, as shown by the moraines — piles of rocks carried downwards by the glacier and left when it melted. As elsewhere in the world the glaciers in East Africa are retreating, and if this continues at the current rate, Uhuru will be without ice in 200 years.

Most East African mountains are cone-shaped volcanoes with steep slopes. The higher the mountain rises, the higher the lava must rise during an eruption in order to reach the surface. Slowly, a volcano begins to discharge less and less lava, until it ceases. It may then happen that the internal pressure becomes so great that the whole mountain is torn open by a terrific explosion, blasting away the peak and leaving a deep crater in its place. Explosions of this type were responsible for the shape of today's Meru and Hanang mountains and one of the Uhuru peaks.

More often, however, a new breach opens in the side of the mountain and a new, lower cone forms on the side. In East Africa there are various stages of this development. The Ruwenzori Range, however, the famous 'Moon Mountains', are not of volcanic origin.

The climate on these mountains resembles summer during the day and winter at night.

After dawn the temperature rises within a few minutes and the night frost retreats. Then the sun shines fiercely for a couple of hours. Fog begins to form lower down on the slopes in the morning, rising slowly to the summit. By noon everything is usually shrouded in fog, and in the afternoon snow or hail often falls. As evening comes the weather usually clears up on the

A large African Elephant on the plains at the foot of Uhuru (Kilimanjaro) in Kenya is completely reddened, having just sprinkled itself with red mud. The breadth of the 'ear-span' corresponds to the height of the animal at the shoulder.

peaks, and from the surrounding lowlands one can observe the peaks emerging from the clouds. After sunset the frost comes down in a few minutes.

The slopes are covered with fairly regular vegetation belts. Among the foothills extends a belt of rain forest, which resembles true tropical rain forest but is poorer in wildlife. A large number of Elephants still live on the slopes, as well as rhinos. In drier places great juniper cedars grow, often covered with Beard Lichens. Under the trees is a carpet of ferns, shrubs and

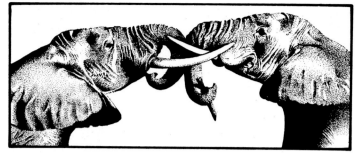

Beginning of an elephant courtship. The animals stand with their foreheads facing, touch each other's trunks and intertwine them in gentle caressing. One partner often feeds the other with its trunk.

Three male East African Elephants drinking on the edge of the swamps of Lake Amboseli, at the foot of Uhuru (Kilimanjaro).

Only humans and elephants are able to destroy giant Baobabs. A starving elephant will ram its tusks into the strong bark of the tree, drag it into the long grass and try to reach the soft pulpy wood.

Even during elephant combat the trunk plays an important role. Each tries to get a firm hold on the other's trunk, which is a very sensitive organ.

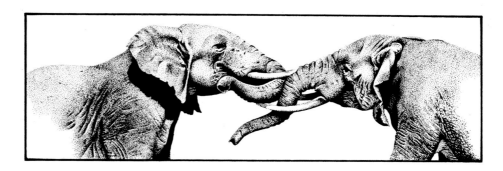

sometimes grass. In river valleys and rocky places there are many clearings carpeted with Tasty Pennisetum (*Pennisetum clandestinum*), which makes excellent pasture. St John's Wort (*Hypericum*) is also abundant. The small brooks have cool water, in which few fish live; trout were introduced there. Many Buffalo also dwell in the foothill forests, and they are larger specimens than anywhere else. The best place for observing them is probably the Ngurudoto Crater, which lies in the forest between Mount Meru and Uhuru. Bushbuck are also common.

A belt of Arundinaria Bamboo (*Arundinaria alpina*) can be found on almost all slopes, looking from a distance like a drab green belt above the dark forest and below the belt of heather. This bamboo grows for several years and goes to seed, then remains standing, like a forest of gigantic dead grass stems. Walking there is a difficult and eerie business: the wind moans through the holes in the bamboo, the stems rattle against one another, and everything is covered in cold fog. Apart from Elephants and Bongo, few other animals live in this bamboo.

Above the bamboo belt are large meadows vegetated with millet, Common Lion's Foot (*Alchemilla vulgaris*) and high Hagenias (*Hagenia abyssinica*). Higher still these give way to tree-like heathers. On the meadows live Buffalo and Bushbuck, while Defassa Waterbuck and Cape Eland graze there. The Giant Forest Hog is common, but rarely seen. The gigantic heathers grow to heights of 20 metres, covering the lower mountain tops. They are sparse and in places there is sufficient grass under them for animals to graze. It rains almost every day, and the heather belt is hidden in a misty haze even when the tops are clear. Leopards hunting at these heights are coloured dark to black. A special sub-species of the Lion, large and spotted, is said to have lived there long ago. Nowadays the common Lion strays to these heights by chance and it is a rare sight.

The belt of tall heather forms the upper boundary of the area in which large animals still live. Only duikers and the Steenbok (*Raphicerus campestris*) can penetrate higher. The bigger animals do not generally go above 3,800 metres, as they cannot withstand the rapid changes in temperature between day and night. Nevertheless even at these heights giant heather, lobelias, *Helichrysum* and Groundsel (*Senecio barbatipes*) attain heights of up to 10 metres.

ELEPHANTS

The African Elephant (*Loxodonta africana*) is the largest land animal, being 600 to 750 centimetres long, measuring up to 400 centimetres at the shoulder, and weighing perhaps 7,500 kilogrammes. There are a number of geographical

sub-species. The Bush Elephant (*L. a. africana*) lives only in southern Africa, in reservations, being somewhat smaller than the Steppe Elephant, which inhabits woodland or open savannahs. The smallest sub-species is the Forest Elephant (*L. a. cyclotis*) of the forests west of the Great Trench Depression. It has rounded ears,

An adult female elephant, the leading mother and a younger female escort their young through flowing water.

The eyes of adult female elephants are covered with long thick lashes. The elephant's eye wrinkles are not arranged elliptically, as in the rhino, but as irregular layers in the shape of an arch above the eye.

the edges of which meet on the nape (as in the Steppe Elephant). They usually measure about 210 to 250 centimetres at the shoulder and their tusks are weaker and yellowish in colour, grow-

ing more vertically and less curved. On the front feet there are five toes, on the back feet four.

The largest elephant is the Steppe Elephant (*L. a. oxyotis*), which usually has only four toes

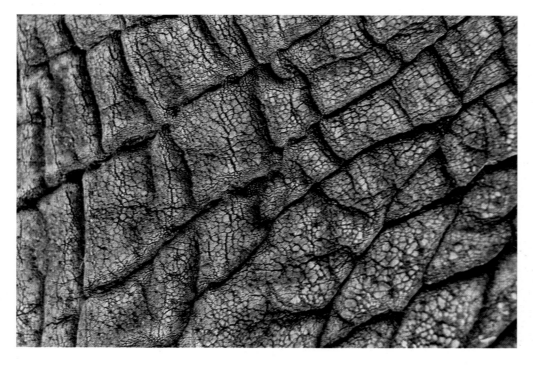

Detail of the hide on the upper parts of the hind legs of a 10-year-old East African Elephant, showing the various shapes formed by furrowing. Individual areas are divided into even smaller irregular patches. These wrinkles in the hide permit the elephant to move easily, as the hide is in places four centimetres thick.

on the front feet and three on the back. It inhabits the great African savannahs and forest edges, but will climb to higher places. In regions where individual sub-species overlap, various transitional forms also exist.

The trunk has many functions. It is the beast's organ of smell and touch, as well as be-

The maternal elephant herd is led to the pasture by the oldest, strongest and most experienced cow, who has the highest position in the hierarchy of the herd. Immediately after her goes her small calf, then the older calves. The other adults with their young follow in the same order. The leading female constantly touches her calf's head with her tail in order to keep it under control and to ensure that it keeps up with her pace. This touching gives the young a feeling of protection and safety.

Another form of elephant combat, in which the elephants try to push each other backwards using their foreheads.

ing used for grasping. The animal uses it to pass food to its mouth, and is able to suck up to six litres of water into it in one go, which it then squirts into its mouth or over its body. A trunk has over 4,000 muscles and African Elephants

When male elephants become adult, they leave the maternal herd and form male herds of various sizes. Young, less experienced males usually walk near the front of the herd, the leader usually being the most experienced male. ▶

157

The African Python (*Python sebae*) transported to the Dvůr Králové Zoo in 1971, from Uganda, now measures four metres.

have at the end of the trunk two small 'fingers' well supplied with blood and equipped with touch cells (Indian Elephants have only one such small finger). A calf is not able to use its trunk until about four months of age, and it gets in the way constantly. The calf curls it up in various ways and swings it; sometimes it treads on it by mistake and becomes startled, crying with pain and falling over.

The tusks are the elongated incisors of the upper jaw. They are hollow at the roots and continue to grow throughout life. Elephants use their tusks to dig up roots, shatter tree trunks, peel off bark, break up soil and sink wells during the dry season. An individual usually uses one of its tusks more often — left-tusked or right-tusked — so that one is more worn down.

The Elephant is in all respects a giant among animals. It eats up to 400 kilogrammes of plant food daily and drinks from 80 to 150 litres of water. It has over 18 metres of intestines, of which the small measures 12 metres, and the large about six metres. The liver weighs 60 kilogrammes, the stomach is 150 centimetres long, and the heart measures 50 centimetres and weighs up to 18 kilogrammes. Elephants eat for between 15 and 18 hours every day, sleeping hardly four hours inshort 20-minute invervals. On average only 35 per cent of the food they consume is digested, so the amount of excrement is substantial: one animal can produce 200 kilogrammes of dung and 80 litres of urine daily. At an average body temperature of 20 °C the creature produces 75,000 calories of heat in 24 hours!

Elephants breathe two-thirds through their trunks, the rest through their mouths. In places the hide is four centimetres thick and has a great number of sweat and oil glands. Between its eye and its ear, especially in the male, this creature has a special temporal gland which exudes a thick brown secretion, and Elephants are usually aggressive at the time of greatest secretion. The regulation of body temperature is not particularly efficient, and they are better able to withstand cold than excessive heat. The surrounding temperature has a direct effect on the waving speed of the ears, which cools the animal. Each ear weighs up to 90 kilogrammes and is densely supplied with blood vessels. Ear movements also express the ranking position of an individual. Weaker animals do not dare to wave their ears in the vicinity of a higher-placed herd member.

Elephants become sexually mature at around eight to 13 years. In the mating season, the female presses her side and hind quarters against the head of the male. When he places his trunk

The African Python is a very close relation of the Tiger Python of India and Sri Lanka. It is doubtful that reports of the ancient Romans were true, in which these snakes grew to seven or eight metres long. It is one of the few pythons which will chase a prey that it was not able to catch initially.

on her back she quickly sets off running, moving her head and swinging her tail. The male follows alongside, pushing his trunk and tusks against her. They cross each other's paths und stand with heads facing and trunks raised in an S-shape, gently touching the tips. This is repeated several times, with the female frequently

Thousands of wildebeest trek to new pastures in the vicinity of the East African mountains. During their journey they go from one watering place to the next, crossing rivers and shallow lakes, stopping only near water and short grass pastures.

Endless herds of wildebeest trek for days and nights across the African steppe. During the long migration they give birth to their young.

turning her hind quarters to the male, kneeling, raising her tail and the male feeling her vulva with his trunk. At last the female stands still, the male raises himself on his hind legs and supports himself on her back with his front legs. Mating takes several minutes and may be repeated after half an hour. Pregnancy lasts for 18 to 22 months for a baby female, 21 to 23 months for a male. Mothers suckle their young for up to three years. The elephant's rate of reproduction is slow. During her lifetime a female elephant bears 7 to 11 young, of which only about 60 per cent reach maturity. Because roughly half of the offspring are males one mother produces only

After long years of migrating regularly to new pastures the wildebeest tread down large numbers of trails to every watering place.

two or three females capable of continuing the line. That is why excessive shooting of elephants may readily devastate their population and it then takes decades for them to attain their original number.

Elephants are among the most intelligent of land mammals. They likewise have the largest, perfectly structured, brain of them all. The brain of males weighs between 4.6 and 5.9 kilogrammes that of females somewhat less. The most perfectly developed in elephants is their sense of smell. They are able to detect even quite faint smells from a great distance. The large cavities in the skull serve as resonators, amplifiers and transmitters of sounds and the large ear lobes likewise play an important auxiliary role. The elephant's sense of taste is also excellent. They are able, for example, to discern a pill in the tastiest of morsels without fail and spit it out. The elephant's eyesight is as good as that of zebras, to give an example. The structure of the eyes is no different from that of other mammals even though they are relatively small. The iris and pupil are round, the lens 7.2 millimetres in diameter. The eyes of elephants are generally brown or greenish-brown, very occasionally blue. They evidently see much more clearly in dim light than in bright light. The sense of touch also plays an important role in the life of elephans. The main tactile organs are the finger-like appendages at the tip of the trunk but there are many more very sensitive spots on the elephant's body comprising large numbers of tactile cells. Knowledge of these spots is put to excellent use by elephant trainers in making the beasts obey their commands.

Elephants are typical social animals. They generally form small family groups consisting of the mother and her variously aged offspring. Several families often join to form a clan, headed by the highest-ranking female. Sometimes, however, families come together to form huge herds, generally accompanied by one or sometimes several adult males. Such herds then travel throughout the countryside destroying everything in their paths. Bands composed exclusively of males of various ages are another type of group, one that is much more loosely-knit; these are headed by the strongest and highest-ranking bull.

At present there are about 30,000 elephants in Africa.

PYTHONS

Among many African peoples snakes are the subject of many myths and legends. In Daho-

The migration of thousands of wildebeest has been repeating itself regularly for centuries on the plains of the Serengeti, Ngorongoro and neighbouring Masai territories. Over half a million animals cover distances of many kilometres annually.

mey the snake used to be worshipped as a god; in Tanzania it was believed that a python spat out a precious stone before its death, and if such a stone was not found near the dead snake the people accused one another of theft.

There are three python species in Africa. The largest, best-known and most revered is the African Python (*Python sebae*), which can grow to an exceptional length of seven metres. The smallest and most beautifully coloured is the Royal Python (*Python regius*), which grows to 130 centimetres. Slightly larger and less striking is the Angola Python (*Python anchietae*), which is about 150 centimetres long.

The body of a snake is equipped with a strong and elastic musculature, and friction is the basis of its movement. The more uneven and rough the ground, the less the snake's body undulates and the faster it moves. The movement arises from opposing contractions of the muscles on the left and right sides. A wave of undulation proceeds from the front to the back, pushing the snake's body forwards. Snakes use another form of movement in narrow clefts or hollows, or when climbing trees; they contract and expand the body regularly, like a worm, and move forwards in this way. They can combine both types of movement.

In the slender body of a snake, the left parts of the lungs, liver and kidneys are stunted, with the right parts of these organs fully developed. The eyelids are transparent and are renewed when the old skin is shed. The eyes themselves are only slightly moveable and snakes are short-sighted, able to discern only movements at a distance. Hearing is also poor. The best developed sense is smell, for which they use their nostrils and tongues. On the constantly flicked-out tongue they pick up scents from the air, inserting the tip of the tongue into special cavities on the roof of the mouth which serve as scent analyzers (Jacobsen's organ).

The African Python lives throughout Africa south of the Sahara. It can swim and climb trees, and it hunts birds and animals up to the size of small antelope. Pythons are not big eaters, consuming only about twice their own body weight in food annually. The female lays up to 100 eggs and curls her body round them, warming them to 10 °C above the surroundings by means of slow rythmic contractions of her muscles which raise her body temperature to 11 °C higher than that of the male.

The Royal Python lives in tropical Africa as far as the Sudanese province of Bahr el Ghazal. It prefers to seek out low bushes and branches, constantly ready to hunt rodents, frogs or other small prey. If startled it instantly rolls into a ball and hides its head inside; it remains curled up even if immersed in water.

RHINOS

Rhinos are odd-toed ungulates. Of the three toes, the middle toe is the most fully developed. These large, heavy animals, like the Elephant, have a high springy cushion on the sole of the foot. The horn does not grow out of the skull bone, but is a product of the skin. It is formed of horny tissue, similar to the coat hairs. These 'hairs' are compressed into a hard substance, and when a rhino is skinned the horns come away with the hide. Some rhino horns are one and a half metres long. Frequently the horn is broken off leaving a bloody patch on the skin, out of which a new horn begins to grow. The rear horn, situated closer to the brow, is usually weaker and shorter.

The rhino is an unpredictable animal. It may run away or turn and attack with its head lowered. It is very short-sighted, which explains some aspects of its behaviour. Its sense of smell is better than its sight, and its hearing is out-

The eyes of a rhino are covered with thick, strong eyelashes. The creature has relatively bad eyesight but is able to sense movement well. It has excellent hearing and a relatively good sense of smell.

standing. If it senses by hearing or smell that there is something nearby and that it cannot see well, it will attack. Sometimes it even attacks a tree or termite mound. In regions such as Masai country where rhinos are not persecuted by people, they behave more calmly and peaceably. In Wakamba in Kenya, where the locals hunt them with poisoned arrows, or in regions where they are poached, they are more aggressive.

Two species of rhinos live in Africa. The smaller is the Black Rhinoceros (*Diceros bicornis*), at 300 to 375 centimetres long, 160 centimetres high at the shoulder, and weighing 2,000 kilogrammes. The White Rhinoceros (*Ceratotherium simum*) is 360 to 400 centimetres long, 160 to 200 centimetres high and 3,200 kilogrammes in weight. These two species differ in several respects. The Black Rhinoceros has a pointed upper lip which takes a firm hold of

Black Rhinoceros male near Lake Amboseli, in the reservation of the same name in Kenya, feeding on shrub twigs only a few hundred metres from the hotel. Rhinos are accompanied by Cattle Egrets, ox-peckers and various storks.

twigs from trees and shrubs, which form its staple diet. It holds its head horizontally. The White Rhinoceros always holds its head low near the ground, giving the impression of searching for something. Its broad, straight lips are designed for grazing on grass, its chief food.

The Black Rhinoceros is almost solitary, ranging through its territory. If it meets another rhino on its trail they both stop, raise their tails in the fighting posture, scrape their hind feet several times, snort and lower their heads, and

165

An older adult female Black Rhino weighs approximately 1,400 kilogrammes. When disturbed it may turn with light-ning speed and attack out of the blue — or gallop away with its tail and head raised.

Various species of groundsel (*Senecio*) grow at altitudes of up to 4,000 metres. Sometimes they form sponge-like trunks up to three metres high, completely covered with dried bunches of leaves, at other times simple or branched small trunks which grow long velvety leaves with lath-shaped flowers. When the flowers fade new rosettes appear, so that a spreading plant can live for up to 200 years.

then charge at each other. When it seems almost inevitable that they will collide, they brake and raise their heads, staring at each other. Then they slowly turn aside and each continues on its way. A rhino behaves in a similar way if it comes across the fresh prints of another rhino, making as if to attack it. White Rhinos live more gregariously, groups of up to six animals grazing peacefully or resting near each other. These creatures have no enemies apart from humans. Lions occasionally manage to kill a young calf, but generally rhinos take little notice of them. Occasionally a rhino coming to a river to drink is attacked by a crocodile or hippo.

The mating season lasts all year. The male and female stand face to face, smelling each other and making bubbling noises. The female usually attacks the male, knocking into his side, which he tolerates. If another male appears, the first makes dancing steps around the female; males do not fight over females, however, and the female herself decides which she prefers. During courtship they snort, grunt and sometimes even squeak. Actual mating can last 35 minutes, during which the pair turn slowly in a circle. Sometimes the female and male separate after mating, at other times they remain together for several months. Pregnancy lasts for about 17 months. Mothers take great care of their young for three to five years.

AFRICAN BUFFALO

A large herd of Cape Buffalo presents an unforgettable sight. These massive, dark animals stand motionless, as if hewn out of stone, powerful and dangerous. It was once believed that no other herbivore killed so many of its enemies — Lions and people — as the Buffalo. Careful observation has revealed a different story: as long as this animal is left alone it is docile and peaceable.

The Cape Buffalo (*Syncerus caffer caffer*) is almost black, has large horns, stands about 160 centimetres high at the shoulder, and weighs around 600 to 900 kilogrammes. It lives on open savannahs, bush country and forest edges south of the Sahara, and will climb high into the mountain belts of East Africa. It is the largest of the three sub-species of African Buffalo.

The Short-horned Buffalo (*S. c. brachyceros*) is usually smaller, reaching 600 kilogrammes and a shoulder height of 140 centimetres. It is greyish-brown and has shorter horns. It inhabits northern savannahs west of Sudan.

The smallest buffalo is the Dwarf Forest Buffalo (*S. c. nanus*). This typical forest dweller is reddish-brown, 120 centimetres tall at the shoulder and weighs up to 400 kilogrammes. It lives

Even when disturbed, Cape Buffalo are reluctant to leave the cooling mud in the noonday heat. When danger passes they immediately return to their much-loved mud. There are ample wallows in the shrubby valley in the Kabelega National Park, Uganda.

The Forest Buffalo (*Syncerus caffer nanus*) has long black hair on the nape, along the back and on the lower edges of the ears. Even the brush on the tail is coloured black. It has noticeably light-orange long hairs on the upper edges of the ears. This species is considerably smaller than the Cape Buffalo, but no less dangerous.

The Cape Buffalo's sense of herd responsibility is highly developed. With their apparently ponderous movements, they are constantly on the alert for any hint of danger. They can scent an enemy 500 metres upwind. When this happens the leading bull becomes immobile and the herd grows restless, turning their heads into the wind. Several animals move forward and stand watching the horizon; females with young remain at the back. If the herd takes flight the bulls run last, thus protecting females with young. Occasionally, in a herd on the alert, the males begin to fight among themselves, apparently to release tension. Males sometimes also fight fiercely for females on heat. They stand about 10 metres apart, stamp their feet and

in small groups. Whereas a huge herd of Cape Buffalo will invariably take to its heels in one body, charging across the savannah like an avalanche, the Dwarf Forest Buffalo has a small, unusually nimble body and short legs for creeping under dense growth. Its horns are short and curved backwards in a sickle shape. The body shape is a few centimetres taller at the rump than the shoulder, so enabling it to creep through forest undergrowth like a wedge. A group of Dwarf Forest Buffalo never dash at random through the forest when afraid, but run in single file. Although much smaller than the other two sub-species, if wounded it can nevertheless be very dangerous.

Cape Buffalo live in herds of about 50 to 150, although on rare occasions it is still possible to see herds numbering thousands on the Serengeti plains and in the Kigezi region. The majority of the herd consists of females with calves, young males and a few large adult males. A bull calf is born and reared in the herd, protected by its mother, the other cows and even by adult bulls. When it is old enough to take care of itself it joins a group of contemporary males and gradually leads an increasingly settled life. When a bull reaches the peak of its physical development it goes off to a small pasture of its own, where there is sufficient grass for night grazing, enough shade from the midday sun, and, if possible, a watering place and muddy spot where it can wallow for hours on end. If a group of young, playful bulls intrudes into its territory, it will graze with them contentedly. Solitary bulls often meet at watering holes but there is little aggression. Only some exceptional danger will drive a bull off his territory.

snort noisily, and throw their heads around; then they charge at each other. The impact is so violent that they appear stunned for a second or two, but then they separate and attack again. Usually the weaker of the two hangs his head after several charges, indicating his subordination. The victor does not attack again but proudly raises and shakes his head, turns and returns to the herd.

Pregnancy lasts for 11 months. The birth itself can take more than half an hour and is evidently very painful, as is the case with the majority of ruminants. Bulls sometimes form a protective circle around a female giving birth, although this is not the norm. Disease is the worst enemy of African Buffalo, and they are particu-larly susceptible to the cattle fever introduced into Africa with domestic cattle from Asia, at the end of the last century. At the time an epidemic of cattle fever across Africa nearly made the African Buffalo extinct. Obtrusive, parasitic insects are unpleasant pests: ticks, flies, lice and mosquitoes bother them wherever they go. This is why they wallow in mud. Red-billed Ox-peckers (*Buphagus erythrorhynchus*) and Cattle Egrets live with the herds, to rid them of parasites and warn them of approaching danger.

Part of a Cape Buffalo herd on the edge of a swamp in the great Ruwenzori National Park in Uganda.

THE LAND OF LAKES AND VOLCANOES
The Great Trench Depression

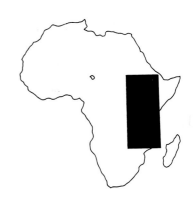

The Great Trench Depression (Rift Valley) is a unique natural formation, beginning in the Taurus Mountains in Turkey and running south through the Jordan Valley as far as the bay of Aqaba. At this point it is submerged in the Red Sea; it reappears on the African continent as the Afar depression in north-eastern Ethiopia. It runs through the Ethiopian mountains and the Kenyan and Tanzanian highlands as far as the southern borders of Tanzania, where it disappears. The majority of the depression is scattered with old and recent volcanoes, alkaline lakes and hot springs.

The second branch of the depression begins at Lake Albert in Uganda, curving in a wide arch to the highlands in Kivu, where its path is blocked by a high cluster of volcanic mountains — some of which are still active. It continues through a deep ravine, in which Lake Tanganika is situated. At Lake Nyasa the two branches of the depression meet.

The Great Trench Depression is unlike any

normal valley. It is the result of movements and cracks in the earth's crust, whereas most valleys are carved out by rivers or glaciers.

The Afar depression in Ethiopia forms one of the harshest wildernesses in the world. In the valley of the upper River Avache, however, there is still an abundance of animals; oryxes, gazelles, Grévy's Zebras and the last groups of Wild Asses all live there. The Afar is situated almost 100 metres below sea level, and is one of the hottest places on earth. The bottom of this depression is covered with razor-sharp volcanic rocks. Salty hot springs have formed enormous salt and potash deposits occupying almost 3,000 square kilometres. Quarried salt bricks have served as currency here for centuries.

Farther into Kenya the depression continues as a hot, arid plain which contrasts starkly with the cool heights on either side. The bottom is covered with pebbles of volcanic rock or a fine white or red sand. The flat dusty plains are the remains of lakes and swamps. The drying-out process has not yet finished and the lakes are still shrinking as their water becomes more alkaline. The underground waters in Tanzania are heated by the volcanic cores and gush out in the form of bubbling, highly salted springs. This spells death for numerous fish species and makes the water undrinkable for large herbivores. Yet life exists here. The high carbonate content, along with the warmth and sunshine, create ideal conditions for blue-green algae in particular; these feed millions of flamingoes. It is estimated that there are approximately six million flamingoes, of four species, in the world and more than half live on the alkaline lakes of the East African Depression. Only in 1954 did

On the sodium-rich Lake Magadi in southern Kenya lives a population of Lesser Flamingoes. From there they fly to nearby Lake Natron in Tanzania, which is the main nesting place of flamingoes, as well as to other lakes in the area.

The Roseate Flamingo has long legs but is short on stamina, being unable to run for any length of time. Apart from African lakes it nests in small numbers in southern Spain, the south of France and in Asia.

Leslie Brown determine that enormous numbers of Lesser Flamingo (*Phoeniconaias minor*) and Roseate Flamingo (*Phoenicopterus ruber*) were living in the middle of the warm Lake Natron.

The crystalline beds of the alkaline lakes are brilliant white, or sometimes slightly pinkish; the shallow water is usually wine-red, blue-green or coffee-brown. The flamingoes build their nests on the steaming mud. They are

On the permanently green plain by one of the five source tributaries of Lake Nakuru, in Kenya, lie millions of feathers moulted by flamingoes.

hunted not only by eagles and vultures but also by big cats. Among predatory birds the Osprey (*Pandion haliaetus*) is common, nesting in tall solitary trees. Poor grass grows in the area around the lakes and small numbers of White-bearded Wildebeest, Giraffe, rhinos, oryxes, antelopes and zebras can live there. In other places in the depression, such as in the swamps of Uaso Nyiro, live Buffalo and hippopotami. In the main, though, the animals are of the semi-desert savannah habitat. In the Olduvai Gorge have been found bones of giant hippopotami, hogs as large as rhinos and sheep the size of cattle. The remains of prehistoric humans have also been discovered, predominantly *Homo habilis* and also the slightly larger, more recent *Homo erectus*.

In the freshwater lakes live nearly 120 species

Lake Nakuru, 1,849 metres above sea level, was in 1970 completely covered by more than two million Roseate and Lesser Flamingoes. The lake and its environs form the Nakuru National Park with an area of 62 square kilometres. Apart from flamingoes, 370 other bird species also live there. Nakuru is a world-famous ornithological research station.

of cichlid fish, as well as an abundance of mouthbrooders of the genus *Tilapia*. In the swamps dwells the African Lungfish (*Protopterus annectens*), a representative of the group Dipnoi; the Water Cobra (*Boulengerina annulata*) inhabits Lake Tanganika. The Great Depression forms a world of its own. Millions of birds migrate there annually and in times long past herds of animals from the north and south met there. To this day it is one of the most important migratory routes in Africa.

FLAMINGOES

I shall never forget the magnificent sight of hundreds of thousands of flamingoes glowing a soft pink in the morning sun on Lake Nakuru, in Kenya. Flamingoes have long necks and long, slender legs with webbed toes on the feet. The bill is relatively long, and bent downwards at an angle. Its edges are notched with horny slats through which the flamingo strains food from the water and mud with its bill closed. Small animals caught on the slats during sieving are licked up with the horny knobs on the tongue and swallowed. Algae and small aquatic creatures form the mainstay of the diet. Flamin-

goes are able to hunt in water at temperatures of 50 °C.

These ungainly birds build cone-shaped nests about 50 centimetres tall, constructed of mud. Each pair has only one nestling, which is fed at first on a red liquid formed in the digestive tract of the parents. When the nestlings have grown they crawl out of the nest and run about; if star-

Around Nakuru there is good agricultural soil, on which African farmers have begun to use chemical fertilizers with the aim of increasing productivity. The lake, however, has no outflow, and its five sources are supplemented by water in the rainy season. Chemicals were washed into the lake water, reducing the level of plankton and algae reproduction, and with this the levels of fish, crustaceans and molluscs. The result is that more than two-thirds of the flamingoes and pelicans have moved away to another lake. This picture was taken in 1976.

The Lesser Flamingo flying over the sodium lakes in Tanzania. In ancient times flamingoes ranked among the greatest culinary delicacies; the ancient Romans particularly liked their tongues.

tled, they quickly seek refuge in any nearby nest. The parents always return to their own nest, and will accept any nestling that comes into it. In their collective lifestyle, an attachment to their own nestling would seem to be superfluous. The roseate flamingo (*Phoenicopterus ruber*) has a wingspan of up to 165 centimetres, and the lesser flamingo (*Phoeniconaias minor*) of around 145 centimetres.

PELICANS, CORMORANTS AND ANHINGAS

Pelicans are large-framed birds with very strangely shaped bills. The lower part consists of two narrow, flexible branches connected at the tip, between which hangs an expandable sack. All four toes on the short legs are webbed. Pelicans are excellent fish catchers and they can co-operate in the hunt. They nest in reeds, bushes and on open spaces. Nestlings are almost bald when hatched and have small bills.

A species of pale violet water-lily, *Nymphaea capensis*, covers almost the whole area of the freshwater Lake Naivasha in Kenya.

Cormorants feeding their young. The parents, after flying in, alight close to the nest, and, with swinging movements of the head, announce to the young that they have brought food. The hungry nestlings push their way upwards, open their bills and reach out to the crop of the parents. The chick that can reach the highest gets the food.

Long-tailed Cormorants rest on the edge of Lake Victoria. Every evening at sunset they fly low over the surface of the water to nearby small islands, where they spend the night in trees. In the morning before dawn they return to their daytime fishing grounds.

The parents feed them with semi-digested fish, which the nestlings take out of their throat pouches. The legendary enormous flocks in Africa are formed from two species, the Eurasian White Pelican (*Pelecanus onocrotalus*), with a body length of 165 centimetres and a wingspan of 255 centimetres, and the Pink-backed Pelican (*Pelecanus rufescens*), which is 135 cm long and with a wingspan of 215 centimetres.

Since time immemorial there have been numerous legends concerning pelicans. The ancient Egyptians domesticated this bird. Muslims declared it to be sacred, as it was alleged to have helped to build the Ka'aba in Mecca. In Christian symbolism the pelican is revered as an example of self-sacrificing love, as parents are said to tear open their own breasts in order to let the hungry nestlings drink their blood. This legend probably originated from the fact that, during the nesting season, pelicans have a pink spot below the neck which looks like a wound.

Cormorants have long necks and the long

In solitary trees a few hundred metres from Lake Turkana are the nesting colonies of Long-tailed Cormorants. In a short time the originally green tree is completely littered with droppings.

The Long-tailed Cormorant is almost completely black, although maturing birds are brownish-white on the underside. This is a common bird of the Ethiopian region and is also found on the lakes of Uganda and Tanzania, on Lake Turkana in Kenya, and the East African coast.

narrow bill is curved into a hook on the upper jaw. The short legs are sited towards the back of the body, and all the toes are webbed. A small throat pouch and a circular area around the eyes are usually without feathers and generally brightly coloured. Cormorants live in watery places in the interior as well as on the coast. They dive below the surface for fish, but must swim up to the surface to swallow. They nest in trees, in colonies of varying size. They continue to eat until the stomach and expandable gullet are full, being able to digest food very quickly.

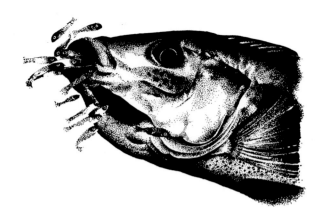

The Mozambique Mouthbrooder (*Tilapia mosambica*) belongs to the family Cichlidae. Over 200 species live in the lakes of the Great Trench Depression.

Pink-backed Pelicans on Lake Nakuru catch fish in large organized flocks. They form themselves into a row and then swim into a circle, which gradually reduces in size as their bills force the fish into the centre. Sometimes they also drive fish from deeper water into the shallows on the edge of the lake.

The Long-tailed Cormorant (*Phalacrocorax africanus*) has a wingspan of 120 centimetres and a body length of 75 centimetres. The Pygmy Cormorant (*Phalacrocorax pygmaeus*) is smaller, with a wingspan of 70 centimetres.

The Anhinga (*Anhinga rufa*), 85 centimetres long and 110 centimetres across the wings, resembles a slender cormorant with a long, snake-like neck. The thin bill has a sharp tip and harpoons fish under water. Anhingas often float almost completely submerged under water, with only part of the neck and head protruding above the surface. They are excellent swimmers and superb divers.

A young Pink-backed Pelican is quite easy to catch from a boat. We let it fly away several times, so as to tire it to the point where it could only swim, and then we trapped it in a net sack attached to a bamboo stick.

The African lungfish is dark brown, the underside of the body lighter and studded with inconspicuous grey spots. The eyes are chestnut brown. In captivity it will even attack members of its own species, biting off tails and fins — but these grow again.

THE SUN-SCORCHED BUSHVELD
The southern savannah and bush

South of the extensive tropical forests, a belt of sun-scorched country stretches from east to west across the whole of Africa. From north to south the landscape slowly changes from dense forest into acacia groves, and then into low shrubs. The region is divided into two by a mountain ridge extending north, from the Drakenberg Mountains across the Transvaal to the eastern slopes of Zimbabwe. However, numerous passes and valleys lead through these mountains and so the wildlife is common to both regions. The eastern part is covered by dense bush, the western part with more sparse acacia savannah or bushveld that extends from the Transvaal and Zimbabwe to south-west Africa. Many permanent rivers flow through this fertile well-irrigated country, mainly eastwards. The largest is the Limpopo. The western part of the belt is situated on sandy ground typical of the Kalahari desert, where there is no surface water, and some rivers disappear into the sand before they can reach the sea.

The Quagga: one of the many examples of the barbarity of humans. About 160 years ago there were hundreds of thousands of quaggas on the South African plains. Today it is an extreme rarity in the collections of museums of the world — there are 19 quagga hides and a few skulls and bones. As documentation of its conduct, humanity may place in its album the three last remaining quagga photographs.

The majority of this area is plagued by Tsetse Fly, so that suitable pasture for domestic cattle is rare. Rain is too unreliable for agriculture: some years it is abundant, in other years there is terrible drought. The grass does not grow tall and so fires are not particularly extensive. There is not enough water for large trees and the acacias are usually less than six metres. At first glance the landscape is similar to the East African bush but it differs in having only one rainy season, from November to April. A cool, dry winter, with many months of cloudless sky, is typical for the western upland plains.

From the eastern foothills of the Transvaal Mountains, as far as the ridge of Lebombo, extends the famous Kruger National Park — one of the few African parks that constitutes a complete ecological habitat. The animals are able to find subsistence all year round within the park's boundaries. Both browsers and grazers co-exist: there are substantial numbers of Elephant, Giraffe, Cape Eland and Greater Kudu, as well as small Impala herds, rare Lowland Nyala, zebras, Roan and Sable Antelope, Blue Wildebeest, Sassaby Hartebeest and many other species. There are no gazelle species, however. The main large predators are the Lion, Leopard, Cheetah, hyaenas and the African Wild Dog. The abundant wildlife, dense bush and watering places give them easier hunting than on the open Serengeti plains.

In the bush there are small hills known as 'kopje', inhabited by hyraxes and baboons. In the undulating country of Matopo, in Zimbabwe, piles of stones of fantastic shapes extend for several kilometres, crowned in places with enormous whale-backed boulders. Around the kopje are dense forests in which large numbers of birds live, particularly the black Verreaux's Eagle (*Aquila verreauxi*).

West of the Transvaal Mountains is an almost flat landscape which descends gently westwards towards the Kalahari basin. Among the low shrubs and grass are as many large animals as

in the Ngorongoro Crater. Although exact figures are not known, I would estimate a quarter of a million wildebeest on these plains. In the dry season they congregate near the Makarikari basin and the River Okovango, where there is permanent water; in the rainy season they disperse over the enormous Kalahari.

In the Angolan highlands, where there is abundant precipitation, are the sources of the great Rivers Zambezi, Cuanda and Okovango. The latter flows through the Kalahari, forming extensive swamps frequented by hippopotami, Buffalo, Lechwe, Defassa Waterbuck, Sitatunga, Sable and Roan Antelope, White-tailed Wildebeest, zebras, Kudus and hartebeest. From the Kalahari, oryxes and Springbuck will also

Rare Hartmann's Zebras live in the mountainous and rocky regions of south-west Africa, on the edge of the Namib Desert. Their foot and hoof structures differ from other zebras. They tread on their toes vertically at right angles. In the rocky granite tablelands these zebras have, over centuries, trodden small trails 20 centimetres deep to the watering places.

come to the edge of a swamp. There are even a few elephants here. There used to be many crocodiles in the rivers, but these have been hunted out for their hides: those that remain are very dangerous. Flocks of storks, herons, ibises,

Black and white stripes are unique to zebras, these patterns being characteristic of:

1 Burchell's Zebra (extinct);
2 Damara Zebra;
3 Chapman's Zebra;
4 Boehm's Zebra;
5 Cape Mountain Zebra;
6 Hartmann's Zebra;
7 Grévy's Zebra.

ducks, geese and predatory birds live along the riverbanks. In the swamps of northern Botswana numerous migrating birds spend the winter, particularly ducks from southern Africa. In the Angolan and Namibian highlands two vast swampy basins, the Etosha and the Makarikari, each cover areas of many thousands of square kilometres. These extensive areas of muddy wilderness originate from the settled sludge carried by rivers. West of the Etosha is the mountainous region of Kaokoveld, a wild landscape with rocky peaks and shrubby valleys. A good

Pattern on the hindquarters of:
1 Boehm's Zebra;
2 Chapman's Zebra;
3 Grévy's Zebra;
4 Mountain Zebra.

Grévy's Zebra stallions have long, aristocratic heads and exceptionally large, rounded ears.

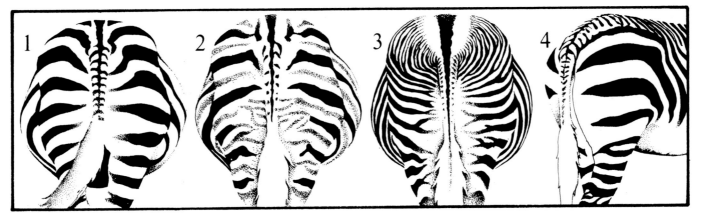

number of elephants, rhinos and over 10,000 zebra live there.

Farther to the west there is arid shrubby country dotted with sparse grass. Farther still this becomes the Namib desert. In recent years farmers in the whole of this bushveld region have introduced many antelope species to their farms and improved supplies of water, so that some wild animals have increased in number. These farmers keep mainly Greater Kudu, Cape Eland, Red Hartebeest, oryxes and Springbuck. On some farms they are even successfully rearing the rare Blesbok and the Blue Wildebeest.

ZEBRAS

The zebra is strikingly covered with black and white stripes forming superb patterns. This colouring forms an excellent camouflage, which is less effective during the day than on clear nights when zebras are completely lost to view in the silver-grey bush. This black-and-white patterning in fact serves two purposes: firstly it conceals the zebras from predators, and secondly it identifies them to members of their own species.

Zebras are mostly found on open savannahs;

only two sub-species of mountain zebra live in rocky terrain. During the day the herds stand close together in the sparse bush, keeping out of the hot sun. As the sun sets they move out onto the steppe, walking in single file to the watering place, led by a stallion. Zebras usually move in the company of antelope and Hartebeest.

At one time in southern Africa lived zebras striped only on the front part of the body, known as Quaggas (*Equus quagga*). When the Boers decided to convert the bush into pasture, they killed these animals in droves. According to reports from 1758 such enormous numbers of

In western Botswana, southern Angola and Damaraland in south-west Africa live the lightest-coloured zebras, the Damara Zebras. They are almost without stripes on the legs and also most closely resemble the now-extinct Burchell's Zebra. The herds of this type of zebra, living in the Etosha National Park in Namibia, regularly go to watering places during the day, together with other animals.

The eyes of young Grévy's stallions are dark brown. On the upper lid grow dense long eyelashes which protect the eye. The head has fine stripes; the nostrils are light-brown, delicate and exceptionally wide.

them were shot that the hunters ran out of ammunition. Exactly one century later the last wild Quagga was shot in the Cape province. There remained a few on farms, but these had died by 1879. Only a few years later Burchell's Zebra (*Equus burchelli burchelli*) met the same fate, the last one dying in 1911 in Hamburg Zoo. People have tried to tame zebras, but they do not have

as much stamina as horses and are not suitable for carrying either people or goods.

There are two types of herd among Steppe Zebras. These are maternal, or family, groups and small stallion herds. Family groups consist of several mares with foals, led by a strong and experienced male and helped by an experienced mare during the day. Such family groups are

This apparent idyll has an important basis, being an expression of herd membership and also riding hygiene. One animal cleans another in places where it cannot itself.

Threatening grimace of a stallion. With erect head and half-raised ears, he shows his incisors in order to ward off his adversary. This posture usually precedes combat.

usually permanent, with relations between individuals maintained by mutual care and greeting rituals. Zebras call each other constantly while grazing, and at least one is always on watch when the others are resting. Mares remain in their own group throughout their lives, even when they grow weak and old. This is not the case, however, with a leading stallion. If he becomes old or sick he is driven out of the herd by a younger, stronger stallion. The deposed leader usually joins another stallion herd. This is led by a strong male but in other respects there is no evidence of a hierarchy.

Grévy's Zebras and Mountain Zebras have harems, in which stallions defend their territory. Grévy's (*Equus grevyi*) is the largest zebra and also lives farthest to the north, in the shrubby regions of Ethiopia, Somalia, southern Sudan and Kenya. Its fine striping extends as far as the hooves. The abdomen is white, with a dark spinal stripe and a small crest of longer hair, and the ears are large and rounded. It differs from other species in having a pregnancy of 13 months; other zebras carry young for 11 months. Grévy's was first described in 1882 on the basis of a specimen sent as a present to the French president of the time, J. Grévy, by the Abyssinian Niegush Menelik.

Among the sub-species of Mountain Zebra (*Equus zebra*) is the Cape Mountain Zebra (*E. z. zebra*) and Hartmann's Zebra (*E. z. hartmannae*). The Cape Mountain Zebra sub-species inhabits a small area in the Cape Mountains. It has somewhat wider striping than Grévy's, is 125 centimetres tall at the shoulder, and has a pronounced dewlap (fold of skin under the

There is great variation in the colouring of Boehm's Zebra. In one herd it is possible to see light-coloured animals with narrow black stripes and the rarer, almost black zebra with striking wide stripes, as on this picture from the Selous Reservation in Tanzania.

Stallion combat: each animal tries to catch hold of the front legs of the other, which are very sensitive and vulnerable. The opponent escapes immediate danger with a leap, at the same time attacking its adversary on the neck from above.

The stallion succeeds in catching his adversary on a sensitive part of the neck. The grip is persistent and sometimes forces the adversary to submit.

throat). On the rear part of the back it has conspicuous transverse stripes in the shape of a small tree. The Mountain Zebra sub-species lives in two strictly-protected reservations in the Republic of South Africa, with a total number of about 120 animals. Hartmann's Zebra is slightly larger than the Mountain Zebra sub-species, and has wider-spaced striping on a lighter background. It inhabits the mountainous region of Namibia.

Among Steppe or Plains Zebras (*Equus burchelli*) are three sub-species, all having more delicately shaped heads and shorter ears than other zebras. Boehm's Zebra (*E. b. boehmi*) lives farthest north, from Lake Turkana to the River Zambezi and from Lake Tanganika as far as the Indian Ocean. It has beautiful black striping down to the hooves, against a pure white background. South of the Zambezi, in the Transvaal, Botswana and the southern part of Mozambique, lives Chapman's Zebra (*E. b. chapmani*), which is the same size as Boehm's Zebra but has brown 'shadow striping' between the dark stripes on the hind quarters, while the stripes on the limbs are finer and more widely spaced. The base colour of the coat has a yellowish-brown tinge in adults.

In southern Angola, western Botswana and northern Namibia lives the least-striped sub-species, the Damara Zebra (*E. b. antiquorum*).

Typical situation during stallion combat: both animals kneeling on their front legs and ramming each other's heads.

The opponents try to kick each other with their front hooves. The stallion with the lower jump tries to catch the neck of its opponent in order to recover its disadvantage.

The striping on the hind quarters is almost completely faded, the limbs and abdomen likewise almost white. The Damara is the rarest of all Steppe Zebras. In fact the populations of zebras are currently dropping catastrophically in the wild, and they will soon rank among the rarest species, threatened with extinction.

On the Karamoja plains live Boehm's Zebras, which lose their manes as they become adult. First it disappears between the ears and then it is all lost; adult males have only a narrow growth of short black hair. These are also called Maneless Zebras.

ANTELOPE

The Bongo (*Boocercus euryceros*), a shy and rare animal, is the largest forest antelope in Africa. Its movements are inconspicuous and it goes almost unnoticed. Bongos live on leaves, need a great deal of water, and use their horns (both males and females are horned) for digging up plant roots. The animal is a magnificent orange-brown, the coat being white on the insides of the legs. There are also white spots on the face and neck, some 12 to 14 white stripes on the sides and rump, and a dark-brown coat on the face, neck and chest. The species has a wedge-shaped body, making it easier to crawl under

obstacles. It lives alone or in small groups, ranging from Cameroun and Gabon across Zaire to the Central African Republic. A small population in the Aberdare Mountains, in Kenya, is separated from the rest by the Great Depression.

Cape Eland (*Taurotragus oryx*) live in herds of up to 60 in open forest. In the wild they are very timid but they can be tamed, behaving like domestic cattle. As in many other antelope species, they run with an ambling gait. From a distance, a herd grazing quietly looks like a herd of cows, some walking to and fro while others sun themselves or rest and chew the cud in the shade of acacias. When moving to new pasture

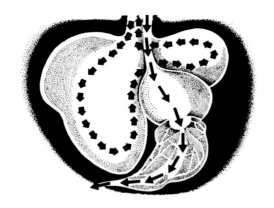

How a ruminant's stomach works. Freshly torn-off and swallowed food enters the first stomach for temporary storage. Later, via the reticulum or second stomach, it returns partly digested to the mouth (short thick arrows). Only after rumination or 'chewing the cud' is the food thoroughly pulverized by the strong molars and thoroughly mixed with saliva. Then it returns to the second stomach, enters the abomasum (rennet stomach) via the third stomach (omasum), and after processing continues into the intestine (long thin arrows).

they are led by an old female in an enclosed group, thus giving the impression of a cavalry formation. When pursued they set off at a trot, which changes to a full gallop in serious danger.

The largest antelope is the Giant Eland (*Taurotragus derbianus*). It differs from Cape Eland with its large horns and black neck bordered by a small white collar. The ears are broad and rounded; the yellowish to rufous body has some 10 to 15 white stripes on the flanks and rump. Large males weigh up to 1,200 kilogrammes. This eland inhabits the region from Senegal across Cameroun and the Central African Republic as far as western Sudan, living in woodland savannah in herds of perhaps 20 individuals.

On the plains of the Makarikari swampy basin, which changes from low shrub into grassy steppes and finally into the Kalahari Desert, lives the large Cape Eland. It is one of the largest antelope in the world.

JACKALS

The Common Jackal (*Canis aureus*) prefers dense reeds and shrubs on the banks of rivers and lakes, but it can also live in dry regions, sparse forests and even on the edges of human

The Giant Eland is the largest antelope species in the world. A record male, hunted in Cameroun, weighed 1,082 kilogrammes and had horns 122 centimetres long. The numbers of this antelope are decreasing rapidly. The last export to Europe was in 1973, from the Central African Republic.

The Cape Eland is an impressive beast, only slightly smaller than the Giant Eland.

settlements. It is widespread in North and East Africa, South Asia and southern Europe. Jackals live in family groups, only occasionally forming larger packs. They excavate shallow burrows in which they hide during the day, hunting at night. Jackals are scavengers; they eat the remains left by large predators, as well as taking mice, lizards, snakes, birds, fish and fruit. In packs they will attack an animal the size of a sheep.

The Side-striped Jackal (*Canis adustus*) is widespread from Ethiopia as far as southern Africa, and is more common in forests than on open savannahs. It is a timid animal, living alone or in small groups. It hunts mainly small animals, although it will eat almost anything — even the fatty fruit of the oil palm. This jackal makes long and mournful howls in the morning and evening.

The Black-backed Jackal (*Canis mesomelas*) has a silver, brown or black saddle, or 'caparison', which differs strikingly from the colour of the back. Its senses are excellent and it usefully disposes of carcasses and exterminates rodents.

The Black-backed Jackal has the most varied colouring of all jackals. These dogs have a unique position in African fairy stories and tales, appearing as clever advisers of the lion-king, the shrewd counsellors of the animal assembly, and adroit and nimble messengers.

The Side-striped Jackal lives both on open savannah and in mountains. It is a very timid animal, living either alone or in small packs and hunting only small prey.

It will eat anything edible, plundering hen-houses and stealing even from larders, killing lambs and goats and ransacking gardens. This jackal is persecuted mercilessly. It is widespread from Nubia across Ethiopia and along the African coast as far as southern Africa. It lives on savannahs and in forests, preferring hilly country.

VULTURES

Vultures regularly scavenge the banquets of the big cats and other predators and consume animal carcasses. They have superb eyesight and fly at great heights, usually within sight of one another. If one spots prey, it immediately swoops down and this is a signal for the others. Within minutes vultures from a wide radius have gathered at the carrion. These birds are capable of going without food for long periods, but once they find it they gorge themselves until they are almost too heavy to fly. As long as a banquet lasts they remain close by, even if they are no longer able to eat. Vultures can fly quickly and far, and are skilful gliders.

The most famous vulture is the Egyptian Vul-

Hooded Vultures circle high in the clouds or rest in solitary trees. As soon as they catch sight of a fellow vulture swooping down, they immediately fly to join one another at the prey.

ture (*Neophron percnopterus*). The ancient Egyptians often depicted this bird in their paintings, revering it as a symbol of parental love. It can be found almost throughout Africa, in western and South Asia, and even in southern Europe, for example in Bulgaria. In good weather it flies at great heights, resting on rocks, towers and tall houses, but avoiding trees. Sometimes these birds occur in groups, amusing themselves by indulging in their superb flying displays as they look out for prey. The Egyptian Vulture takes anything edible: even excrement or soil soaked in blood. It will also accompany desert caravans for whole days at a time. With the aid of stones it can break open large ostrich eggs — the only vulture species able to do this.

When a Griffon Vulture (*Gyps fulvus*) happens upon a fresh carcass, it tears out mainly entrails. A few cuts with its beak open up the abdominal cavity, and then it thrusts in its long neck as far as it will reach. It gulps down softer entrails without even taking out its head. The ruff is white in old individuals, brown in young ones.

The White-headed Vulture (*Trigonoceps occipitalis*) inhabits unforested regions of Central Africa. It has a red beak, and apart from the white down on its head, neck and throat it is completely brown. The Hooded Vulture (*Necrosyrtes monachus*) lives in Central, East and West Africa. There is a brownish-white 'hood' on its nape; otherwise it is dark brown in colour, the wing and tail feathers being black.

The Palm-nut Vulture (*Gypohierax angolensis*) resembles an eagle in appearance, but the white patches on the sides of the head show its membership of the vulture family. It is the smallest species measuring scarcely 60 centimetres long. Its favourite food is the palm nut, but it will also hunt small vertebrates, molluscs and crabs, and will not disdain any form of carrion. It inhabits West and Central Africa. The most beau-

Vultures and Marabou Storks fly away sated from the remains of a Grévy's Zebra, which they have gulped down in 32 minutes. The zebra was killed by Lions, which attacked our animal enclosures at night.

tifully-coloured vulture is Rueppell's Griffon (*Gyps rueppelli*), measuring 100 centimetres in the body and with a wingspan of up to 225 centimetres. It ranges across open country from Senegal, Nigeria and Cameroun as far as Ethiopia and beyond, across Uganda and Tanzania — in fact, in all places where large animals are found.

The Bearded Vulture (*Gypaetus barbatus*) is rare in Europe but still common in the mountains of Western and Central Asia, North and East Africa, and in the Drakenberg Range. It has a striking black band across the eyes and a long black beard on the mandible. It is up to 110 centimetres long, and 250 centimetres from wingtip to wingtip. It prefers to eat the bones of big animals, forcing quite large ones down its expandable gullet. It will carry bones and turtles high into the air and drop them onto rocks in order to break them open. It also eats carrion.

The Griffon Vulture has its head and neck covered with fine white plumage. It nests in Spain, north-west Africa, the Balkans, the Near East and Central Asia.

FROM THE DRAKENBERG MOUNTAINS TO LEMURIA
The southern mountains and coast, and Madagascar

From the coast of the Indian Ocean the steep slopes of the Drakenberg Mountains ascend dramatically to heights of over 3,000 metres. Moisture-laden winds from the ocean beat against them, releasing most of the rains they carry. From here rushing rivers flow eastwards, carrying eroded sediments into the Indian Ocean. To the west the mountains are transformed into gentle grassy slopes — the plateaux known as the 'Roof of Africa'. Here it rains much less, and almost all the local water drains into a single river, the Orange, which flows westwards into the Atlantic. A high-altitude mountain climate, with severe winters in which the ground freezes for prolonged periods, is typical in Lesotho, although the snowfall is only light.

On the upper plateaux live the last 30 or so pairs of Bearded Vultures. They build their nests on overhanging rocks, lining them with fur and animal remains. Large herds of sheep graze on the mountain pastures, and dead sheep form the staple diet of these vultures. The Bald Ibis (*Geronticus calvus*) is another rare bird of the region. Like eagles, it builds its nest on high rocks. For food these ibises fly to the lowlands; they migrate to milder country in winter.

The original wildlife of the southern mountains has survived in only a few nature reserves. The Blesbok has been reintroduced; in summer the Paradise Crane (*Anthropoides paradisea*), Denham's bustard *(Neotis denhami)* and many small songbirds live there. The tree cover has decreased as a result of constantly recurring fires, which help better quality grass growth to flourish. Hyraxes also play their part in the reduction of forest areas: after total extermination of large cats, jackals and other predators, hyrax numbers have increased to such an extent that they have abandoned their life among the rocks and spread over the whole area. Here they feed on grass, lilies, small shrubs and other plants, and in this way are denuding the ground and accelerating erosion. Watsonia and scilla grow in abundance on the mountain slopes. Farther to the west these slopes become increasingly drier, until they finally merge with the Karru Desert.

The Brush-tailed Porcupine is much more slender than other porcupines. The tail is club-shaped, the spines being flat, extremely sharp and grooved lengthwise. They increase in length from the head towards the hind quarters. The small horny plates on the end of the tail are yellowish-white; the underside of the body is covered with thick, soft fur.

Typical animal species on the upper plains are the Vaal Rhebuck (*Pelea capreolus*) and the Southern Reedbuck. Black Wildebeest, Bubal Hartebeest, Burchell's Zebra, Quaggas, Blesbok and Springbuck lived there in vast numbers in the recent past, and vast animal migrations, called 'treks' by the Boers, took place there. The last such trek was observed in 1896, when a closely-formed Springbuck herd numbering over 50 million trekked to the River Orange — and was never seen again.

As a result of the extermination of predators, water birds and ground-nesting birds have become common. Egyptian Geese are so numerous nowadays that they are a threat to cornfields. The Quelea has also become a disaster for crops, in spite of the fact that several million are killed every year. This whole region is

The Drakenberg Mountains are a magnificent range which drops sharply eastwards to the Indian Ocean and on the western side slowly descends to the Transvaal and the Orange Free State. In the Drakenberg Mountains are many rock paintings several thousand years old.

a prime example of how people and their activities can disturb the balance of nature.

Madagascar, possibly the remainder of the legendary island of Lemuria, separated from the African mainland over 20 million years ago. Most of the animals living there today are the result of immigration. Significantly, Madagascar became an island before the evolution of hoofed mammals and large predators, so these

The medium-sized Denham's Bustard is one of 23 bustard species. The smallest bustards are the size of hens; the largest may reach the greatest weight (up to 16 kilogrammes) of all flying birds. Bustards have only three toes on their strong legs, the back toes being almost absent.

The Blue Crane (*Anthropoides paradisea*) is a soft grey in colour, lighter on the head. The head looks exceptionally large, being completely covered with ruffled plumage. The elongated secondary wing feathers reach down to the ground.

animals are almost completely absent on the island. Malagasy plants in fact bear more similarity to those of India than Africa.

Madagascar has preserved the stages of evolution of its native animals. The island possesses primitive primates, mostly lemurs. Insectivores there mostly belong to the family Tenrecidae. Bats and amphibians display a certain affinity with their Asian cousins; the bird communities are close to those on the African main-

land, since it is fairly easy to fly over the Straits of Mozambique. Even the Madagascan Bush-pig (*Potamochoerus porcus larvatus*) which clearly originates from the African mainland, could have swum there when the straits were narrower than today. Crocodiles probably reached Madagascar in the same way. The only larger predators on the island are six species of the civet family (*Viverridae*). There is also the odd Reuter's Blind Snake (*Typhlops reuteri*), 10 centimetres long, which lives on ants and termites.

In the 19th and 20th centuries extensive areas of Madagascar forest were cleared to make room for pasture, and the exploitation of timber still continues. Before the arrival of people the island was covered with forest, whereas today hardly one-fifteenth of the original cover remains. The ancestors of the present-day inhabitants may have arrived there by boat in the first millenium BC from the Polynesian and Melanesian islands, pushing back the original inhabitants. Nine million people keep almost 10 million cattle and three million smaller domestic animals. These graze freely throughout the year and render attempts to reafforest the island impossible. For this reason the island is drying out and changing into savannah; some areas in the south have already changed into desert.

The animals of Madagascar are also disappearing at a horrifying rate. The only remaining significant area of forest lies in the north of the island, in Angotil Bay. Seven metres of rain falls annually, and the forest is surrounded and covered with swamps which make it inaccessible: this fact may yet save it from destruction.

The Common Horned Chameleon (*Chamaeleo deremensis*) is the best-known of the four 'three-horned' species which inhabit East Africa. Some people are afraid of them, mistakenly believing their horn tips to be poisonous.

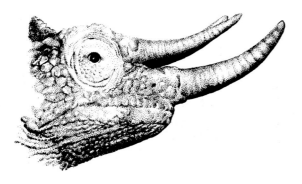

196

PORCUPINES

Porcupines belong to the family Hystricidae. All species have quills, which may be up to 40 centimetres long. A porcupine defends itself by stabbing with its quills, positioning itself with its side towards the enemy and rattling them while stamping, whining and grumbling. Porcupines feed predominantly on plant matter but they will also take meat, as will their rodent cousins. They eat mainly roots, bark, herbs, fruits and bamboo, venturing out to feed after dusk. Porcupines have exceptionally good hearing: a sleeping porcupine can hear a small nut fall off a tree several metres away. They are social and indulge in mutual licking. When a female shows signs of willingness to mate she arches her tail over her back, and the male supports himself on her with his front legs. Pregnancy lasts from 6 to 8 weeks; these animals can live up to 20 years.

In North Africa and near the Mediterranean coast lives the Common Porcupine (*Hystrix cristata*). Similar to this species is the Crested Porcupine (*Hystrix galeata*), which is 70 centimetres long. It inhabits East Africa, ranging across southern Sudan and reaching as far as the Central African Republic and Cameroun. Somewhat larger and with longer spines on its head is the Southern Porcupine (*Hystrix africaeaustralis*). Its range extends across the southern half of Africa. The Brush-tailed Porcupine (*Atherurus africanus*) is smaller and more slender, measuring 45 centimetres long, and has sharp, flat quills which are curved back at the tips. The quills on the shoulders are only about 4 cen-

timetres long, the longest quills on the back and tail measuring 11 centimetres. This species prefers to live in abandoned termite mounds or small burrows in the roots of old trees. It is widespread from Sierra Leone as far as Angola.

CHAMELEONS

Chameleons are among the most beautiful and interesting of lizards. They live almost exclusively in trees and shrubs and have spindly tong-like limbs which are finished off with five toes. These toes are linked as a pair and a trio as far as the final knuckle, and are positioned facing each other for a vice-like grip.

The proverbial ability of chameleons to change colour is in reality not particularly marked. Each species has only a few colour shades at its disposal. Some species cannot go green, while others are unable to turn red. In most cases they can blend in with their surroundings, but they also change colour according to their physical condition or if they fall ill. They have sharp colours during the day, dull at night.

The chameleon's eyes are covered with thick circular lids which leave a small hole for the iris. The eyes can move independently and a chameleon can look upwards with one eye and down with the other. The tongue is unusual: when at rest it lies retracted in the mouth cavity and gullet, but when hunting it quickly shoots forwards as far as 30 centimetres. The sticky gum at the end of the tongue traps insect prey, then the chameleon coils back the tongue and swallows the prey.

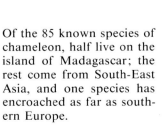

Of the 85 known species of chameleon, half live on the island of Madagascar; the rest come from South-East Asia, and one species has encroached as far as southern Europe.

A female chameleon lays 20 to 35 white eggs in a pit about 20 centimetres deep, which she excavates over several days in the earth. After laying the eggs she covers them with leaves and soil. The young hatch in two and a half months. Some chameleon species are viviparous — they give birth to fully-formed young. These lizards have many enemies, being pursued by snakes, birds of prey and small predatory mammals.

	Body length in cm	Tail length in cm
Common Chameleon (*Chamaeleo chamaeleon*)	25—38	21
African Chameleon (*C. africanus*)	37	20
Oustalet's Chameleon (*C. oustaleti*)	63	35
Panther Chameleon (*C. pardalis*)	40—48	27
Dwarf Chameleon (*C. pumilus*)	10	4

The South African sub-species of Leopard (*Panthera pardus shortridgei*) is the second most powerful African predator after the Lions. Its hunting style shows the state of the art. This cat is so dangerous that when professional hunters are trying to find one they have shot, they protect their faces and abdomens with plexiglass shields.

LEOPARDS

Leopards (*Panthera pardus*) live in Africa and across the southern part of Asia as far as Manchuria and Korea. In Africa they can be found in most habitats, even in the high mountains. If they have sufficient food they will stay in one place, marking their hunting territory with excrement and urine. During the day they rest in tall grass and shrubs or on forked tree branches. At night they creep silently downwind of their chosen prey to within a distance of several metres, and then jump, catch and kill it by biting into the nape or throat, cracking the spine. A Leopard will carry the prey to a quiet spot to eat; when it has satisfied its hunger, it usually pulls the remains into a tree so that jackals and hyaenas cannot feast themselves. For unknown reasons vultures do not touch the kill. A Leopard once carried a young giraffe weighing 90 kilogrammes into a tree, in spite of the fact that it weighed scarcely 60 kilogrammes itself. After feeding the cat usually goes to drink, and it likes to stay near water, although during the dry season it can go without drinking for three days.

Leopards are much more nocturnal than other large cats. They hunt alone and live alone too. Only during the mating season do they meet with a partner. At this time a pair hunts together. After a pregnancy lasting about 100 days, the mother gives birth to between two and four cubs, and these are fully mature at four years.

Leopards are consummate hunters, and fearless. Despite their reputation they are not bloodthirsty, hunting no more than is necessary for their needs. If an individual is injured, however, it can become a man-eater and terrorize the whole region.

LEMURS AND OTHER PROSIMIANS

Of the 35 species of prosimians ('lower' primates related to monkeys and apes), 21 live on Madagascar. The remainder are found in the forests and savannahs of Africa, southern Asia, Indonesia and the Philippines. Prosimians are arboreal (tree-dwelling) animals, and all species are outstanding climbers with unusual strength in their limbs. They are able to lift their entire bodies by one limb, and also to hang by one hand for long periods without any visible signs of tiring. This is because in each muscle a dense network of tiny blood vessels keeps the tissue well supplied with oxygen and nutrients.

A female East African Leopard (*Panthera pardus suahelica*) has hunted down a fairly young male baboon and carried it off to the dried out tree cleft which previously served as a hunting look-out post.

Almost all prosimians are light sleepers, and the buzzing of a fly or a scratching beetle is enough to wake them. As soon as it grows dark they clean themselves, rearrange their dense furry coats, call loudly and then set off in search of food. Some species shriek regularly as they jump with long leaps from branch to branch, running up trunks and along branches with amazing agility. When the troop finds a tree with fruit, the members start to eat and in the process they can destroy a good deal.

Other prosimians prowl with inaudible steps, their large round eyes lit up in the last rays of the setting sun, like burning globes. Their movements are deliberate and quiet, and heaven help the sleeping bird that does not notice them. Noiselessly in the dark the creature makes its way closer, then puts out its hand so close as to almost touch the unwary prey. Then comes a movement faster than the human eye can see. Before the bird has a chance, it is too late.

Lemurs and Indri-type prosimians represent very old groups from the evolutionary viewpoint. They survived solely because Madagascar was separated from Africa before more de-

The Grey Lemur (*Hapalemur griseus*), together with the much rarer Wide-tailed Lemur (*Hapalemur simus*), form the *Hapalemur* genus. All lemur species are rare. A few are on the verge of extinction, including Wide-tailed Lemur, the Mongoz Lemur, the Maki (*Cheirogaleus medius*) and the Fork-crowned Maki (*Phaner furcifer*).

199

The Lesser Mouse Lemur (*Microcebus murinus*) is the smallest member of the Lemuridae. It is between 25 and 30 centimetres long, half of this being the tail. This is a typical nocturnal animal, with great strength in its limbs. It will often cling to a branch by only one hand, pulling itself along with agility. The skull has a high brain cavity, the mouth is small, the eyes large and the external ears bald and easily visible.

The Cape Dassie or Cape Hyrax lives in large numbers in the Drakenberg Mountains. It has become too numerous as a result of the almost total extermination of leopards, jackals and other predators. In zoos the dassie is usually kept on artificial rocks near to elephants, which are their closest living relatives.

veloped predators could colonize the island. At one time they were widespread elsewhere, but became extinct in the course of evolution.

The Aye-aye is an endangered species native to Madagascar. It has a large head with a flat mouth, short neck, slender body and shaggy tail, the latter being longer than the body. Aye-

ayes urinate in a characteristic manner, towards the same spot with the body pressed against a trunk. Many Malagasy fables and tales are told about this ghost-like animal.

Pottos and Angwantibos live in African forests. They sleep during the day in hollow trees or hanging from a secluded branch. Bushbabies live in dry forests, on savannah and in bush country in a substantial part of Africa south of the Sahara. They have striking bald ears and exquisite hearing, living mainly on insects and small vertebrates which they catch by a cat-like pounce.

The front legs of the Aye-aye have long fingers and thumbs. The middle finger is very thin and has a sharp small claw which serves for scraping out and piercing its food, mainly insects.

The Senegal Bushbaby is about the same size as a squirrel. It has thick silky fur which is earthy-grey on the sides, the head and back being slightly reddish and the insides of the limbs and the abdomen yellow-white. It has short, strong fingers.

The Indri is the largest prosimian species. The sturdy body grows to 85 centimetres, although the tail is only five centimetres long. The limbs are the same length. It has long palms, thick thumbs and the fingers are joined by a web. The head is small in relation to the body; the eyes are also small, and the ears are almost hidden by fur and bald inside.

	Body length in cm	Tail length in cm
Gentle Lemur (*Hapalemur griseus*)	28—46	28—46
Ring-tailed Lemur (*Lemur catta*)	30—45	40—51
Ruffed Lemur (*Varecia variegata)*	42—64	50—58
Lesser Mouse Monkey (*Microcebus murinus*)		
Diadem Monkey (*Propithecus diadema*)	50—100	43—53
Indri (*Indri indri*)	60—85	5—6
Aye-aye (*Daubentonia madagascarensis*)	38—45	46—55
Angwantibo (*Arctocebus calabarensis*)	25—30	—
Potto (*Perodicticus potto*)	30—35	5—7
Senegal or Lesser Bushbaby (*Galago senegalensis*)	16—20	23—25
Zanzibar Bushbaby (*Galago zanzibaricus*)	14—16	17—19

The Common Reedbuck is typical of the upper flatlands. Reedbuck live in small groups on rocky ground sparsely vegetated with poor grass. These timid antelope are very difficult to keep in captivity.

THE LAND OF RED SAND
The southern deserts and bushvelds

The whole western part of southern Africa is either desert or semi-desert. The deserts are not quite as intimidating as the Sahara, partly since they are considerably smaller. The largest is the Kalahari, a vast sandy basin, extending from northern Botswana to beyond the River Molopo and from the upper plateaux of Namibia as far as the shrubby plains of the Transvaal. The driest desert, the Namib, is a narrow strip only about 160 kilometres wide extending along the West African coast from the River Orange beyond Mossamedes in Angola. The third desert, the Karru, lies south of the Orange River; it has some sparse shrubs and forms a transition to the sub-tropical Cape region. In winter — from April to September — it has more rain than the other two deserts. Strong winds often blow across these deserts, and there can be substantial differences between day and night temperatures.

The southern African deserts are somewhat cooler than the Sahara, and winter frosts occur in all of them. They are more like semi-desert steppes, with small growths of vegetation here and there. There is only a small amount of rock and so rain drains away into the sand, from where the plants can draw on it with their long roots. Along the ridges of dunes, which are usually deep pink or red to reddish-brown, grow tough grasses (mostly *Eragrostis* and *Aristida*) which dry out to almost white. Acacias also grow there, typically *Acacia giraffae* and *Acacia haematoxylon*, which have hard, heavy, reddish wood.

Typical animals for these deserts are the True Gemsbok, Springbuck, Blue Wildebeest and Cape Eland, and occasionally Greater Kudu or Cape Hartebeest. All these animals must lead a nomadic life. In the Kalahari live many creatures which are rare elsewhere. One is the Ratel or Honey Badger (*Mellivora capensis*), which ocurs scattered south of the Sahara and also in Asia. This mustelid has even been found in the northern border belt of the Sahara, south of the River Orange. The Black-throated Honey Guide (*Indicator indicator*) often shows the Ratel the way to bee nests, also leading people to them. Apart from honey, the Ratel also eats birds, eggs, insects and any small animals it can hunt, and will not even refuse carrion. In the Kalahari the Chanting Goshawk (*Melierax canorus*) also follows the Honey Guide, as well as the Spotted Eagle Owl (*Bubo africanus*). Another unusual animal of the region is the Aardwolf (*Proteles cristatus*), which generally lives alone, spending the day in burrows and coming out to hunt at night. Although it is related to hyaenas and civets, its teeth are adapted solely for eating insects.

Large acacias such as *Acacia giraffae* and *Acacia albida* grow in river valleys, as well as a tamarisk (*Tamaryx austro-africana*) and the Thorny Parkinsonia (*Parkinsonia africana*). Butterpits (*Acanthosicyos horridus*) grows in the sand, its greater part remaining concealed with

The Welwitschia is a rare and strictly protected plant which grows in the Namib Desert. It is about one metre high and has a turnip-shaped 'radical stem' which carries two band-like leaves. These are in fact seed-leaves. The plant never produces any other leaves throughout its whole life. At the top of the 'stem' grow inconspicuous flowers in cones.

only the rough shoots protruding. Baboons and jackals live along the rivers, and at one time there were even small herds of elephants. On the bare dunes grow low bushes (*Zygophyllum stapfii*) and the remarkable Welwitschia (*Welwitschia bainesi*). This plant begins as two inconspicuous leaves which grow larger, the plant then forming a short stem; the leaves remain throughout the whole life of the plant, which may be more than a thousand years.

A large number of beetles and reptiles are at home in these deserts. A nocturnal gecko (genus *Palmatogekko*) has spindly legs and long toes for running quickly over the shifting sand. There are also large, sand-coloured chameleons, three viper species and a dwarf python. At night large nimble spiders of the genus *Cerbalus* come out to hunt, being known locally as the 'white lady of Namib'. Numerous lizards move through the sand as if swimming. In the cooling ocean stream that washes the shores of southern

Angola and Namibia there is a profusion of plankton, which makes life possible for large numbers of fish. These in turn serve as food for cormorants, pelicans, seagulls and other marine birds, as well as for the South African Fur Seal (*Arctocephalus pusillus*). Albatrosses hunt at sea, and during the winter the coast is full of migratory water birds from Europe. The giant nests of Sociable Weaver Birds (*Philetairus socius*) festoon the solitary acacia trees.

The southern part of Namibia is rocky, with aloes growing among the jumbled boulders. The

The Namib Desert extends along the Atlantic coast for a length of 1,300 kilometres and ranges between 50 and 130 kilometres in width. The northern part is rockier, the southern part sandy. Between 20 and 30 kilometres south of the port of Walvis Bay, sand dunes up to 70 metres high form right on the coast.

Hundreds of years ago Springbuck lived in their millions in Namibia and South Africa, mainly in what are now the Transvaal and the Orange Free State. In recent decades farmers have been trying to increase their numbers. They are still plentiful in the Kalahari and Etosha Parks.

River Fish flows through this region, having carved out a canyon up to 300 metres deep. The Karru is a rocky basin which was once a lake bed; the edges of the basin are of volcanic origin. Apart from Karru Acacias (*Acacia karroo*) few other trees grow there. Large herds of White-tailed Wildebeest, oryxes and Quaggas used to live there, but the natural conditions have deteriorated. The grass is receding and domestic cattle have devastated the whole region. Predators, especially eagles and jackals, have also been exterminated, with the result that rodents have become too numerous. Hyraxes, mice and squirrels have become a real menace in the region. Finally, there are scorpions and the Praying Mantis of the *Mantis* genus, which play an important role in many African religions.

The small but remarkable Cape Province, at the southern corner of South Africa, has a subtropical climate similar to that of the Mediterranean in north-west Africa. It rains in winter, from April to September, while the summers are dry and hot. Across the River Orange, southwards, the change in vegetation is astonishing. Shrubs predominate and after rain the whole region is a blaze of orange, yellow and white blossoms. The southern region is formed by coastal lowlands and a number of magnificent non-volcanic mountain belts in which there are harsh winters with snow. Sparse shrubland and forest cloaks the mountain ridges, but they are fre-

quently subjected to fire. The broad valleys among the mountains are cultivated and over 20,000 species of plant bloom there. Many have been introduced into the gardens of the world: gladioli, agapanthas and freesias. These blossoms have made life possible for bird species living on nectar. One of the most beautiful of these is the Malachite Sunbird (*Nectarinia famosa*), its long curved beak and tongue adapted for sucking nectar.

Hardly any of the large animals remain on the coastal plains. The largest sub-species of Lion, the Cape Lion, together with many antelope and zebra species, have disappeared without trace. The Southern Reedbuck, Grimm's Duiker and Cape Grysbok (*Raphicerus melanotis*) live today in small numbers and only in the mountains. There are some baboons and large numbers of Cape Hyraxes or Cape Dassies (*Procavia capensis*), which are larger than their cousins the steppe hyraxes of tropical Africa; the Leopard lives there, but is rare. At the end of the 18th century the magnificent Blaawbok (*Hippotragus leucophaeus*) of the region was completely exterminated.

On the Cape, many bird species spend the winter and even build their nests. They include the White Stork, Black Stork and European Bee-eater (*Merops apiaster*). On river lagoons enormous numbers of aquatic birds congregate, among them several duck species, the Arctic Tern (*Sterna paradisaea*) and various herons.

A common bird is the Southern Black-backed Gull (*Larus dominicanus*), while on the little islands nest the Cape Gannet (*Morus capensis*) and the Jackass Penguin (*Spheniscus demersus*), which is up to 70 centimetres high. Around the Cape of Good Hope sail albatrosses and petrels. Standing on the Cape, one can sense the vast Southern Ocean and Antarctica far beyond.

SCORPIONS

Scorpions do not in general arouse the greatest sympathy in people. Their weapon is a sting with a venom gland, which in fact is a protuberance on the last segment. The hind parts of a scorpion are narrow, with the segments connected in such a way as to form a flexible tail. The scorpion generally holds this rear part erect, permanently ready to sting. With a lightning movement it siezes prey in its pincers; if the victim is not killed by this, the scorpion bends its tail over and stabs its venomous tip into the prey. It then eats the food with its small mandibles. Scorpions are solitary, and even among themselves are dangerous. The female, like the Praying Mantis, not infrequently eats

The Southern Saharan Scorpion ranks as one of the most poisonous scorpions. Like other species, it gives birth to fully-formed young. Scorpions grow very slowly, reaching complete maturity only after several years.

Male Springbuck have strong horns curved into a lyre shape. Farmers often make artificial watering places for them in suitable spots, into which they pump water from deep wells. These watering places serve domestic cattle but also help wild animals in severe droughts.

Kirk's Dik-dik is one of the smallest antelope species. The length of the body is between 55 and 65 centimetres, the height at the shoulder 37 to 45 centimetres, and the weight 4.5 kilogrammes. Females give birth to only one young. Considering how small they are, they have a very long gestation period — between 175 and 185 days. This dik-dik has a mobile muzzle, which apart from the lower part of the nasal partition has a complete growth of fur. It inhabits the denser shrubby bush in Namibia and East Africa.

her partner after mating. Nevertheless she takes good care of her young.

During courtship the male takes hold of the female with his pincers and the pair face each another. He draws the female towards himself, giving the impression that they are dancing. The male then drops his sperm capsule onto the ground and moves the female until her sexual orifice is positioned over it, when she takes it into her body. Some scorpion species are viviparous, while in others the eggs hatch only after being laid. Mothers carry the fully-formed young for a while on their backs, the young holding on with their small claws. A mother will accept even strange young.

The Southern Saharan Scorpion (*Androctonus australis*) grows to a length of 13 centimetres and is highly poisonous. The largest species is the West African Scorpion (*Pandinus imperator*), which grows to 18 centimetres. The venom takes effect slowly, so that there is usually enough time to use an antidote. A scorpion sting is only occasionally fatal, altough it is always dangerous for small children. Interestingly, scorpions are able to withstand enormous doses of radiation — five hundred times more than vertebrates.

The Angolan Impala (*Aepyceros melampus*) differs markedly from other geographical sub-species of Impala. It is larger, has distinctly black facial colouring, black ear tips, a central black stripe of fur from the root to the tip of the tail, and a long tail with a white growth of fur on the underside. This growing male had already been ejected from the native herd as a rival by the leading male.

The foothills of the Drakenberg Mountains, around the source of the River Vaal, are rocky and sparsely vegetated with grass. There are often fogs and, in the winter, severe frosts.

WEAVERS

Weaver birds (Ploceidae) are song birds resembling finches. Their characteristic feature is a short, strong conical beak suitable for cracking open seeds. Of the 259 species, the majority live in the tropical regions of Africa and across Europe, and Asia as far as Australia. Weavers are usually gloriously arrayed in bright colours. Some build spherical nests with holes in the side or base as entrances. Others weave long flight entrances into their remarkable nests. Some species form large colonies; some nest throughout the whole year, but the majority nest in spring and early summer (the rainy season or shortly afterwards). They are friendly, nimble and mobile with a beautiful appearance, but they are not liked as they plunder ripe corn.

The Red-billed Firefinch (*Lagonosticta senegala*) is 10 centimetres long. This thin-beaked finch has a short tail, wine-red plumage and white spots on the breast. The Northern Firefinch (*Lagonosticta brunneiceps*) is as abundant in the Upper Nile region as the sparrow is in Europe. In the last months of the dry season the firefinches moult and collect in flocks. After the first spring rains they divide into pairs. In villages, towns and trees, in any remotely suitable place, they pile up an untidy stack of dry grass, make a round hollow in it, and lay their eggs. The young hatch after 13 days and are fed on insects and grains, which the parents soften in their crops.

The Violet-eared Waxbill (*Uraeginthus granatinus*), at 15 centimetres long, is brownish-red and has grey eye spots behind the carmine beak.

The West African Red Bishop (*Euplectes franciscanus*) has magnificent red and crimson colouring only during the nesting season. At that time it also has, on its back and head, velvety plumage. Most people in Africa take little notice of these birds, so their colossal nests can often be found near villages. In farming regions, however, the people do not like them as their flocks of many thousands can cause considerable damage. The farmers defend their crops by burning out the nests, cutting down the trees, frightening the birds by shooting, spraying with chemicals, and in some places even burning them with flame-throwers.

The lower tail feathers are metallic blue. This bird lives between the Orange and Zambezi Rivers, is not particularly friendly, and builds rounded nests with side entrances.

Whydahs are interesting birds. Courting males have four central tail feathers that are so elongated they are a hindrance to flight. In the nesting season they live in pairs and after leaving the nest and moulting they group into large flocks.

The Pin-tailed Whydah (*Vidua macroura*) has a body up to 13 centimetres long and a tail of nearly 20 centimetres. It is able to fly well even with these relatively long tail feathers. Whydahs mainly keep near to the ground, where they collect seeds and hunt insects. The Paradise Windowbird (*Steganura paradisaea*), 42 centimetres long with the tail, lives in the sparse forests of central Africa. The males wear their magnificent mating dress in the rainy season for about four months, after which they moult quickly, the long feathers falling off at the beginning of the dry season. When the green sorghum begins to ripen in Africa the magnificent West African Red Bishop (*Euplectes franciscanus*) appears on the spikes, looking like a little glowing flame flickering in all directions as it sings its monotonous song. Out of the breeding season the males and females have inconspicuous dress, similar to that of sparrows. The Sociable Weavers (*Philetairus socius*) live mainly in southern Africa, building common nests under a single roof. The following year they build new nests under the old ones. The nesting place grows from year to year, until the branch breaks off and the accumulated homes fall to the ground. On the pastures among herds of African Buffalo, in the company of Splendid Glossy Starlings (*Lamprocolius splendidus*) and oxpeckers, I have often observed the Buffalo Weaver or Alecto (*Bubalornis albirostris*), which is up to 25 centimetres in size. I saw this bird jumping from place to place on a buffalo, scrupulously pecking out as many parasites as possible. In the event of

North of the Brandenberg Mountains in Namibia, out on the open plains, lie fossilized tree trunks — their ages estimated at 200 million years. The longest trunk measures 46 metres. It is not possible to be sure whether the trunks, which were exposed by erosion, are the remains of an original forest or whether they were carried there by water.

A South African female Ostrich shows signs of willingness to mate. The young have an inconspicuous grey colouring. Females remain an inconspicuous light greyish-brown, while males are black with the exception of the wing and tail tips.

danger, it warned its host promptly. I have counted as many as 18 of these weavers' nests in some large trees, each a good metre in diameter. The nest is constructed from thorny twigs and sticks and has a wide, tapering entrance, the nesting chamber being filled with a bunch of fine roots and grass. Inside there might be eight separate nests. The chaos in such a tree is not unlike a cloud of swarming bees.

ALBATROSSES AND PETRELS

Tube-nosed birds (Procellariiformes) — albatrosses and petrels—are typically inhabitants of seas and oceans. They have characteristic nostrils which open out on the upper side of the curved bill into two tube-shaped extensions, longer in petrels than in albatrosses. These web-footed birds spend the greater part of their lives

The Malachite Sunbird is one of 104 glossy, metallic and magnificently-coloured species of the sunbird family (Nectariniidae). Sunbirds are sometimes called the 'humming birds of the Old World', although they are not at all related to humming birds. They do have similar food, narrow beaks and darting flight.

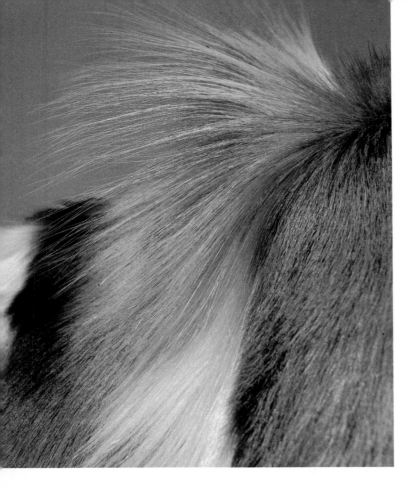

voracious birds is the Southern Giant Fulmar (*Macronectes giganteus*), which is up to 90 centimetres in body length and with a wingspan of 280 centimetres. It attacks the young of other birds, or indeed anything that is edible.

Albatrosses sail through the air with dignity and elegance, rising and falling with no visible effort. They fly against the wind even in the worst storms. They will hang suspended above a ship for hours, only to disappear in the distance with a sudden burst of speed. The Wandering Albatross *(Diomedea exulans)* is up to 135 centimetres long, with a wingspan of up to three and a half metres. It belongs among the species which do not really 'build' nests. Instead they rake their beaks around an area to make a pile of plants, into which they bore a hole with their bodies and then lay a single egg weighing almost half a kilogramme. They sit on the egg for 80 days. Wandering Albatrosses live in large colonies, and along the coast of the Cape Province one can observe seven species of albatross and 28 species of petrel.

AARDVARKS

The Aardvark or 'earth pig' (*Orycteropus afer*) may grow to 200 centimetres long and weigh 100 kilogrammes. It has a remarkable ability to dig itself into the ground, working with the strong claws on its powerful front limbs and throwing clumps of earth out behind. During the day it sleeps in excavated burrows, emerging for food at night. First the creature remains

The Springbuck acquired its name from the strange way it jumps. It springs almost straight up into the air with all four legs, holding the legs rigidly extended and with its head hanging down. While jumping the coat is opened out on the back, from the root of the tail to halfway across the back, forming a magnificent white fan.

in the air and on the water, nesting on the coast or small islands, but do not fly inland. They live in pairs and nest in large colonies. Among them are species the size of swallows, and flying giants with a wingspan of three and a half metres and weighing up to eight kilogrammes. They feed on a wide variety of marine life which they gather from the surface; they also fly round ships and snatch refuse.

The majority of petrels nest in hollows in the ground lined with feathers and grass stalks. They are good swimmers and dive for food. Both parents take turns in sitting on the eggs. They feed the young on an oily liquid regurgitated from the crop. Perhaps the most faithful companion of ships of all marine birds is the Pintado Petrel of Cape Petrel (*Daption capensis*), which has a body 35 centimetres long and a wingspan of 120 centimetres. One of the most

The Aardwolf is similar to the Laughing Hyaena but considerably smaller. Its skeleton partly resembles that of a dog and partly a hyaena. It is not a hunter of large animals, feeding on insects—predominantly termites.

Scientists debated for a long time the Aardvark's position in zoological classification. It is most often put in an order of its own, Tubulidentata, related to elephants and hyraxes.

The Ratel is one of the strongest animals in the world in relation to its size. Approximately 75 centimetres in length, an individual killed with lightning speed three out of four large hunting greyhounds set on it. Its neck seems as strong as steel.

motionless for several minutes in one of the entrances to its burrow, then it leaps out with large jumps. About 10 metres from the burrow it stops, stretches upwards, turns its head in all directions and listens. If it does not hear anything suspicious it leaps farther away and after a while changes to a light trot. It carries its head lowered almost to the ground, with ears folded backwards, back bent and the tail dragging behind. The muzzle is so low that the circle of hairs around the nostrils touches the ground. The Aardvark lives predominantly on termites, digging a hole in the termite hill and flicking its long sticky tongue over the occupants.

The first live Aardvark was transported to

Europe from Cape Town in 1869. At London Zoo its daily menu was a quarter of a kilogramme of minced meat, a handful of ant pupae and three rolls dipped in milk. In its run it used to dig up the corridors. It was never heard to make a sound; it knew its keeper well and allowed him to stroke it.

The Red Hartebeest lives only in the Etosha, Tsitsikama and Kruger National Parks and on a few private farms. The female gives birth to one young in the period between September and December.

CARACALS

The Caracal (*Caracal caracal*) is a relative of the lynx and in general it resembles the other cat predators. It has a strong body and sharp senses, particularly sight. It can be 75 centimetres long, measuring 45 centimetres at the shoulder. It seeks out a hiding place in rock faces, bushes or in holes and during the day it drowses in a semi-sleep, although still alert. As soon as evening draws in, it sets off to hunt — as far as possible, walking in the same tracks. The young are spotted, but later their spots disappear. This species inhabits almost the whole of Africa, as well as south-west Asia and India. It is an outstanding climber and hunts small rodents, gazelles and the young of larger antelope. Like the Cheetah it can be tamed to hunt small animals, foxes, hares and birds.

The Caracal defends its territory enthusiastically, mainly from other members of its own species. It is a fundamental principle of animal communities that a hunting territory must be large enough to sustain the individuals, the pair, the family, or whoever occupies it. For carnivores, the territory must contain sufficient numbers of animals to hunt; for herbivores, it must have enough grazing.

The True Gemsbok lives to an age of 18 or 19 years. It is able to survive in the sparse desert and in semi-desert regions, where it can go without water for several months.

One of the most beautiful antelope species, the Greater Kudu is kept on many farms in southern and south-west Africa. These antelope are strictly protected in the Etosha National Park in Namibia, and in the Kruger, Umfolozi, Hluhluhwe, Mkuzi, Loskop and Dam Parks in South Africa.

The Serval leaves its excrement in conspicuous places on its territory, representing warning notices for members of its own species: No entry! Area occupied!

SERVALS

The Serval (*Leptailurus serval*) grows to 100 centimetres long and 50 centimetres high at the shoulder, and is known as the 'Bush-cat' to the Afrikaaners. It occasionally hunts hares, small antelope and lambs, but mainly birds, which it is able to catch in flight (usually when they are taking off) by jumping as high as two metres. It naps during the day in a hide-out and only sets off to hunt at dusk. The young can be easily tamed and kept in captivity, but they are sensitive to chills.

The sign of wealth among the majority of South African ▶ ▶ tribes is the ownership of cattle, goats and sheep. The disproportionate numbers of domestic cattle kept there for centuries have damaged the vegetation, which has devastated the soil, ending in disastrous erosion.

One of the little streams in the Namib Desert, which even in the driest periods has some water. The annual rainfall here is between 10 and 100 millimetres.

THE CAPTURE AND TRANSPORTATION OF ANIMALS
Safari without gunpowder and bullets

There are more than 800 zoos around the world. The functions of many zoos have changed markedly in recent times. These are cultural and scientific institutions; their main tasks are the protection of species on our planet, scientific research on the species they keep, and education with the aim of the conscious protection of nature and the environment. We set ourselves these tasks in the zoological gardens at Dvůr Králové on the Elbe, of which I was director for many years. More than this, however, I wanted to build up and expand this zoo as a specialized institution for rearing animals from the African continent.

Where could we obtain healthy young animals in such numbers as would allow them to maintain their social systems that they have in the wild? And how could we guarantee long term rearing work without the dangers of inbreeding? There was nothing for it but to set off for Africa to capture and bring home the required animals. In the years from 1967 to 1976 I spent six to eight months in Africa every year with a small number of assistants. At the end of May, when the weather in Europe is already fine, the captured and partially zoo-adapted animals could be brought over.

Our main intention was keep to a minimum any animal losses during capture and enclosure in the hunting camps, as well as during shipment to Europe and quarantine in the zoo — hopefully less than five per cent would be lost. This was a difficult task, as during shipment alone the losses of large animals could average 30 per cent.

During capture we used various methods. On the open, flat plains of Uganda, Kenya and Sudan we caught large animals in lassoos from modified Toyota jeeps, while during the capture of heavy and dangerous animals we used Fords. Chase and capture could not last more than two minutes, so as not to tire the selected animal too much. On the stony terrains of south-west Africa and Botswana we used a helicopter to drive whole herds of animals into enclosures 150 by 200 metres in size, enclosed by awnings two and a half metres high made of synthetic material. In rain forests we dug out dozens of camouflaged pits on animal trails. By watering places or the fields of local farmers we hunted with a rifle that fired hypodermic darts filled with a sedative drug.

Capture of a South African oryx in nylon nets.

On the upper plains and uneven savannahs we drove large animals, using a small aeroplane or helicopter, into nets several hundred metres long with single or double openings. In dense thorny bush we built spiral enclosures up to 40 metres in diameter, with funnel nets over a kilometre long leading to the openings; into this we drove the animals. At night we hunted with the aid of spotlights, and when catching water birds we used boats and nets. Occasionally we also pursued snakes, lizards and monitors, as well as catching various monkey species in cages and nets.

We knew of course that not every animal is suitable for rearing in a zoo. During capture we selected strong young animals without visible defects, with good colouring and the appropriate characteristics of their species. We paid close attention to their psychological characteristics too: animals which defended themselves energetically, attacked us and did not give up were the best.

When transporting captured animals we watched them closely for signs of shock. For instance, if a captured Giraffe began to tremble and breathe heavily with flared nostrils we immediately stopped, quickly unloaded the box and let the giraffe go. Some animals could not

This is how we caught elephants in the equatorial province of southern Sudan, in the sparsely wooded steppe on the east bank of the White Nile.

These tall and slender young relations of the Dinka tribe speak a dialect belonging to the north-west group of Nilotic languages. They are settled herdsmen and farmers. To protect their cattle as well as for self-defence they use a light steel spear and a shield of buffalo hide.

get used to their keepers even after a month in the camp, cowering in fear in the farthest corner: these too were unsuitable for transport or rearing and so they were returned to the wild.

At first we offered all animals the same food that they would have in the wild, gradually weaning them onto the diet they would receive on board ship and in Europe. Some did not eat this new food even after several weeks; others ate well but lost weight in spite of all our care. These animals were also released.

After two months of adapting to capture conditions, we taught the animals to live in transport boxes. Gradually we put their food further into the boxes, until they had become used to

entering, eating and even resting inside. Some animals, however, would never take food in the boxes and others were afraid of them; these were allowed back into the bush. After about four months, during which all the animals had spent at least two months in enclosures, we selected for transport only those which were not afraid of us, were eating well, were in first-class condition and were not afraid of the transport boxes.

Before transportation we de-wormed the animals several times and used sprays to rid them of external parasites. Then we took our charges carefully by lorry and train to the port or airport. The animals were never left unattended for a moment. On board, we loaded the boxes onto the upper deck of the ship, where we attended to them three times daily. It was hard work — from five in the morning until ten at night throughout the whole voyage! If a storm blew up we would stay with the animals throughout, dozing when we could between the boxes.

The length of the journey from Africa to Europe is shown by the following example. In camp we spent three days loading the animals; transportation from Karamoja camp in Uganda to the railway station in Tororo also took three days; the journey from Tororo to Mombasa was six days. One day was spent loading from the wagons to the ship, then 35 days on the voyage around Africa, via the Canary Islands and the Channel to Hamburg. One day saw the transfer of the animals onto river barges; nine days sailing against the current took us up the Elbe to Kolín-on-Elbe in Bohemia. Finally there were two days unloading the animals and transporting them by lorry to quarantine in the zoo at Dvůr Králové. Total journey time was 50 days, and the animals covered a distance of 19,860 kilometres!

On the plains by the River Ngiro in Kenya, in 1974, we caught 25 Reticulated Giraffes without a single loss, using land rovers and a small aeroplane.

MY FIRST GIRAFFE

The first animal I ever caught by jeep was a magnificent female Baringo Giraffe, on 21 December 1967. I write in my diary: 'I haven't

been able to sleep since 5 o'clock; today I am going to try to catch my first giraffe!' The jeep is prepared and a bamboo stick about six metres long has an expandable wire noose at the end, so that the lassoo can be slipped off the stick. The jeep is almost stripped — number plates, lights, roof cover, rear seats and passenger seat have all been removed. Attached to the reinforced roll bars of the roof framework is a tyre

A young female Reticulated Giraffe, separated from the mother herd, is closely followed by a jeep. travelling at almost 70 kilometres per hour. The lassoo for capture is fixed to an eight-metre-long bamboo stick using knitting cotton yarn.

As soon as it becomes possible to slip the loop of the lassoo around the neck of the running animal, the jeep reduces speed and very carefully begins to brake. The Giraffe, caught in the lassoo, is forced to stop. The occupants of the jeep then jump out and the first to reach the captured giraffe hangs on to its tail.

in horizontal position, with the sharp inside edges cut off and a slightly inflated inner tube inserted. I stand on the floor of the jeep with the tyre surrounding my body like a tight ring, giving me a feeling of safety and stability. Above the waist my body can move freely and both my hands can manipulate the stick, to which the lassoo has been lightly attached in several places with cotton thread. A second jeep carries the transport box and eight assistants.

As we catch sight of the first giraffes, we leave the track and set off into the bush. Among the thorny scrub and termite mounds we gradually approach a small herd. Slowly we press them to more open grass cover and select a beautiful, young, magnificently-coloured female. The driver accelerates as I prepare the lassoo. The chosen giraffe runs away, dodges us and runs in circles as we tear along after her. With shouts I indicate the hazards on the ground to the driver, since I can see better from my standing position.

In front of us is a bare, flat square in the middle of the bush. We rush forwards at full speed. We are scarcely eight metres away from the giraffe, so I lean out and the lassoo noose at the end of the bamboo stick moves towards her head. In a moment we shall have her. All of a sudden the jeep swerves abruptly to the left, to avoid a termite hill. We skid for a few moments on two wheels, and I feel as if my back is broken. I now appreciate the valve of that tyre! But the giraffe has got away — after being scarcely half a metre out of my grasp. We have been lucky, though — a collision with a termite hill would have destroyed the jeep.

Once again we drive after the giraffe, which is heading for a belt of dense shrubs. We are at full speed. Somehow I manage to get the noose round the giraffe's neck. With my free hand I flick the lassoo back and pull it off the stick. The driver is beginning to slow down, the lassoo is gradually tightening, and we brake and stop. The soft cotton lassoo is as taut as a string. Suddenly there is silence as we switch off and jump out of the vehicle. The first to reach the rearing

The other hunters go round the animal and hang onto the front legs. As soon as they have a firm hold, the lassoo is quickly released. This picture shows the capture of a still maturing female Rothschild Giraffe on the Karamoja plains in northeast Uganda.

▲
The capture jeep is followed by a back-up jeep which carries the transport box. The box is placed in front of the creature, who is pushed into it. The box is then quickly slammed shut, using a sliding panel, and loaded onto the transport jeep for the trip back to camp.

On the scorched plains south of Karamoja in Uganda we caught a Topi Hartebeest, a Jackson's Hartebeest, a Roan Antelope and Maneless Zebras. It is extremely difficult to catch young male Jackson's Hartebeest in a lassoo. The male runs at a speed of 65 kilometres per hour and makes unexpected movements.
▼

giraffe hangs on to her tail and the second takes a firm hold of the front legs, leaping in from one side. Then we have to free the tight lassoo with a flick, so that the breathless giraffe is not choked. The transport jeep pulls up with the box and backs up to the giraffe. Quickly get the box down! The giraffe is standing as rigid as a statue. We literally push her into the transport box, quickly slide in the rear cover, and that's it.

To lift the box we push tyres under it alternately at the front and behind, until the box is almost level with the floor of the transport jeep. Then one gentle push forwards is enough. We quickly secure the box and off we go. In the camp we release the giraffe into the enclosure, where there are freshly-cut acacia branches with soft green leaves stuck into the ground. The giraffe is relatively calm. My first giraffe!

AN ELEPHANT CALF

We used four vehicles for the capture of elephant calves; two heavy army Fords, a heavy Humber and a lighter Willys as a scouting vehicle. The capture of the first two elephant calves went smoothly. During the capture of the third calf, however, we almost lost a driver and a jeep, as follows. We drove out at dawn to the edge of a forest, to wait for a herd of elephants on their way back from their nocturnal pastures on the open savannahs. Far in the distance I spotted a large herd with three smaller maternal groups. Choosing a suitable elephant calf is no simple matter: the calf should be neither too young nor too large, the tusks should be no longer than 10 centimetres, and ideally their tips should just be visible. Such a calf is about 130 centimetres tall, and although still young it is strong and able to feed itself.

We found a suitable calf in a small herd of elephant cows. The herd was being led by the calf's mother and accompanied by four females, one very old and three young 'aunts' as the Africans call elephant cows without calves. As the animals approached we drove across to cut off their path to the forest. The herd reached roughly 150 metres from us, and we set off.

The herd starts to run, intending to go round us and flee into the forest from the other side. This, however, is exactly what we have been waiting for, as we are much faster. The elephant cows trumpet with raised trunks. We close on the herd and separate the cow and calf between the vehicles. The calf begins to fall behind. From the Ford the lassoo expert hooks the lassoo over the head of the calf at the second attempt, and they slow down. The Willys and my

At the moment when the hunters had nearly reached the hartebeest the animal managed to shake its head out of the lassoo, which had only caught one of its horns. Immediately it rushed to escape, but the quick-reacting driver took a firm hold of its tail.

The capture of a Grévy's Zebra in the half-dried marshes of the Isiolo district.

Even in the lassoo the zebra defends itself, kicks and bites. For this reason it is necessary to hold it firmly underneath by the lower jaw and ear, while the others put their arms round its neck, catch it by the tail and hold its back and flanks. In the meantime the lassoo loop is loosened as quickly as possible. The zebra is forced into the box with the lassoo still on, and only when the box is firmly closed is the lassoo carefully removed from over its head.

Humber continue the chase for a while longer, trying to drive the cows away from the calf and into the forest.

The Ford is now moving at walking speed. All of a sudden, however, the calf trumpets loudly. The mother is still only a short distance in front of us; she turns, runs between the vehicles like a storm and rushes to help the calf. We turn quickly, but the elephant reaches the Ford first. There is a violent collision. The enraged mother pierces her tusks through the radiator and the left mudguard, lifts the heavy car with her enormous strength, and turns it on its side. We are still 10 metres away from the elephant. The moment seems to last an eternity — the lives of four people are at stake.

I distract the cow from the disabled car and she turns on me. My jeep, however, is protected from attack by an armoured bonnet and protec-tive bodywork. I literally push her away from the Ford and the calf. The calf falls over, stands up again and trumpets, but the cow moves aside, backs off and suddenly turns and flees. There is no time to turn my jeep round so I reverse to the calf and, with it lying close by, I jump out of the car with my co-driver and tie the calf's feet with my short lassoo. The others run to assist the driver of the overturned car. The hunters had jumped down from the back of the vehicle and fled, but the driver had been trapped in the cabin; it turns out he is only shaken, with a bump on the head, a gashed knee and cut fingers. At least we had our calf.

A RHINOCEROS MOTHER

We were making preparations for the capture of White Rhinos. Working with us was Ken Randall, one of the most experienced hunters in Kenya, who selected the camp site and hunting grounds. Looking after the camp and us was Ken's wife Jenny, a cheerful, good-hearted lady and an excellent cook.

We had a full working programme. Apart from rhinos we were also after young Cape Buffalo and elephant calves. We had promised that we would first obtain one large male and two adult female rhinos for the national parks, then elephant calves for an American, Don Hunt, and finally we would hunt rhinos, elephants and Cape Buffalo for our zoo. Ken was full of optimism and assured us that we would see several rhinos, elephant herds and large buffalo herds every day.

For capture we had prepared two armoured military Fords. Yet, although we went out daily, getting up when it was still dark, we managed in the course of the first 10 days to catch only one elephant calf and two buffalo. Jenny was teasing us, Ken was unhappy, and I calculated that if things carried on the expedition would have to be extended into the next rainy season.

'Ken, where are all these herds of animals?' I asked him almost daily.

'I don't know, I can't understand it, it just isn't possible,' he would answer. 'I caught animals here six years ago for the East African national parks and we would meet between 10 and 15 rhinos a day. In three days we had fourteen of them in the enclosures!'

In the last few years, however, the situation had changed. The territories inhabited by wild animals are diminishing, and poaching is on the increase. Rhino horns, elephant tusks and zebra, antelope and monkey skins still sell well. The numbers of people are growing rapidly, they are hungry, and wild animals have good meat.

We needed help. We turned to Murray Watson, an outstanding pilot, ethologist (student of animal behaviour) and expert on Africa. He promised to fly over in two weeks with his small two-seater plane. There was just one small thing he needed: a landing strip behind the camp. So, just behind the camp we built a landing strip and even sewed a windsock from a sheet. As we had no air-to-ground radio contact we agreed on a system of signals for co-operation between ground and air.

While it was still dark, before dawn, we drove out to a gigantic baobab on the edge of a great plain, about 10 kilometres from the camp. There we unloaded the boxes for the buffalo and elephant calves and waited for Murray. Just at dawn, when it was possible to see a little,

he took off and flew over to reconnoitre the area. When he found animals he flew back to the baobab and gave us a signal: waving of the wings meant rhino, a spin was for elephant, a figure-of-eight for buffalo. Then he would fly off in the direction in which the animals were to be found and circle above them at greater height, while we drove slowly through the bush towards the spot below the centre of the circle. Murray would do a nose dive towards the

In the mountainous and hilly terrain of Namibia, above the half-dry Swakop stream, we caught a small herd of Hartmann's Zebras. Using a small helicopter we drove them into prepared enclosures surrounded by plastic foils two and a half metres high. The foil was at the top and the bottom, reinforced on tense wires attached to trees or to steel posts dug into the ground.

Capture of a Black Rhinoceros in a sisal lassoo 3 centimetres thick, using heavy jeeps.

ground like an eagle, to show us precisely where the animals were.

Thanks to Murray, capturing began to be successful. We caught several young rhinos, and then we decided to hunt for adults. We changed the cotton lassoos for strong sisal ropes and prepared rifle darts with sedative drugs. First we caught a large male about 10 years old with magnificent strong horns. We looked for a non-leading female but had no luck, although we did manage to catch another almost full-grown adult. We were unfortunate in the capture of another young rhino. Its mother kept attacking us fearlessly and in the end, when we almost had the young in the noose, she ran round our jeep and lifted the rear of the vehicle in the air, leaving its wheels turning aimlessly. Meanwhile the young rhino had run off. With Murray's help, we managed later to catch both the young rhinoceros and its fearless mother.

We were short of time, so we decided to take the rhinoceros mother back to camp and eventually donate her to the national park. That was our mistake. We put the female in the strongest large enclosure, fetched her fresh branches, dug her a hollow and filled it with water. She was still angry and attacked us, and would not touch a thing. Her offspring, a female about three years old, had already been transported to quarantine in Langata, near Nairobi, so that she would not sense it nearby. The next day we went after an adolescent rhino weighing roughly 500 kilogrammes. When we had it firmly in the lassoo we jumped out of the vehicle and ran towards it. The young defended itself fiercely but finally we managed to loop one of its back legs with a second, short lassoo. We rushed at it and tried to knock it over but the young rhino turned round abruptly, one of the hunters fell over and unfortunately he broke his leg. As he cried out with pain the others started and loosened their hold; the rhino immediately took advantage of this and went for me with its horn. It struck me in the left side and jerked its head upwards. I felt a sharp pain in my side and left shoulder and I had to let the rhino go.

At the hospital in Nairobi it was discovered that I had two broken ribs, a fractured collarbone, a torn shoulder ligament and a dislocated shoulder joint. Three days later I returned to camp. The large female rhino had still eaten nothing, and cried out every few minutes for her young. As I was unable to go out, I sat by her and talked to her day and night. She was restless, and kept making a thorough check of the enclosure.

In the province of the upper Nile we hunted the rare Northern White Rhinoceros (*Ceratotherium simum cottoni*) using narcotic rifles. After doses of about 2.5 millilitres of Immobilon sedative the rhino would stop and fall over within five to eight minutes, so that we were able to put the lassoo around it and tie its feet.

Early next morning as I approached the enclosures near the female I could see that something was wrong. They were empty. All night she had been tearing up and shaking out the posts, which were dug 60 centimetres into the ground, letting the four young rhinos come to her. She was lying contentedly in the middle of her enclosure on a pile of branches, and the young were resting around her. We were afraid for the young, so with great difficulty we separated them from her and repaired and reinforced the enclosures.

The following night the situation repeated itself. The female rhino rooted up the enclosures and regained the young, one by one. As soon as she had them round her she was content, eating and resting happily. She never tried to break her enclosure on the side towards the bush, although the walls were all the same strength.

'I don't want that young of hers at Langata,' I said at last. 'I can't take it away from her; we'll have to take her to Langata, return her young and let them go to the national park. She is a superb mother.'

So this female rhino and her young may still be living to this day, somewhere on the Masai steppes of Kenya. I hope that they are still alive, and not slaughtered just because someone can get a few dollars for the horns growing on their noble heads.

The drugged rhino was placed in the jeep as quickly as possible, and taken to the camp. We ensured that it was lying comfortably, covered it with a wet blanket and protected it from the glare of the sun. After unloading into the compound we gave the same dose of Revivon, which works as an antidote. The rhino came to within a few minutes, and in an hour behaved as if it had never been drugged.

TREACHEROUS TERRAIN

During the capture of Cape Eland, I found what human beings can withstand. These eland are strong animals, although not as pugnacious as, for example, Roan Antelope. As soon as we

We constructed the compounds for captured animals from local materials. Thick trunks made posts, digging them 60 to 80 centimetres into the ground. The cross poles were made of such hard wood that we could not nail them to the post, tying them instead with strong double binding wire. The system was vindicated: not even elephant calves or rhinos damaged the enclosure during the entire expedition.

caught a young eland in the lassoo, it would give in straight away. Three people were able to hold it and shut it in the box; sometimes it was not even necessary to take down the box from the back-up vehicle. Only a few times did an eland kick unexpectedly with its hind legs — although it was powerful kicking, and unpleasant.

We preferred catching eland on the vast flat

Kopenek plains in Karamoja, in north-east Uganda. We selected one of these beautiful antelopes and chased after it in the jeep at full speed. About 50 metres in front of us a long strip of tall grass loomed up, which is very dangerous for a jeep since the grass can conceal boulders, termite mounds or holes. (Normally we first burned an area so that we could spot obstacles; short green grass grows on the area and animals gather there.)

'Look out, grass, slow down!' I shouted to the driver. He took no notice, however, and did not slow down. His face was in a trance, his eyes were on fire; he had been siezed by hunting fever. We were nearing the antelope, but the grass cover was rapidly approaching. Then the

Elephant herds on the right bank of the Nile, in the equatorial province of southern Sudan. These vast plains are sparsely wooded with tree-type acacias, in the shade of which elephants like to stand at midday.

engine roared and I waited with lassoo at the ready. The antelope veered and ran into the dense grass, and we raced after it. The distance between us narrowed... five metres... three... I stretched forward as far as I could with the lassoo, but at that moment a tremendous force threw me backwards, knocking my shoulders against the stabilizing iron cage. It took me several seconds to come to and realise what had happened. The jeep had run at full speed over a sloping termite hill, flown into the

Hunting camp on a gentle slope above a stream, which always had water, even in the dry season. We put up the tents a little distance away from the animal enclosures so as to have them all in sight at all times. The tents of the local hunters were placed below the enclosures. The camp was dominated by a large Baobab tree, which was without leaves in the dry season.

In an enclosure of the Nabiswa camp a captured Cape Eland female gave birth. The birth lasted nearly three hours. As soon as the young was born the mother cleaned it. A six-day-old young, whose mother had been killed by predators during the night, ran to this antelope mother and began to suck from her. The new mother reared both young.

air as if from a ski-jump and landed rear wheels first, then front wheels. The vehicle survived, the driver changed to a lower gear, and we were back in pursuit.

I straightened up, took the lassoo stick in both hands and at the first attempt managed to catch the antelope. The cord gently slipped round her neck and she slackened pace, as if realizing there was no point in putting up a struggle. But we discovered that the back-up lorry with the boxes and assistants was nowhere in sight. The driver drove off to look for it, while one assistant and myself desperately held on to the antelope for about 20 minutes. I have no idea how I survived — on the way back I could neither sit nor stand. My back was gashed and bleeding and I had a couple of broken ribs, so once again I ended up in hospital.

CAPTURING ZEBRAS

While capturing Boehm's (Maneless) Zebras in Uganda, we caught a strong young stallion. Two of our hunters ran to hold it and release the noose of the lassoo, but the stallion turned and bit one in the back. He cried out with pain, but the stallion did not let go. With a flicking movement I undid the lassoo and ran to help. From the side I gave the stallion a hard slap with my open hand and he let the hunter go, turning instead on me. I fastened the end of the lassoo to the tree trunk around which he was chasing me. Finally the other hunters managed to subdue the stallion. In our zoo the keepers gave him the name 'Devil'. To them he behaved reasonably, but he would never allow anybody to separate a single mare from his herd.

Two days later we managed to catch a beautiful young mare which we put for a couple of days into a small isolated enclosure. In another large enclosure we had 14 zebras captured earlier. The new mare refused food, so we let her join the herd. Even in the group she was clearly not well, ate badly, stood about in the corner with her head hanging, and she lost weight. We thought she might improve but her condition grew steadily worse, and we decided to let her back into the bush. Although she ran out of the enclosure into an open space of the camp, that was all. She would not let us drive her away at any price. She would walk around the camp, go into the stream to drink, and graze nearby, yet return to the outside of the enclosure each evening. Somehow she identified herself with the herd standing inside. When this pattern repeated itself on subsequent evenings, we gave her a bowl of oats and a little hay. In about three

After capture, and before release into the quarantine enclosures, animals must be examined and treated for any injury. Some, for example South African oryxes or Blue Wildebeest, had rubber fittings put over their sharp horns so as not to injure one another.

weeks she seemed well again. One day I opened the enclosure and she went inside of her own accord.

From that moment the mare was content to be with other zebras. She was not afraid of us, came when she was called and allowed us to stroke her. We took the herd to the zoo and the keepers named her 'Uganda'. This magnificent, docile zebra was the first to produce a foal — a stallion which is now fully grown and leading his own herd in the zoo. The mare lived with us for 14 years, producing a beautiful healthy foal each year.

During the capture of Grévy's Zebra in the semi-deserts of northern Kenya we put up a large camp behind the village of Sericho. In this region there were not enough poles and sticks and so the enclosures were prefabricated from strong deal planks. We wanted to capture 40 Grévy's Zebras and among them we wanted a young, strong, adult stallion. We managed to capture him when we already had over 30 mares in the enclosures. We put the stallion into a separate smaller enclosure between the mares. In the middle of the night we were woken by a banging noise. The stallion was jumping up in the air and, with powerful blows of his head and feet, breaking the planks in the roof and

The hunting enclosure of the Nabiswa camp in Uganda had connecting corridors through which Giraffes, zebras and Cape Eland walked continuously. The corridors served primarily as release tunnels, later for the transfer of animals from one enclosure to another, and lastly when Giraffes were driven through them in transport boxes.

sides and trying to escape. Before we had the chance to return with the tools, he had run off into the night. There was nothing we could do.

Within a few days we spotted a small herd in which there was a strong young stallion. We caught him and, as we were putting him into the box, I noticed he had some unusual gashes on the forehead and a tear wound, as if from a nail. It was the same stallion that had escaped. We let him straight among the mares this time and he was docile, behaving as if he had always belonged there. Evidently he had not liked his initial isolation. He soon got used to us and became our best stallion.

THE OBSTINATE MONITOR

I managed to catch my first Nile Monitor at the beginning of December 1967, in Uganda. I was staying in a small house on the shore of Lake Victoria, about five kilometres from Entebbe. Every late afternoon after work I would walk along the lake shore, and sometimes I would go by boat to the nearby bay to watch the otters swimming or the cormorants skimming low over the water. I would often sit on a tall termite hill until it was dark, watching the beautiful sunsets.

Once, as I was going as usual to my termite hill, I suddenly caught sight of the monitor, over a metre in length, breaking into the mound. Without much thought I leapt towards

In the camp by the River Ewase Ngiro our tents stood in the shade of a large acacia. One night a Leopard visited our camp and pulled its freshly-killed Grant's Gazelle into a tree, eating it with snarling noises. After a warning shot it ran away, leaving its prey in the tree, and did not appear again.

it and caught it by its strong tail, pulling it out of the hole and catching its head with my other hand. The monitor defended itself fiercely, and somehow it jerked round and gripped the back of my hand with the sharp claws on its front limbs. Neither of us would loosen our grip. I ran back and two hunters came up, but they were afraid to take hold of the lizard. Eventually they took a front leg each and tried to pull the claws out of my hands. It did not work. Then they both took one foot and levered the claws out of my muscles, pulling it away, and then freeing the other.

In the New Year of 1968 I sent the monitor to Czechoslovakia by plane, together with a crocodile and several poisonous snakes. The next day

Transport of the animals on the upper deck of the *Vogtland*. The journey round Cape Town, across the Atlantic and round the Canary Islands to Hamburg lasted 28 days. Every day we had to uncover the animals, feed them and water them, clean their boxes and cover them again with canvas for the night.

◀ All the large animals we hunted in East Africa were taken to the port of Mombasa, and from there by ocean-going ships to Hamburg and up the Elbe to Czechoslovakia.

I received a telex from Zurich, informing me succinctly: 'Monitor and crocodile broke open box and ran round luggage hold. Discovered during stopover in Zurich. Employees of our company quickly closed compartment, and plane took off for Copenhagen. Employees from Copenhagen Zoological Gardens caught animals, repaired box. Reptiles immediately dispatched to Prague. Cargo received in Prague in perfect order.'

These are just a few incidents from the early days of our work. What were the results, and why do we do it at all? We captured in Africa a total of over 2,500 mammals, birds and reptiles, from which, after careful selection, we transported 1,963. The total losses, including quarantines, were 2.8 per cent. Using ocean-going ships from various African ports we organized six large transportations and three smaller ones. On four occasions we hired a Boeing 707 plane from Lufthansa, filled it with animals and

flew with them to Prague. The longest flight took 16 hours 34 minutes, from Windhoek via Johannesburg and Nairobi. During air transportation we lost only two animals.

The animals we brought over formed the nucleus for the creation of breeding pairs, groups and herds — not only at our zoo, but also in others around the world. Within 10 years of breeding, for example, we succeeded in rearing 138 young from 11 transported Roan Antelope; 87 foals of various species from 68 zebras; 94 young from 17 Sable Antelope; and in addition we solved the problem of snake breeding. We were also the first zoo in the world to breed the rare northern race of the White Rhinoceros, which we had obtained with extraordinary difficulty. Although we did not succeed in breeding all species, nevertheless the majority are now reproducing successfully. The offspring from our zoo are taken to zoos and parks all over the world.

We have built up a research institute for the breeding and care of zoo animals which in the years from 1980 to 1983 processed over 30,000 items of often quite unique data. We are also extremely pleased that we were able to present Algerian, Moroccan and Tunisian zoos with dozens of young and beautiful African animals. The third generation of Cape Buffalo reared at our zoo will form, in Johannesburg, the basis for new breeding herds in the wild.

We ourselves owe a great debt to Africa. Although zoos and wildlife parks have an important place in the global strategy for nature conservation, they are not the decisive factor. The main factors in this respect are people, their governments and the industrial-military complexes and gigantic technological installations which are capable of changing the landscapes of entire regions. Surely, however, we cannot transform everything into towns, factories, airports, motorways and gigantic fields cultivated by mechanical and chemical means.

In places our world must remain as it was, in its natural beauty and balance, and with its animals — our partners in life. The planet belonged to them long before it became ours. In this respect, many of the African states are far ahead of the rich and industrially-developed states of the world, since there are many large national parks in Africa where wild animals have a chance of survival. The greatest task ahead is our struggle for awareness among human beings. The current levels of biological consciousness and human understanding lag behind an unlimited faith in crude technology mechanization, industrial processes and nuclear power — which could annihilate humankind and the whole of planet Earth.